Contemporary American Architects

Volume II

Philip Jodidio

Contemporary American Architects

Volume II

TASCHEN

KÖLN LISBOA LONDON NEW YORK OSAKA PARIS

Page 2 · Seite 2
Steven Holl: D.E. Shaw and Company Office (detail), New York, 1991–92
© Photo: Paul Warchol

This book was printed on 100% chlorine-free bleached paper in accordance with the TCF-standard

© 1996 Benedikt Taschen Verlag GmbH
Hohenzollernring 53, D-50672 Köln

Edited by Angelika Muthesius, Cologne
Text edited by Silvia Kinkel, Cologne
Design: Frank Schwab, Schwäbisch Gmünd
Cover Design: Angelika Muthesius, Cologne; Mark Thomson, London
French translation: Jacques Bosser, Paris
German translation: Franca Fritz, Heinrich Koop, Cologne

Printed in Italy
ISBN 3-8228-8589-4

Contents
Inhalt
Sommaire

Brave New World
American Architects in the 1990s

Schöne neue Welt
Amerikanische Architekten in den 90er Jahren

Le meilleur des mondes
Architectes américains des années 90

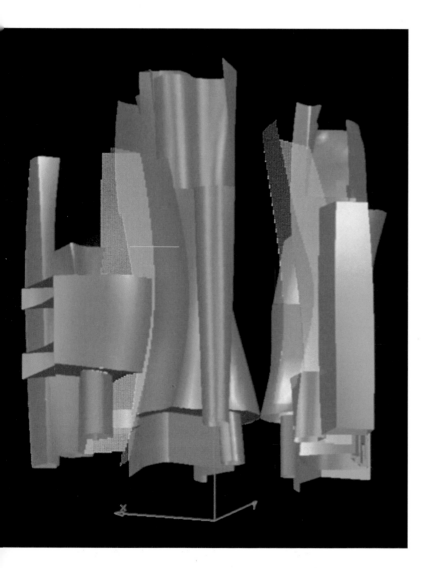

Frank O. Gehry, Guggenheim Museum, Bilbao, Spain, 1991–97. Computer drawing.

Frank O. Gehry, Guggenheim Museum, Bilbao, Spanien, 1991–97. Computerzeichnung.

Frank O. Gehry, Guggenheim Museum, Bilbao, Espagne, 1991–97. Dessin par ordinateur.

American architecture in the 1990s has been confronted with a number of powerful forces. Foremost amongst these have been the coupled effects of a recession, and the speculative frenzy of the preceding decade. Not only have these factors led logically to a slowing of construction, but they have also had a more profound, psychological impact. As Peter Eisenman says, "The world has changed. It has all become very conservative." Economic considerations were always important in modern architecture, but aside from a few, exceptional clients, the trend today is not only toward "cost-effective" buildings, but also toward structures which are not esthetically challenging. In clear terms, what little work there is usually goes to the architect a client knows he can "rely on." Since inventive contemporary architects have often been associated with a self-indulgent or overtly individualistic approach, corporate or government work is rarely given to them. In some instances such decisions may proceed from a political bias. It should be noted, at least in passing, that some commentators have equated the new conservatism – as evidenced, for example, in the 1994 Congressional elections, or in the strong position of the "religious right" – with a marked reticence toward certain types of contemporary art or architecture. The case of architecture is naturally less clear than that of more overtly provocative art, but conservatism naturally finds its equivalent in the built form as well. Fortunately, the private entrepreneurial spirit which made for much of the success of the United States still exists, and many of the buildings published in this book were built thanks not only to the talent of the architects, but also thanks to the open minds and spirits of the clients.

Another significant element of change which has already begun to substantially alter the built environment is the generalization of the use of computer assisted design. Not only does such technology, which has progressively become more affordable and easy to use, facilitate design in its technical aspects, it also invites architects to explore hitherto unheard of possibilities in creating new forms. The enthusiasm of a number of the architects cited in this book for computer techniques is a sure indication that this electronic revolution will have a growing influence on design.

Die amerikanische Architektur wird seit Beginn der 90er Jahre mit einer Reihe gravierender Einflüsse konfrontiert, an deren erster Stelle die wechselseitige Wirkung der Wirtschaftsrezession und des Spekulationswahns des vorangegangenen Jahrzehnts steht. Diese beiden Faktoren haben nicht nur zu einer Rezession der Bauindustrie geführt, sondern auch tiefgreifende psychologische Auswirkungen gezeigt. Peter Eisenman formulierte es so: »Die Welt hat sich verändert. Es ist alles sehr konservativ geworden.« Wirtschaftliche Überlegungen spielten in der modernen Architektur schon immer eine bedeutende Rolle, aber abgesehen von einigen wenigen außergewöhnlichen Auftraggebern geht der Trend heute nicht nur in Richtung »kosteneffizienter« Bauwerke, sondern favorisiert Bauten, die in ästhetischer Hinsicht keinerlei Herausforderung darstellen. Mit anderen Worten: Das bereits geringe Auftragsvolumen wird im allgemeinen an Architekten vergeben, von denen der Kunde weiß, daß er sich »auf sie verlassen kann«. Da erfindungsreiche zeitgenössische Architekten häufig mit einem maßlosen oder übertrieben individualistischen Ansatz assoziiert werden, erhalten sie immer seltener staatliche oder große Firmenaufträge. In manchen Fällen beruhen solche Entscheidungen auf einer Voreingenommenheit von Seiten der Politik. Bei der Architektur ist das natürlich weniger ersichtlich als bei eher offenkundig provokativer Kunst, aber der Konservatismus findet sein Äquivalent auch in der gebauten Form. Glücklicherweise existiert der private Unternehmergeist noch, der in hohem Maße zum Erfolg der Vereinigten Staaten beitrug, und viele der in diesem Buch beschriebenen Gebäude konnten nicht nur dank des Talents ihrer Architekten errichtet werden, sondern auch dank der Unvoreingenommenheit und Aufgeschlossenheit der Bauherren.

Ein weiterer bedeutender Faktor im Wandel der Architektur – der die Bauindustrie bereits grundlegend verändert – ist die allgemeine Verwendung von computergestütztem Design. Diese immer erschwinglichere und leichter zu handhabende Technologie fördert nicht nur die eher technischen Aspekte des Designs, sondern lädt die Architekten auch dazu ein, bis dato ungeahnte Möglichkeiten zur Gestaltung neuer Formen zu erforschen. Die Begeisterung

L'architecture américaine s'est trouvée confrontée à un certain nombre de fortes pressions au cours des années 90. Parmi celles-ci figurent au premier plan les effets de la récession économique et de la frénésie spéculative de la décennie précédente. Ces facteurs ont naturellement conduit à un ralentissement de la construction et ont eu un profond impact psychologique. Comme le fait remarquer Peter Eisenman: «Le monde a changé. Il est devenu conservateur.» Les considérations économiques ont toujours joué un rôle important dans l'architecture moderne, mais en dehors de quelques clients aussi exceptionnels que peu nombreux, la tendance actuelle est à la fois aux bâtiments «rentables», et aux constructions qui n'ont guère d'ambitions esthétiques. En clair, les rares commandes vont généralement à l'architecte «prévisible». Comme les architectes contemporains créatifs ont souvent été accusés de narcissisme ou d'individualisme forcené, les commandes officielles ou des grandes entreprises ne leur sont plus que rarement attribuées. Ces décisions s'expliquent aussi parfois par des considérations politiques. Certains commentateurs ont ainsi relevé que le nouveau conservatisme, conforté par les élections au Congrès américain de 1994 ou la montée en puissance de la «droite religieuse», se montre très réticent vis-à-vis de certaines expressions artistiques ou architecturales contemporaines. Le cas de l'architecture est naturellement moins évident que celui de l'art contemporain qui se veut souvent provocant, mais le conservatisme n'épargne naturellement pas l'art de construire. Il est heureux que subsiste encore l'esprit d'entreprise individuel auquel la réussite des Etats-Unis doit tant. Un grand nombre des réalisations présentées dans cet ouvrage ont été rendues possibles grâce à la fois au talent des architectes et à l'ouverture d'esprit de leurs clients.

Autre élément significatif de changement: la généralisation de la CAO (conception assistée par ordinateur). Non seulement cette technologie de plus en plus accessible et commode facilite l'établissement des plans dans leurs aspects techniques, mais elle pousse les architectes à une exploration jusque – là impossible de formes encore jamais vues. Cette révolution technologique va incontestablement jouer un rôle grandissant dans l'architecture des années à venir.

Doubt and Readjustment

Aside from overriding economic and political considerations
which may influence contemporary architecture, there are
other regional or individual factors which play a strong role.
The older practicing American architects, such as Frank
O. Gehry (born in 1929), or Richard Meier (born in 1934)
have reached a degree of international notoriety which for
the time being eludes the younger generation. Both Meier
and Gehry are completing large buildings in Europe, but
they are not receiving the number of commissions which
might be expected in the United States. As Frank O. Gehry
has said, "In L.A., I've long been considered strange and
odd, a maverick. For years, no big corporation or major
developer gave me a commission of any size. Disney Hall,
which I won in close competition with Stirling, Hollein and
Böhm is the first big thing I've been given to do in my
home town. In Los Angeles, despite all its freedom to
experiment, the avant-garde remains peripheral to the
mainstream of most of what's being built." Construction of
Gehry's Disney Concert Hall in Los Angeles, once hailed as
a breakthrough for Gehry, and for contemporary architecture in general, is now indefinitely halted, and Meier's
office has certainly contracted from the heady days of the
1980s. Simply put, in the best of times, "quality" architecture is seen as self-indulgent or uneconomical by many
potential clients. The American economy has suffered a
substantial recession and conservatism has become the
political and esthetic watchword. The net result is that even
the best-known non-corporate architects receive few commissions. Richard Meier's Getty Center is nearing completion in the Brentwood area of Los Angeles but it has long
appeared to be a project born of an era of unlimited expectations, coming to fruition in a new period of doubt and
substantial readjustment.

Without suggesting, as one of their prominent New York
colleagues does, that Meier and Gehry have been fundamentally unable to make the transition to the larger-scale
work that their reputation permitted them to attempt, it is
interesting to note that, despite the overall climate of conservatism, some younger, admittedly "flashy" architects
have recently obtained large commissions. Such is the case

einer Reihe in diesem Buch zitierter Architekten für die
Möglichkeiten der Computertechnologie ist ein eindeutiges
Anzeichen dafür, daß diese elektronische Revolution einen
immer stärkeren Einfluß auf das Design haben wird.

Zweifel und Neuorientierung

Abgesehen von vorrangig wirtschaftlichen und politischen
Überlegungen, die die zeitgenössische Architektur beein-
flussen, spielen auch regionale oder individuelle Faktoren
eine wichtige Rolle. Architekten wie Frank O. Gehry
(geboren 1929) oder Richard Meier (geboren 1934) haben
einen Grad an internationaler Bekanntheit erreicht, der die
jüngere Generation vorläufig in den Hintergrund drängt.
Obwohl Meier und Gehry an großen Bauwerken in Europa
arbeiten, erhalten sie in den Vereinigten Staaten keines-
wegs die Anzahl von Aufträgen, die man vermuten könnte.
Frank O. Gehrys Kommentar dazu: »In Los Angeles galt ich
lange als verschroben und sonderbar, ein Außenseiter, und
habe deshalb jahrelang weder von größeren Unternehmen
noch von bedeutenden Stadtplanern auch nur einen einzigen Auftrag erhalten. Die Disney Concert Hall, deren Ausschreibung ich in einem harten Wettbewerb gegen Stirling,
Hollein und Böhm gewann, ist der erste große Auftrag, den
man mir in meiner Heimatstadt erteilte.« Die Bauarbeiten
an Gehrys Disney Concert Hall in Los Angeles, die einst als
sein internationaler Durchbruch bejubelt wurde, aber auch
die zeitgenössische Architektur im allgemeinen sind auf
unbestimmte Zeit zum Stillstand gekommen. Und auch
Meiers Büro kennt nicht mehr solch hektische Tage wie in
den 80er Jahren. Mit anderen Worten: Selbst in guten Zeiten wird »Qualitäts«-Architektur von vielen potentiellen
Kunden als maßlos oder unwirtschaftlich betrachtet. Die
amerikanische Wirtschaft erlebte eine schwerwiegende
Rezession, und der Konservatismus wurde zum politischen
und ästhetischen Schlagwort – mit dem Ergebnis, daß
selbst die bekanntesten der freien Architekten kaum noch
Aufträge erhalten. Richard Meiers Getty Center in Brentwood, Los Angeles, nähert sich zwar der Fertigstellung,
aber es hat sich als ein Projekt herausgestellt, das in einer
Zeit der unbegrenzten Möglichkeiten konzipiert wurde,
aber in einer neuen Ära voller Zweifel und umfassender

Doutes et réajustements

En dehors du contexte économique et politique, d'autres puissants facteurs régionaux ou individuels peuvent influencer l'architecture contemporaine. Les architectes américains dans leur maturité, comme Frank O. Gehry (né en 1929) ou Richard Meier (né en 1934) ont atteint une notoriété internationale qui manque encore à la jeune génération. Si Meier et Gehry mènent tous deux d'importants chantiers en Europe, ils ne reçoivent pas aux Etats-Unis le nombre de commandes qu'ils auraient pu espérer. Comme le dit Gehry: «A Los Angeles, j'ai longtemps été considéré comme étrange et même bizarre... un non-conformiste. Pendant des années aucun grand promoteur ou entreprise importante ne m'a passé la moindre commande. Disney Hall, que j'ai remporté de justesse dans un concours auquel participaient Stirling, Hollein et Böhm, est la première grande réalisation qui m'ait été confiée dans ma ville. A L.A., malgré toute notre apparente liberté d'expérimentation, l'avant-garde reste périphérique au courant principal qui anime l'essentiel de ce qui est construit.» La construction de la salle de concert Disney au centre de Los Angeles, naguère saluée comme un triomphe pour Gehry et l'architecture contemporaine, est aujourd'hui arrêtée pour une durée indéfinie, et l'agence de Meier compte certainement moins de collaborateurs aujourd'hui que lors des années 80. Bref, on considère souvent l'architecture «de qualité» comme nombriliste ou anti-économique. L'économie américaine a souffert d'une forte récession et le conservatisme est devenu le mot d'ordre politique et esthétique. Résultat: même les architectes les plus connus reçoivent peu de commandes. Si le Getty Center de Richard Meier, à Brentwood, sera bientôt achevé, il a depuis longtemps l'image d'un projet né au cours d'une période d'espoirs illimités, qui ouvrira ses portes au cours d'une nouvelle phase, marquée par le doute et des réajustements fondamentaux.

Sans suggérer pour autant, comme le fait l'un de leurs éminents confrères new-yorkais, que Meier et Gehry n'ont pas su s'adapter aux grands projets que leur réputation leur aurait permis de remporter, il est intéressant de noter qu'en dépit du climat conservateur général quelques architectes plus jeunes, dotés d'une «vision», ont récemment reçu

Steven Holl, Storefront for Art and Architecture, New York, 1994. View of pivoting panels in the facade.

Steven Holl, Storefront for Art and Architecture, New York, 1994. Bewegliche Platten der Fassade.

Steven Holl, Storefront for Art and Architecture, New York, 1994. Panneaux de façade pivotants.

of the Miami-based Arquitectonica group. They have just completed the spectacular headquarters of the Banque de Luxembourg in Luxembourg, and if all goes according to plan, they will inaugurate their most visible project – a multi-building complex located on the corner of Eighth Avenue and 42nd Street in New York on January 1, 2000. This 47 story, 680 room convention hotel, sheathed in colored glass. designed to resemble the tail of a comet crashing into Times Square will hardly go unnoticed. Whatever criticism can be leveled at Arquitectonica, the 45 year old principal Bernardo Fort-Brescia has certainly managed to bring an exuberant style and a measure of quality to a type of project normally reserved to much less flamboyant "corporate" architects. The fact that the 42nd Street project is a collaborative venture between the Tishman Urban Development Corporation and Disney does much to explain the choice of Arquitectonica, as well as the fact that the other two finalists were Michael Graves and Zaha Hadid. Disney chairman Michael Eisner is a well-known "fan" of contemporary architecture.

An ability to create forms adapted to new constraints of the 1990s is certainly a hallmark of the rising figures in American architecture. For the Los Angeles architect Eric Owen Moss (born in 1943), success has come through an ability to make spectacular designs out of existing warehouse space in Culver City. An innovative use of ordinary materials such as water pipes transformed into columns or bolts bent into light fixtures are features of the style of an architect Philip Johnson once called a "jeweler of junk." With the unfailing support of the developer Frederick Norton Smith, Moss has managed to turn a desolate stretch of practically abandoned buildings into an exciting and economically viable area for offices. On the opposite side of the United States, New Yorker Steven Holl (born in 1947) has achieved a substantial degree of international recognition with projects which challenge assumptions about architectural space, light and durability. His Storefront for Art and Architecture, a collaborative project with the artist Vito Acconci is a radical design which has neither windows nor doors in the traditional sense of the words. Rather, this is an adaptive response to the "nomadic" conditions of contem-

Eric Owen Moss, Ince Theater, Culver City, California, 1994. Computer drawing for this project which is not yet under construction.

Eric Owen Moss, Ince Theater, Culver City, Kalifornien, 1994. Computerzeichnung des geplanten Projektes.

Eric Owen Moss, Ince Theater, Culver City, Californie, 1994. Dessin par ordinateur pour ce projet dont la construction n'a pas encore commencé.

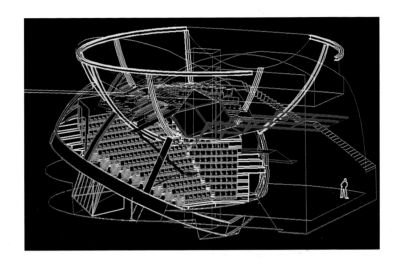

wirtschaftlicher Neuorientierungen zur Vollendung gelangt. Ohne – wie einer ihrer berühmten New Yorker Kollegen – behaupten zu wollen, daß Meier und Gehry im Grunde nicht in der Lage sind, den Schritt von ihren bisherigen Aufträgen zu den Großprojekten zu vollziehen, ist es doch interessant, daß trotz des allgemein konservativen Klimas in letzter Zeit diverse bedeutende Aufträge an jüngere, zugegebenermaßen »modische« Architekten vergeben wurden – wie etwa an die Architekturgruppe Arquitectonica in Miami. Sie haben gerade die aufsehenerregende Zentrale der Banque de Luxembourg in Luxemburg fertiggestellt, und wenn alles nach Plan verläuft, werden sie am 1. Januar 2000 ihr herausragendstes Projekt – ein mehrere Gebäude umfassender Komplex auf einem Eckgelände an der Eighth Avenue und der 42nd Street in New York – einweihen können. Dieses 47 geschossige, buntglasverkleidete Kongreßhotel mit 680 Zimmern, das an den gebogenen Schweif eines auf den Times Square herabstürzenden Meteors erinnern soll, wird zweifellos Aufsehen erregen. Unabhängig davon, wieviel Kritik man an Arquitectonica üben mag, ist es dem 45-jährigen Leiter dieser Architektengruppe, Bernardo Fort-Brescia, gelungen, diesem Bauprojekt einen überschwenglichen Stil und einen außerordentlichen Grad an Qualität zu verleihen. Die Tatsache, daß es sich bei diesem Gebäudekomplex um ein Gemeinschaftsunternehmen der Disney Corporation und der Tishman Urban Development Corporation handelt, erklärt, warum die Wahl auf Arquitectonica fiel und warum die beiden anderen Finalisten Michael Graves und Zaha Hadid hießen. Der Vorsitzende der Disney Corporation, Michael Eisner, ist ein bekannter »Fan« zeitgenössischer Architektur.

Ein Kennzeichen der aufstrebenden Persönlichkeiten in der amerikanischen Architektur ist ihre Fähigkeit, Formen zu schaffen, die sich den neuen Beschränkungen der 90er Jahre anpassen. Bei dem Architekten Eric Owen Moss aus Los Angeles stellte sich der Erfolg aufgrund seiner Fähigkeit ein, bereits vorhandene Lagerhäuser in Culver City in spektakuläre Bauten zu verwandeln. Die einfallsreiche Verwendung herkömmlicher Materialien – wie z.B. Abwasserrohre, die als Säulen dienen oder Leuchtstofflampen in Form von U-förmig gebogenen Bolzen – sind typische

d'importantes commandes. C'est le cas du groupe Arquitectonica de Miami. Il vient juste de terminer le superbe siège social de la Banque de Luxembourg, et si tout se passe bien, il inaugurera un complexe de bâtiments à l'angle de la 8ème avenue et de la 42ème rue à New York, le 1er janvier 2000. Cet hôtel de 47 étages gainé de verre teinté, comprenant 680 chambres et un centre de congrès, et ressemblant à la queue d'une comète plantée dans Times Square ne risque pas de passer inaperçu. Quelles que soient les critiques adressées à Arquitectonica, son associé principal, Bernardo Fort-Brescia a certainement réussi à imposer un style exubérant et un niveau de qualité élevé à un type de réalisation normalement attribué à des architectes bien moins flamboyants. Le fait que ce projet soit né de l'association entre Tishman Urban Development Corporation et Disney explique pour une bonne part le choix d'Arquitectonica, et que les deux autres finalistes du concours aient été Michael Graves et Zaha Hadid. Le président de Disney, Michael Eisner, est un «fan» d'architecture contemporaine bien connu.

La capacité à créer des formes adaptées aux nouvelles contraintes des années 90 est certainement le signe caractéristique des figures montantes de l'architecture américaine. Pour l'architecte de Los Angeles Eric Owen Moss (né en 1943), le succès est venu du talent qu'il a déployé pour mener à bien des projets spectaculaires de reconversion de vieux entrepôts à Culver City. L'utilisation créative de matériaux ordinaires est caractéristique du style d'un architecte qualifié un jour par Philip Johnson de «joaillier de la ferraille». Avec le soutien sans faille du promoteur Frederick Norton Smith, Moss a réussi à transformer une zone désolée de bâtiments pratiquement abandonnés en un quartier de bureaux séduisant et économiquement viable. De l'autre côté des Etats-Unis, le New-Yorkais Steven Holl (né en 1947) s'est fait connaître avec des projets qui remettent en question les préjugés classiques sur l'espace, la lumière et la pérennité de l'architecture. Son Storefront for Art and Architecture, créé en collaboration avec l'artiste Vito Acconci, est un projet radical qui ne possède ni portes ni fenêtres au sens traditionnel du terme. Il s'agit plutôt d'une réponse adaptée aux conditions «nomades» de la vie

porary urban life, accomplished with a very limited budget, and destined to be replaced with a new design very quickly.

Nowhere is the client-architect relationship more at issue than in the design and construction of private houses. Economic circumstances have not made for a shortage of new millionaires in the United States, and a number of these individualistic figures have seen architecture as a way to realize their dreams or confirm their success. At their best, at least in terms of appearance, if not always in terms of comfort, such houses can become works of art in their own right. In this book, two remarkable houses by very different architects indicate the range of architectural responses which can be made to this peculiarly American quest for the "great" private dwelling. Cesar Pelli, born in Argentina in 1926 is one of the best known designers of large buildings in the world. His recent work ranges from the World Financial Center in New York, to twin 85 story towers in Kuala Lumpur, yet Pelli accepted an exceptional commission for a house situated in the western United States. As Paul Goldberger of *The New York Times* wrote about this residence, "The design merges worlds that by all normal measure have nothing to do with each other: the sleekness of modernism married to the embracing warmth of a log cabin. And for the all the hugeness and luxury (the house costs several million dollars) in the end it celebrates the land far more than it defies it. The house possesses human warmth but also the essential quality of all art, which is the ability to make us see the world in a slightly different way."[1]

Simon Ungers, born in Cologne, Germany in 1957 approached his client's desire for a combined house and library in a very different way, creating the T-House, which has been rightfully compared to a sculpture by Richard Serra. Ungers has actually completed more works of installation art than he has buildings, but the trend toward architecture as art, which has indeed been a factor throughout the 20th century, seems, if anything, to have been reinforced by the new circumstances of the 1990s. Architecture, more than art, is naturally obliged to evolve rapidly in the face of changing economic circumstances. Recession and penury may not be the most pleasant of constraints,

Kennzeichen für den Stil eines Architekten, den Philip Johnson einst als »Juwelier des Schrotts« bezeichnete. Dank der unermüdlichen Hilfe des Bauunternehmers Frederick Norton Smith war Moss in der Lage, ein trostloses Gebiet mit praktisch verlassenen Gebäuden in ein aufregendes und wirtschaftlich lebensfähiges Areal für Büroräumlichkeiten zu verwandeln. Auf der anderen Seite der Vereinigten Staaten gelangte der New Yorker Architekt Steven Holl (geboren 1947) aufgrund einiger Projekte zu internationaler Berühmtheit, die herkömmliche Auffassungen in bezug auf Raum, Licht und Beständigkeit architektonischer Werke in Frage stellen. Holls Storefront for Art and Architecture, ein Gemeinschaftsprojekt mit dem Künstler Vito Acconci, zeigt ein radikales Design, das weder Fenster noch Türen im traditionellen Sinne besitzt. Vielmehr handelt es sich hierbei um eine anpassungsfähige Reaktion auf das »Nomaden«-Leben im modernen Großstadtdschungel, die mit einem sehr schmalen Budget verwirklicht wurde und dazu bestimmt ist, schon bald durch einen neuen Entwurf ersetzt zu werden.

Nirgendwo ist das Verhältnis zwischen Auftraggeber und Architekt von größerer Bedeutung als beim Entwurf und der Fertigstellung von Privathäusern. Eine Reihe Individualisten betrachtet die Architektur als einen Weg zur Verwirklichung ihrer Träume oder zur Bestätigung ihres Erfolgs. Im besten Falle können diese Häuser zu eigenständigen Kunstwerken werden – wenn auch nicht immer im Hinblick auf ihren Grad an Komfort und Bequemlichkeit, dann doch zumindest in Bezug auf ihr Erscheinungsbild. Zwei in diesem Buch vorgestellte bemerkenswerte Häuser von sehr unterschiedlichen Architekten verdeutlichen die Bandbreite architektonischer Reaktionen auf die eigentümliche Suche der Amerikaner nach »eindrucksvollen« Privathäusern. Der 1926 in Argentinien geborene Architekt Cesar Pelli ist einer der bekanntesten Schöpfer großer Bauten. Obwohl zu seinen jüngsten Projekten u.a. das World Financial Center in New York und zwei 85-stöckige Türme in Kuala Lumpur gehören, nahm er den Auftrag für dieses ungewöhnliche Privathaus im Westen der Vereinigten Staaten an. Paul Goldberger kommentierte das Gebäude in der »New York Times« folgendermaßen: »Das Design verschmilzt Welten

Cesar Pelli, Kuala Lumpur City Center, Phase 1,
Petronas Towers, Kuala Lumpur, Malaysia,
1992–96.

Cesar Pelli, Kuala Lumpur City Center, Phase 1,
Petronas Towers, Kuala Lumpur, Malaysia,
1992–96.

Cesar Pelli, Kuala Lumpur City Center, Phase 1,
Petronas Towers, Kuala Lumpur, Malaisie,
1992–96.

urbaine contemporaine, réalisée pour un budget très limité,
et destinée à être remplacé rapidement par une autre solution.

Nulle part la relation client-architecte n'est plus délicate
que dans l'élaboration des plans et la construction de résidences privées. Les difficultés économiques n'ont pas fait
diminuer le nombre des nouveaux milliardaires américains,
et un certain nombre de ces personnages hautement indi-
vidualistes voient dans l'architecture le moyen de réaliser
leurs rêves ou de confirmer leur réussite. En termes
d'apparence si ce n'est toujours de confort, leurs habita-
tions peuvent parfois prétendre à un véritable statut
d'œuvre d'art. Dans les pages qui suivent, deux remar-
quables demeures signées de deux architectes très différents montrent la gamme des réponses que l'architecture
peut apporter à cette quête typiquement américaine de la
«grande» résidence privée. Cesar Pelli, né en Argentine en
1926, est l'un des créateurs d'immeubles de grande hauteur les plus connus au monde. Ses récentes réalisations
vont du World Financial Center à New York, à des tours
jumelles de 85 étages à Kuala Lumpur. Pelli n'en a pas
moins accepté la commande exceptionnelle d'une maison
située dans l'Ouest des Etats-Unis. Comme Paul Goldberger, du «New York Times», l'a écrit: «Le design fusionne
deux univers qui normalement n'ont rien à voir: le style
profilé du modernisme marié à la chaleureuse intimité d'un
chalet de bois. Malgré son gigantisme et son luxe (elle a
coûté plusieurs millions de dollars), cette demeure finit par
célébrer la terre plus qu'elle ne la défie. Elle possède non
seulement une réelle chaleur humaine, mais aussi la qualité
essentielle de tout art, c'est-à-dire la capacité à nous faire
voir le monde d'une façon légèrement différente.»[1]

Avec sa maison «T», comparée à juste titre à une sculpture de Richard Serra, Simon Ungers, né à Cologne, en Allemagne en 1957, a mis en forme de façon très différente le
désir de son client d'une maison-bibliothèque. Ungers a en
fait davantage réalisé d'œuvres d'art – sous forme d'installations – que de constructions, mais la tendance à l'architecture en tant qu'art, notable au cours du XXe siècle,
paraît, entre autres, avoir été renforcée par la conjoncture
des années 90. Plus que l'art, l'architecture est naturelle-

13

but it is not to be excluded that such a difficult period might prove to be far more productive and innovative than one of expansion and excess.

Home on the Range

Another variable of considerable importance in the evolution of contemporary American architecture is the geographic diversity of the country. When the dynamism of one area slows, another may well be in a period of expansion. The example of the city of Phoenix, Arizona is interesting in this respect. A quiet provincial city of 100 000 inhabitants after World War II, this southwestern urban center now has a population of 2.25 million people and covers an area of over 5000 square kilometers. With such a phenomenal rate of expansion, the cultural and municipal facilities lagged behind the growth of Phoenix. It took the will of an individual, Terry Goddard, who was mayor from 1984 to 1990, to launch a number of projects in keeping with the new status of Phoenix as America's eighth largest city. Despite subsequent cutbacks, one of the most ambitious projects of that period, the new central library has just been completed by the architect Will Bruder. Bruder thus joins the growing ranks of architects from the southwest who have gained a national reputation recently. Like Antoine Predock, now considered one of the foremost American designers, Bruder bases his concept in the very particular light and forms of the desert. Like Predock, he also seeks an almost mystical relationship between this region, whose history should be measured less in terms of European settlement, than of the vast expanses of geological time, and his architecture. Although Predock has already built in California, or even at EuroDisney in France, the strong message coming from the southwestern United States is that architecture must now project a strong sense of place and time. The monolithic esthetics of Modernism, willfully divorced from any precise notion of history, give way to a wide variety of approaches, almost all aware of the past, and each firmly rooted in local circumstances.

Although energy conservation is not necessarily a concern for the architects of southern California, where the year-round mild climate makes the use of chainlink fence

miteinander, die unter normalen Gesichtspunkten nichts miteinander gemein haben: Die Eleganz des Modernismus in Kombination mit der umschmeichelnden Wärme einer Blockhütte. Und trotz seiner Größe und luxuriösen Ausstattung (das Haus kostete mehrere Millionen Dollar) ist es letztendlich viel mehr ein Hohelied auf das Land und die Umgebung, als ein sich ihr widersetzender Fremdkörper. Das Haus besitzt menschliche Wärme, aber auch die unentbehrliche Eigenschaft eines jeden Kunstwerks: nämlich die Fähigkeit, uns die Welt mit etwas anderen Augen sehen zu lassen.«[1]

Der 1957 in Köln geborene Simon Ungers näherte sich dem Wunsch seines Kunden nach einem kombinierten Wohn- und Bibliotheksgebäude auf völlig andere Weise, indem er das T-House schuf, das zu Recht mit einer Skulptur von Richard Serra verglichen wurde. Tatsächlich hat Ungers bis heute bedeutend mehr Installationskunstwerke als Gebäude geschaffen, aber der Trend, Architektur als Kunst zu betrachten – der sich durch das gesamte 20. Jahrhundert zieht – scheint durch die neuen Gegebenheiten der 90er Jahre verstärkt worden zu sein. Die Architektur unterliegt natürlich (stärker als die Kunst) dem Gebot, sich angesichts der sich verändernden wirtschaftlichen Bedingungen rasch weiterzuentwickeln. Rezession und Armut mögen nicht die angenehmsten Konditionen sein, aber es ist nicht auszuschließen, daß sich eine solch schwierige Zeit als erheblich produktiver und innovativer erweist als eine Periode des Überflusses und der wirtschaftlichen Expansion.

»Home on the Range«

Von beachtlicher Bedeutung für die Entwicklung der amerikanischen Architektur ist die geographische Vielfalt des Landes. Während in einer Region das Wirtschaftswachstum nachläßt, kann sich eine andere Region gerade in einer Phase der Expansion befinden. In diesem Zusammenhang ist das Beispiel der Stadt Phoenix in Arizona besonders interessant. Diese nach dem Zweiten Weltkrieg 100 000 Einwohner zählende, ruhige Provinzstadt im Südwesten der Vereinigten Staaten ist heute eine Großstadt mit 2,25 Millionen Menschen, die sich über eine Fläche von

ment obligée de s'adapter rapidement à l'évolution économique. La récession et la pénurie ne sont peut-être pas des
contraintes agréables, mais il n'est pas exclu que cette
époque difficile se révèle bien plus productive et innovante
que celle de l'expansion et des excès.

Retour à la terre

La diversité géographique des Etats-Unis a marqué l'évolution de l'architecture américaine contemporaine. Lorsque
le dynamisme d'une région s'essouffle, une autre peut très
bien connaître une période d'expansion. L'exemple de
Phoenix, en Arizona, est intéressant à cet égard. Tranquille
et banale ville de province de 100 000 habitants à la fin
de la seconde guerre mondiale, elle compte maintenant
2 250 000 habitants et s'étend sur plus de 5 000 km². Les
services municipaux et les équipements culturels n'ont pas
suivi ce rythme phénoménal. Il a fallu la volonté d'un indi-
vidu, Terry Goddard, maire de 1984 à 1990, pour lancer un
certain nombre de projets à l'échelle du nouveau statut de
huitième ville des Etats-Unis. Malgré certaines coupes budgétaires, la nouvelle bibliothèque centrale, l'un des plus
ambitieux projets de cette période, vient d'être achevée par
Will Bruder, qui rejoint du même coup le cercle de ces
architectes du Sud-Ouest américain qui se sont fait récemment connaître au niveau national. Comme Antoine Predock, Bruder a fondé ses travaux sur la lumière et les
formes du désert. Comme son confrère, il recherche une
relation presque mystique entre une région dont l'histoire
se mesure moins en termes de peuplement qu'à l'aune des
ères géologiques, et son architecture. Si Predock a déjà
construit en Californie, et même en France, le message fort
que nous envoie ce Sud-Ouest est que l'architecture doit
projeter un sens puissant du temps et du lieu. L'esthétique
monolithique du modernisme, volontairement coupée de
référent historique, cède la place à une grande variété
d'approches, presque toutes conscientes du passé, chacune fermement enracinée dans les contextes locaux.

Bien que l'économie d'énergie ne soit pas forcément un
souci primordial dans cette Californie du Sud où la douceur
du climat justifie l'utilisation de la clôture légère et du
carton ondulé, la pression économique évidente sur l'archi-

Will Bruder, Phoenix Central Library, Phoenix,
Arizona, 1988–95. View of the main entrance.

Will Bruder, Phoenix Central Library, Phoenix,
Arizona, 1988–95. Haupteingang.

Will Bruder, Phoenix Central Library, Phoenix,
Arizona, 1988–95. Entrée principale.

Peter Forbes, House on Mount Desert Island,
Maine, 1991–93. View of the main stairway.

Peter Forbes, Privathaus, Mount Desert Island,
Maine, 1991–93. Haupttreppe.

Peter Forbes, maison sur Mount Desert Island,
Maine, 1991–93. Vue de l'escalier principal.

and corrugated board something less than laughable, the obvious economic pressure on contemporary architecture, together with a desire to counter the excesses of the 1980s, have brought a resurgence of "green" buildings. Ecological concerns had their time of popularity in the 1970s and some ideas, and figures who were already prominent then, have returned in strength. The SITE group, founded by James Wines and his partners in the early 1970s have turned their attention largely to structures which are overtly ecological. A recent project, a scheme to assist the decommissioning of a nuclear power station in North Wales is a fascinating attempt to link the possibilities of architecture to the resolution of one of the most serious global pollution problems. It seems that James Wines's natural tendency to want to drape green plants all over buildings, might actually speed the decontamination of radioactive sites in a process known as "phyto-remediation."

The concern about the possibility of recycling building products, of being energy conscious, and of enjoying nature itself is a declared aim of much contemporary architecture across the world. Reputed as one of the worst offenders in the world insofar as energy waste is concerned, Americans, albeit in small numbers, have again become aware of the potential for catastrophe inscribed in their habits. Despite its large glass surfaces, the house designed by Peter Forbes on Mount Desert Island, Maine published in this book is an example of this trend, especially because of its open, simple design.

Forms in Mutation
In his acceptance speech for the 1989 Pritzker Prize, Frank O. Gehry described some of the factors which formed his style: "My artist friends, like Jasper Johns, Bob Rauschenberg, Ed Kienholz and Claes Oldenburg, were working with very inexpensive materials – broken wood and paper – and they were making beauty. These were not superficial details, they were direct, and raised the question in my mind of what beauty was. I chose to use the craft available, and to work with craftsmen and make a virtue out of their limitations. Painting had an immediacy that I craved for in architecture. I explored the process of new construction

über 5000 Quadratkilometern erstreckt. Bei dieser Expansionsrate konnten die städtischen und kulturellen Einrichtungen dem Wachstum der Stadt nur hinterherhinken. Es bedurfte des Durchsetzungsvermögens eines Terry Goddard (1984–90 Bürgermeister von Phoenix), um eine Reihe von Projekten in Gang zu bringen, die dem neuen Status von Phoenix als achtgrößter Stadt Amerikas gerecht werden. Trotz der nachfolgenden Kürzungen und Einschränkungen konnte eines der anspruchsvollsten Projekte dieser Zeit, die neue Zentralbibliothek, kürzlich von dem Architekten Will Bruder fertiggestellt werden. Bruder zählt somit ebenfalls zur wachsenden Gruppe von Architekten aus dem Südwesten, die sich in jüngster Zeit einen nationalen Ruf erworben haben. Ebenso wie bei Antoine Predock, der heute als einer der führenden amerikanischen Architekten gilt, basiert auch Bruders Konzept auf dem ganz speziellen Licht und den Formen der Wüste. Und genau wie Predock strebt auch Bruder ein nahezu mystisches Verhältnis zwischen dieser Region und seiner eigenen Architektur an. Obwohl Predock bereits in Kalifornien und sogar für Euro-Disney in Frankreich tätig war, lautet die unüberhörbare Botschaft der Architekten im Südwesten der Vereinigten Staaten, daß die Architektur heute ein deutliches Gefühl für Ort und Zeit vermitteln muß. Die monolithische Ästhetik des Modernismus, der bewußt auf jedwede exakte historische Anspielung verzichtet, macht einer Vielzahl von Ansätzen Platz, die nahezu alle die Vergangenheit miteinbeziehen und fest in den örtlichen Gegebenheiten verwurzelt sind.

Obwohl Energiesparmaßnahmen nicht notwendigerweise in die Überlegungen eines Architekten in Südkalifornien einfließen müssen, hat der starke wirtschaftliche Druck auf die zeitgenössische Architektur zusammen mit dem Wunsch, die Auswüchse der 80er Jahre wieder auszugleichen, den Ruf nach »grünen« Gebäuden wieder aufleben lassen. Die Architektengruppe SITE, Anfang der 70er Jahre von James Wines und seinen Partnern gegründet, konzentriert ihre Aufmerksamkeit hauptsächlich auf Bauwerke, die als offenkundig ökologisch bezeichnet werden können. Ihr jüngstes Projekt, ein Entwurf für die Stillegung eines Atomkraftwerks in Nordwales, stellt den faszinierenden Versuch dar, die Möglichkeiten der Architektur mit der

tecture contemporaine, et, dans le même temps, le désir de contrer les excès des années 80, ont conduit à une résurgence des bâtiments «verts». L'écologie avait connu une relative faveur dans les années 70, et certaines idées et personnages éminents de cette époque sont revenus au premier plan. Le groupe SITE, fondé par James Wines et ses associés au début des années 70, a beaucoup travaillé sur des bâtiments qui se voulaient écologiques. Un de ses récents projets, un programme de démantèlement d'une centrale nucléaire du nord du Pays de Galles, est une fascinante tentative de mobilisation des ressources de l'architecture pour résoudre l'un des plus sérieux problèmes actuels de pollution globale. Il semble que la tendance naturelle de Wines à couvrir de verdure ses réalisations puisse en l'occurrence réellement accélérer la décontamination des sites radioactifs grâce à un processus bio-chimique, le phyto-traitement.

Recyclage des matériaux de construction, économies d'énergie, protection de la nature: tels sont les objectifs déclarés de beaucoup d'architectes contemporains partout dans le monde. Réputés être les plus grands gaspilleurs d'énergie du monde, les Américains commencent à mesurer le risque de catastrophe inscrit dans leurs habitudes de vie. Malgré ses larges surfaces vitrées, la maison dessinée par Peter Forbes sur Mount Desert Island (Maine), reproduite plus loin, illustre cette nouvelle conscience, en particulier dans la simplicité de son plan ouvert.

Formes en mutation
Dans son discours d'acceptation du Prix Pritzker en 1989, Frank O. Gehry avait décrit quelques éléments de son style: «Mes amis artistes, comme Jasper Johns, Bob Rauschenberg, Ed Kienholz et Claes Oldenburg travaillaient avec des matériaux bon marché – bouts de bois et papier – et savaient en tirer de la beauté. Il ne s'agissait pas de détails superficiels. Leurs propositions étaient directes, et soulevaient en moi des questions sur la nature même de la beauté. J'ai choisi d'utiliser des techniques à ma portée, de travailler avec des artisans, et de faire de leurs limites vertu. J'ai analysé les nouveaux matériaux de construction pour tenter de leur conférer un sentiment et un esprit de

SITE, Trawsfynydd Nuclear Power Station Decommissioning Project, North Wales, 1994. Watercolor drawing by James Wines.

SITE, Trawsfynydd Nuclear Power Station Decommissioning Project, Nordwales, 1994. Aquarellzeichnung von James Wines.

SITE, Projet de mise hors service de la centrale nucléaire de Trawsfynydd, nord du Pays de Galles, 1994. Dessin à l'aquarelle de James Wines.

materials to try giving feeling and spirit to form. In trying to find the essence of my own expression, I fantasized that I was an artist standing before a white canvas deciding what the first move should be." This description is in many ways faithful to the appearance of the built work of Gehry. As Thomas Fisher wrote recently, "Not only do his buildings assert the fundamentally artistic nature of architecture, but their forms draw almost literally from other arts, sculpture and theater especially."[2]

Despite the considerable difficulties raised by the Disney Concert Hall in Los Angeles, Gehry is forging ahead with what will be his most sculptural and perhaps largest building. The 24000 square meter Guggenheim Museum in Spain is scheduled to open in the summer of 1997. Located in the center of a cultural district formed by the Museo de Bellas Artes, the University of Duesto and the Opera House this $100 million titanium, limestone and glass "metallic flower" will take a form which rarely if ever has been imagined in architecture. Using a highly advanced three dimensional modeling program called CATIA, devised by the French aerospace company Dassault to map the curved surfaces of fighter planes, Gehry's office has been able to give life to forms so complex that they would have been unimaginable in architecture just a few years ago. By coupling his own penchant for the arts and sculpture in particular to such powerful computer tools, Frank O. Gehry is opening a new horizon in architecture. Where the economics of manufacturing once imposed linear geometric designs on architects, the affordability of computer technology and the manufacturing capacity that has sprung up with it now make almost any design, no matter how apparently complex, possible. This is a real revolution, but one which may not yet have been fully mastered by Frank O. Gehry or anyone else. Speaking of the "Santa Monica School" as a whole, John Morris Dixon has written, "One of the serious criticisms directed at this body of work is that its sculptural preoccupation takes precedence over the shaping of effective interior space. We don't necessarily want to carry on our lives inside tilted cones or angular crystalline forms."[3]

Although his body of completed work is quite limited, the New York architect Peter Eisenman has actively

Bewältigung eines der schwerwiegendsten umwelttechnischen Probleme der heutigen Zeit zu verbinden. Der Wunsch, Baumaterialien weitestgehend zu recyclen, energie- und umweltbewußt zu bauen und sich an der Natur zu erfreuen, ist weltweit das erklärte Ziel zeitgenössischer Architekten. Die in bezug auf Energieverschwendung als schlimmste Missetäter gebrandmarkten Amerikaner werden sich – wenn auch bisher nur in kleinen Gruppen – mehr und mehr des hohen Katastrophenpotentials ihres Verhaltens bewußt. Das in diesem Buch vorgestellte, von Peter Forbes auf Mount Desert Island in Maine entworfene Haus ist (trotz seiner großen Glasflächen) aufgrund des offenen, schlichten Designs ein gutes Beispiel für diesen Trend.

Formen im Wandel
Bei seiner Dankesrede für den Pritzker Preis 1989 beschrieb Frank O. Gehry einige der Faktoren, die seinen Stil prägen: »Meine Künstlerfreunde – Jasper Johns, Bob Rauschenberg, Ed Kienholz und Claes Oldenburg – arbeiteten mit sehr preiswerten Materialien wie Abfallholz und Papier und schufen damit Werke von großer Schönheit. Die Malerei besitzt eine Unmittelbarkeit, nach der ich in der Architektur vergebens suchte. Ich erforschte die Herstellung neuer Baumaterialien, in dem Versuch, Formen Gefühl und Geist zu verleihen. Auf der Suche nach dem Wesentlichen in meinem eigenen Ausdrucksvermögen stellte ich mir vor, ich wäre ein Künstler, der vor einer weißen Leinwand steht und darüber nachdenkt, wie der erste Schritt aussehen soll.« Diese Beschreibung entspricht dem Erscheinungsbild von Gehrys Œuvre. Thomas Fisher kommentierte seine Bauwerke kürzlich folgendermaßen: »Nicht nur seine Gebäude dokumentieren die grundlegend künstlerische Natur der Architektur, sondern auch ihre Formen sind von anderen Künsten, insbesondere der Bildhauerei und dem Theater, buchstäblich inspiriert.«[2]

Trotz der beträchtlichen Schwierigkeiten, die die Disney Concert Hall in Los Angeles bereitete, macht Gehry bei seinem skulpturalen und wahrscheinlich größten Gebäude allmählich Fortschritte. Das 24000m² große Guggenheim Museum in Bilbao, Spanien, soll im Sommer 1997 eröffnet werden. Die in der Mitte eines durch das Museo de Bellas

Left and below: Frank O. Gehry, Vitra Headquarters, Basel, Switzerland, 1988/1992–94.

Links und unten: Frank O. Gehry, Vitra Headquarters, Basel, Schweiz, 1988/1992–94.

A gauche et ci-dessous: Frank O. Gehry, siège social de Vitra, Bâle, Suisse, 1988/1992–94.

forme. En essayant de trouver l'essence de ma propre expression, j'ai imaginé que j'étais un artiste debout devant sa toile blanche, libre de décider du premier mouvement qu'il allait entreprendre.» Cette description est à de nombreux égards fidèle à l'aspect de ce que construit Gehry. Comme l'a récemment noté Thomas Fisher: «Non seulement ses bâtiments affirment la nature fondamentalement artistique de l'architecture, mais leurs formes sont littéralement tirées d'autres expressions artistiques, en particulier du théâtre et de la sculpture.»[2]

Gehry poursuit actuellement la réalisation de ce qui sera son bâtiment le plus sculptural, et peut-être le plus vaste. Les 24000m[2] du musée de Bilbao (Espagne) devraient ouvrir au public en 1997. Implantée au centre d'un ensemble culturel formé par le Museo de Bellas Artes, l'Université de Duesto et l'opéra, cette «fleur métallique» de 100 millions de $, en titane, verre et calcaire, prendra une forme sans doute inédite dans l'histoire de l'architecture. A l'aide d'un logiciel perfectionné travaillant en trois dimensions, CATIA, mis au point par le constructeur d'avions français Dassault pour tracer les courbes de ses chasseurs, l'agence de Gehry a donné vie à des formes si complexes qu'elles auraient été inimaginables en architecture il y a quelques années seulement. En associant ses propres penchants pour les arts – et la sculpture en particulier – à un outil informatique de grande puissance, Frank O. Gehry ouvre de nouveaux horizons. Là où l'économie de fabrication imposait aux architectes des plans géométriques et linéaires, l'avènement de la technologie informatique et les capacités de réalisation qui en découlent rendent n'importe quel projet presque possible. Nous sommes en présence d'une véritable révolution, mais qui n'a peut-être pas encore été maîtrisée par Frank O. Gehry, ou qui que ce soit d'autre. Parlant de l'Ecole de Santa Monica, John Morris Dixon a ainsi pu écrire: «L'une des critiques les plus sérieuses adressées à ce projet est que sa préoccupation sculpturale prend le pas sur la mise en forme efficace de l'espace intérieur. Nous ne souhaitons pas particulièrement vivre à l'intérieur de cônes tronqués ou de formes cristallines anguleuses.»[3]

Bien que le corpus de ses œuvres achevées soit assez

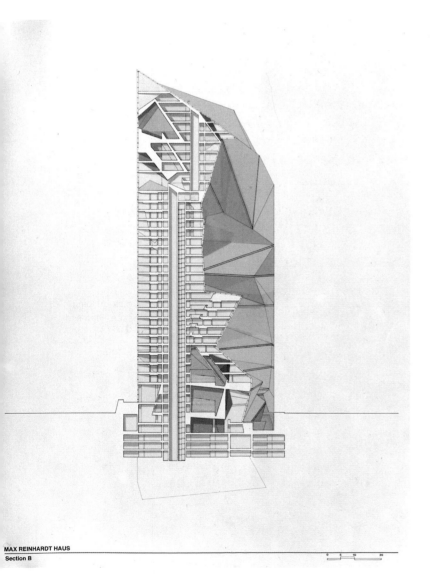

MAX REINHARDT HAUS
Section B

0 5 10 20

explored the area of computer assisted design in recent years. One of his most controversial unbuilt works is the Max Reinhardt Haus in Berlin. The highly unusual shape of this twin tower was derived from the manipulation of a Möbius strip (a band having only one side, made by turning one end of a rectangular ribbon 180° and then fastening it to the other end) on a computer. Though the end result is sculptural, Peter Eisenman's approach is much more theoretical than it is esthetic. As he says, "I am interested in internal questions such as those of profile, repetition, movement, of the relation of object to subject perception. This is what I would call a fluid architecture. It has a gelatinous quality. We are using a computer technique called morphing. There is very little philosophy that I can read today which is going to help me with the internal problems of memory – that is to say the memory of the computer versus that of the human brain. The random access memory of the computer gives you enormous possibilities which human memory does not have access to."[4]

Peter Eisenman is undoubtedly even less interested than Frank O. Gehry in Vitruvian commodiousness; in fact he proudly declares his desire to make buildings "uncomfortable." In the case of the Max Reinhardt Haus he has also flaunted local height restrictions to an extent that its actual construction, at least in the original form, seems unlikely. Eisenman declares a desire to "break critical ground" in his work, and his exploration of the theme of the random access memory of the computer as opposed to that of even the most inventive unassisted human designer is certainly fertile ground to break. Whether Frank O. Gehry or Peter Eisenman are really the architects who will show what impact computers can have on design remains to be seen, but so many of their colleagues are interested in the same subject that it seems that architecture is on the threshold of a new era.

Contemporary interest in technology or in new ways to design and use light are also a common point between two younger architects mentioned above. Eric Owen Moss, who has proven his capacity to generate new types of spaces not only in his Culver City renovation projects, but also in the Lawson-Westen House in Brentwood has used

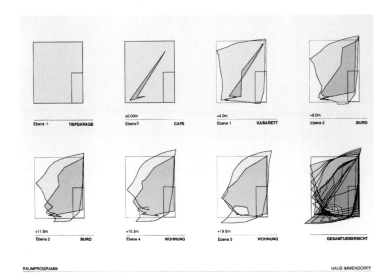

Pages 20/21: Peter Eisenman, Max Reinhardt Haus, Berlin, Germany, 1992. Computer drawings.

Seite 20/21: Peter Eisenman, Max Reinhardt Haus, Berlin, Deutschland, 1992. Computerzeichnungen.

Pages 20/21: Peter Eisenman, Max Reinhardt Haus, Berlin, Allemagne, 1992. Dessins par ordinateur.

Artes, die Universidad de Duesto und das Opernhaus stark kulturell geprägten Viertels gelegene, 100 Millionen Dollar teure »Metallblüte« aus Titan, Kalkstein und Glas wird sich durch eine Form auszeichnen, die man sich bisher in der Architektur kaum vorstellen konnte. Mit Hilfe eines hochentwickelten dreidimensionalen Computerprogramms namens CATIA, das die französische Flugzeuggesellschaft Dassault zur Kartographie der geschwungenen Oberflächen von Kampfflugzeugen entwickelt hat, war Gehrys Büro in der Lage, hochkomplexe Formen zum Leben zu erwecken, die noch vor wenigen Jahren in der Architektur völlig undenkbar gewesen wären. Durch die Kombination solch mächtiger Computerwerkzeuge mit seiner eigenen Vorliebe für die Künste im allgemeinen und die Bildhauerei im besonderen öffnet Frank O. Gehry neue Horizonte in der Architektur. Während früher die Fertigungsökonomie den Architekten lineare geometrische Entwürfe abverlangte, ist heute dank der erschwinglichen Computertechnologie und der damit verbundenen Produktionskapazität nahezu jedes Design möglich – unabhängig von seiner Komplexität. Das ist die eigentliche Revolution, die aber wahrscheinlich weder von Frank O. Gehry noch von jemand anderem bisher vollständig beherrscht wird. Zur »Santa Monica School« befragt, schrieb John Morris Dixon: »Einer der Hauptkritikpunkte an diesen Bauwerken ist die Tatsache, daß die vorwiegende Beschäftigung mit dem Skulpturalen Vorrang erlangt vor der Gestaltung effektiver Innenräume. Wir möchten unser Leben nicht notwendigerweise in schräggelegten Kegeln oder winkligen kristallinen Formen fristen.«[3]

Obwohl Peter Eisenman bisher nur relativ wenige Bauwerke errichtet hat, beschäftigte sich dieser New Yorker Architekt in den letzten Jahren sehr intensiv mit dem Thema »CAD« (Computer assisted design). Eines seiner kontroversesten, noch nicht gebauten Projekte ist das Max Reinhardt Haus in Berlin. Die in hohem Maße ungewöhnliche Form dieses Doppelturms entstand durch die computergesteuerte Abwandlung eines Möbinsschen Bandes (einer einseitigen Fläche, die entsteht, indem man einen rechteckigen Streifen um 180° dreht und am anderen Ende befestigt). Obwohl es sich bei dem Endergebnis um eine skulpturale Form handelt, ist Eisenmans Ansatz weniger limité, l'architecte new-yorkais Peter Eisenman explore activement depuis quelques années les possibilités de création assistée par ordinateur. L'une de ses propositions les plus controversées – et non encore construite – est la Max Reinhardt Haus à Berlin. La forme très inhabituelle de ces tours jumelles vient de la manipulation d'un ruban de Möbius (forme constituée d'un ruban de papier dont on tord une extrémité à 180° avant de la fixer à l'autre, ce qui permet d'obtenir un anneau à une seule face) sur ordinateur. Bien que le résultat final soit spectaculaire, l'approche de Peter Eisenman est beaucoup plus théorique qu'esthétique: «Je m'intéresse aux problèmes internes, comme le profil, la répétition, le mouvement, la relation entre l'objet et le sujet dans la perception. C'est ce que j'appellerai une architecture fluide. Elle possède une qualité «gélatineuse». Nous utilisons une technique informatique appelée le *morphing*. Il n'y a pas grand-chose dans la philosophie d'aujourd'hui qui puisse m'aider à explorer les problèmes intrinsèques de la mémoire, c'est-à-dire la mémoire de l'ordinateur face au cerveau humain. La mémoire à accès aléatoire de l'ordinateur vous donne d'énormes possibilités hors de portée de la mémoire humaine.»[4]

Peter Eisenman est sans aucun doute encore moins intéressé que Frank O. Gehry par la spatialité vitruvienne. En fait il affiche fièrement son désir de réaliser des bâtiments «inconfortables». Dans le cas de la Max Reinhardt Haus, il s'est également joué de la réglementation locale sur les hauteurs, ce qui rend la construction de ces immeubles assez improbable, du moins sous leur forme originale. Il parle de son désir de «dépasser le seuil critique» dans son travail, et son exploration du thème de la mémoire à accès aléatoire de l'ordinateur, opposée à celle du créateur humain le plus inventif et non assisté, ouvre certainement la voie à de nouvelles percées. Que Frank O. Gehry ou Peter Eisenman soient réellement les architectes qui vont illustrer l'impact des ordinateurs sur la création architecturale reste à prouver, mais le nombre de leurs confrères intéressés par le même sujet est si élevé qu'il semble bien que l'architecture se trouve ici à l'aube d'une ère nouvelle.

L'intérêt contemporain pour la technologie ou les nouvelles techniques de dessin et d'utilisation de la lumière

Steven Holl, Storefront for Art and Architecture,
New York, 1994.

computer assisted design to imagine the Ince Theater. This 450 seat theater has a form created by the interaction of three spheres. Not as far blown out of proportion as the Max Reinhardt Haus or the Guggenheim Museum, this project seems to represent a more modest and probably more viable approach to the use of the computer. Even more modest and thoughtful, Steven Holl's renovation of the D.E. Shaw and Company offices in New York, makes use of a painterly system of color refraction, and an unusual sense of space. Holl who was selected to design the new Helsinki Museum of Modern Art, has often written about the direction of contemporary architecture, taking into account not only the emerging possibilities of the "information society," but also the realities of local conflict and degeneration. As he says, "as in Ovid's *Metamorphoses*, 'Knowledge of the world means dissolving the solidity of the world.' So in the paradigm shifts of today all material heaviness seems to disappear. The devices propelling this world of information-flow utilize non-material impulses in a visual field. Computer aided design, motion control, virtual reality, magnetic resonance imaging, computer animation, synthetic holography – to name a few of the present means – are all rapidly developing vectors of information which are characterized by motion and light. The horrors of current events are projected into domestic living rooms everywhere. Likewise, a soulless fashionable commercialism characterizes many of the arts. As we allow ourselves to be victims of unconscious habits, skipping from gesture to final image, we leap over the simmering of feelings and thoughts that carries a slow-developing intensity of ideas and forms and their interior spatial consequences. An architecture fusing these worlds of flow and difference is inconsistent by nature. As the differences of individual circumstance are essential, this architecture must accept Emerson's admonition, 'consistency is the hobgoblin of little minds.' Rather than conforming to technological or stylistic uniformity, this architecture would be open to the irrationalities of place. It would resist the homogenizing tendencies of standardization... A new architecture must be formed that is simultaneously aligned with transcultural continuity and with the poetic expression of individual situations and communities."[5]

ästhetisch als vielmehr hochtheoretisch: »Ich interessiere mich für interne Aspekte wie etwa die Frage nach dem Profil, dem Wiederholungsgrad, der Bewegung, dem Verhältnis zwischen Objekt und subjektiver Wahrnehmung. Das würde ich als fließende Architektur bezeichnen. Sie besitzt eine gallertartige Qualität. Wir verwenden dazu eine Computertechnik namens ›Morphing‹.«[4]

Peter Eisenman zeigt zweifellos noch weniger Interesse an vitruvscher Geräumigkeit als Frank O. Gehry. Statt dessen verkündet er stolz den Wunsch, seine Gebäude »unbequem« zu konzipieren. Im Falle des Max Reinhardt Hauses hat Eisenman sich darüber hinaus auch derart über die örtlichen Bauhöhenvorschriften hinweggesetzt, daß eine Durchführung des Vorhabens – zumindest der Originalpläne – sehr unwahrscheinlich ist. Eisenman betont, daß er mit seinen Werken »Neuland erschließen« will, und seine Erforschung des Direktzugriffsspeichers des Computers, im Gegensatz zum Gehirn eines noch so erfindungsreichen, nicht computergestützten menschlichen Designers, ist zweifellos sehr fruchtbares Neuland. Es bleibt abzuwarten, ob Frank O. Gehry und Peter Eisenman wirklich diejenigen Architekten sind, die den Einfluß des Computers auf das Design veranschaulichen werden; aber es interessieren sich so viele ihrer Kollegen für das gleiche Thema, daß der Eindruck entsteht, daß sich die Architektur an der Schwelle zu einer neuen Ära befindet.

Das heutige Interesse an Technologie und neuen Wegen der Gestaltung und der Verwendung von Licht sind ebenfalls typische Kennzeichen zweier bereits zuvor erwähnter, junger Architekten. Eric Owen Moss, der nicht nur mit seinem Sanierungsprojekt in Culver City, sondern auch mit dem Lawson-Westen House in Brentwood seine Fähigkeit zur Gestaltung neuer Raumtypen bewiesen hat, griff beim Entwurf des Ince Theater ebenfalls auf CAD-Programme zurück. Die Form dieses 450 Sitze umfassenden Theaters basiert auf der computererzeugten Interaktion dreier Kugeln, und da es lange nicht so überproportioniert ist wie das Max Reinhardt Haus oder das Guggenheim Museum, scheint dieses Projekt einen bescheideneren und wahrscheinlich lebensfähigeren Ansatz einer computergestützten Architektur darzustellen.

sont également un point commun entre deux jeunes architectes déjà cités plus haut. Eric Owen Moss, qui a prouvé
sa capacité à générer de nouveaux types d'espaces non
seulement dans ses projets de rénovation de Culver City,
mais également dans sa Lawson-Westen House (Brentwood), s'est servi de l'ordinateur pour imaginer le Ince
Theater. Cette salle de 450 places doit sa forme à l'interaction de trois sphères. Beaucoup moins gigantesque que la
Max Reinhardt Haus ou le musée de Bilbao, ce projet
semble représenter une approche plus raisonnable et probablement plus viable du recours à l'ordinateur.

Encore plus modeste et réfléchie, la rénovation des
bureaux de la société D.E. Shaw & Company par Steven
Holl, à New York, fait appel à un système pictural de réfraction de la couleur, et à un sens peu habituel de l'espace.
Holl, qui a été retenu pour réaliser le nouveau musée d'art
moderne d'Helsinki, a longuement réfléchi au devenir de
l'architecture contemporaine, en prenant en compte non
seulement les nouvelles possibilités de la société de l'information, mais également la réalité des conflits locaux et les
risques de dégénération. Il écrit ainsi: «Dans les ‹Métamor-
phoses› d'Ovide, connaître le monde signifie dissoudre la
solidité du monde. Ainsi dans les glissements paradigma-
tiques d'aujourd'hui, toute pesanteur matérielle semble
disparaître. Les techniques qui permettent de gérer cet univers de flux d'information se servent d'impulsions non
matérielles dans un champ visuel. Le dessin assisté par
ordinateur, le contrôle du mouvement, la réalité virtuelle,
l'imagerie par résonance magnétique, l'animation par
ordinateur, l'holographie de synthèse, pour ne citer que
quelques – uns des moyens actuels, deviennent rapidement des vecteurs d'information caractérisés par le mouvement et la lumière. L'horreur des événements actuels se
retrouve dans la salle de séjour de tout un chacun, partout.
De même, un esprit mercantile à la mode et sans âme
caractérise de nombreuses expressions artistiques. En
nous laissant aller à être les victimes d'habitudes inconsci-
entes, glissant du geste à l'image finale, nous court-circui-
tons la lente élaboration des sentiments et des pensées
qui, en un développement mûri, véhicule l'intensité des
idées et des formes et leurs conséquences spatiales inté-

Steven Holl, D.E. Shaw and Company Office,
New York, 1991–92.

Steven Holl, D.E. Shaw and Company Office,
New York, 1991–92.

Steven Holl, bureaux de D.E. Shaw and
Company, New York, 1991–92.

23

Pages 24/25: Agrest and Gandelsonas, House on Sag Pond, Sagaponack, Long Island, New York, 1990–94.

Seite 24/25: Agrest and Gandelsonas, House on Sag Pond, Sagaponack, Long Island, New York, 1990–94.

Pages 24/25: Agrest and Gandelsonas, maison sur Sag Pond, Sagaponack, Long Island, New York, 1990–94.

Houses as works of art

It would seem that the laws of nature, or at least the laws that govern contemporary architecture can occasionally be suspended when American private houses are concerned. When the right architect and the right client get together, almost anything can happen. The case of Cesar Pelli, builder of skyscrapers and a wealthy, anonymous client in the Western United States has already been mentioned. Another, almost mythical case, a sort of Loch Ness monster of architecture, is the house which Frank O. Gehry is designing for a Cleveland insurance company owner named Peter Lewis. If it is ever built, this 3000 square meter house will cost more than $ 30 million. Despite his declared reticence at being associated with such a blatant display of wealth, Gehry says of Lewis, "he wants to push the limits. He has paid for experiments in technology so that we can use the most advanced materials; he has commissioned Philip Johnson to work along with me doing a guest house; he brought in Richard Serra, Larry Bell and other artists." And what does Lewis have to say? He admits that the house design, which has been eight years in the making "is a blatant bid for immortality on my part – it could be another Fallingwater." As Paul Goldberger, the chief cultural correspondant of *The New York Times*, points out, the rich no longer commission paintings or sculpture as such. Rather, in the United States at least, they look to architecture. "Houses," says Goldberger, "may be the last form of private artistic patronage."[6]

Another astonishing residence, which in this instance actually has been built, is the house on Sag Pond, Long Island designed by Diana Agrest and Mario Gandelsonas for Richard Ekstract. Both born in Argentina, Agrest and Gandelsonas also shared the experience of attending the Ecole Pratique des Hautes Etudes in Paris, studying under Roland Barthes. Respectively professors at Columbia and at Princeton, their approach is undoubtedly theoretical, as evidenced in their own description of this house, which they compare to a "cluster of found objects." Making use of an "analytical decomposition" of architecture based partially in Diana Agrest's study of the films of Sergei Eisenstein, the house, again according to its architects "resists stylistic, typologi-

Noch bescheidener und durchdachter ist Steven Holls bauliche Neugestaltung der Büroräume von D.E. Shaw and Company in New York: Ihr liegt ein malerisches System der Farbbrechung und ein ungewöhnliches Raumgefühl zugrunde. Holl, der für den Entwurf des Museums für zeitgenössische Kunst in Helsinki ausgewählt wurde, schrieb mehrfach über die Richtung, die die zeitgenössische Architektur einschlägt, und berücksichtigte dabei nicht nur die wachsenden Möglichkeiten einer »Informationsgesellschaft«, sondern auch reale Probleme wie örtliche Kontroversen und Degeneration: Wie in den Metamorphosen Ovids bedeutet die »Kenntnis der Welt die Auflösung der Festigkeit dieser Welt«. Also scheint in den heute immanenten paradigmatischen Verschiebungen jegliche materielle Schwere aufgehoben zu sein. Die Mechanismen, die diese Welt des Informationsflusses vorantreiben, nutzen immaterielle Impulse auf einem visuellen Feld. Computergestützte Entwurfstechniken, Bewegungskontrolle, virtuelle Realität, magnetische Resonanzbilder, Computeranimation, synthetische Holographie, um nur einige der heutigen Mittel zu nennen, bei denen es sich um sich rasch entwickelnde Informationsvektoren handelt, deren Charakteristika Bewegung und Licht sind ...

Der Horror der gegenwärtigen Ereignisse wird überall in häusliche Wohnzimmer übertragen. Ebenso ist für etliche Bereiche der Kunst ein seelenloser, modischer Kommerzialismus kennzeichnend. Wenn wir uns erlauben, Opfer unterbewußter Gewohnheiten zu werden und von der Geste zum endgültigen Bild zu springen, übergehen wir das Gären der Gefühle und Gedanken, von dem die sich langsam entwickelnde Intensität der Ideen und Formen sowie ihre inneren räumlichen Folgen getragen werden ...

Eine Architektur, die die Welten des Flusses und der Differenzierung verbindet, ist ihrem Charakter nach inkonsequent. Da die Unterschiede individueller Gegebenheiten wesentlich sind, muß diese Architektur mit Emersons Mahnung »Konsequenz ist das Schreckgespenst der Kleingeister« leben. Anstatt sich technischer oder stilistischer Uniformität anzupassen, würde sich diese Architektur den Irrationalitäten des Ortes öffnen. Sie würde sich den Homogenisierungstendenzen der Standardisierung wider-

rieures. Une architecture fusionnant ces univers de flux et de différences est par nature contradictoire. Comme les différences des situations individuelles sont essentielles, cette architecture doit accepter l'avertissement d'Emerson selon lequel ‹la cohérence est le hochet des petits esprits.› Plutôt que de se conformer à une unité technologique ou stylistique, cette architecture serait ouverte aux irrationalités du lieu. Elle résisterait à la force uniformisante de la standardisation... Une nouvelle architecture doit apparaître, simultanément alignée sur la continuité transculturelle et l'expression poétique des situations individuelles et des communautés humaines.»[5]

La maison en tant qu'œuvre d'art

Il semble que les lois de la nature, ou du moins celles qui gouvernent l'architecture contemporaine peuvent être momentanément abolies pour les résidences privées américaines. Lorsque se produit une vraie rencontre entre un architecte et un client, tout ou presque peut arriver. Le cas du constructeur de tours Cesar Pelli et d'un riche client anonyme a déjà été mentionné. Un autre, presque mythique, est la maison que Frank O. Gehry dessine pour le propriétaire d'une compagnie d'assurance de Cleveland, Peter Lewis. Si elle est jamais construite, ses 3000 m² auront coûté plus de 30 millions de $. Malgré sa réticence déclarée à s'associer à un tel étalage de richesse, Gehry dit de Lewis: «Il veut repousser les limites. Il a financé des expériences dans certaines technologies pour que nous puissions utiliser les matériaux les plus avancés, il a demandé à Philip Johnson de travailler avec moi pour construire la maison des invités; il a amené Richard Serra, Larry Bell, et d'autres artistes.» Et qu'en dit Lewis? Il admet que le dessin de la maison en gestation depuis huit ans est une «prétention affichée à l'immortalité; elle pourrait être une autre Fallingwater.» Comme le fait remarquer Paul Goldberger, principal critique culturel du «New York Times», les gens riches ne commandent plus seulement des peintures ou des sculptures. Aux Etats-Unis du moins, il regardent plutôt du côté de l'architecture. «Les maisons, dit-il, sont peut-être la dernière forme du mécénat artistique privé.»[6]

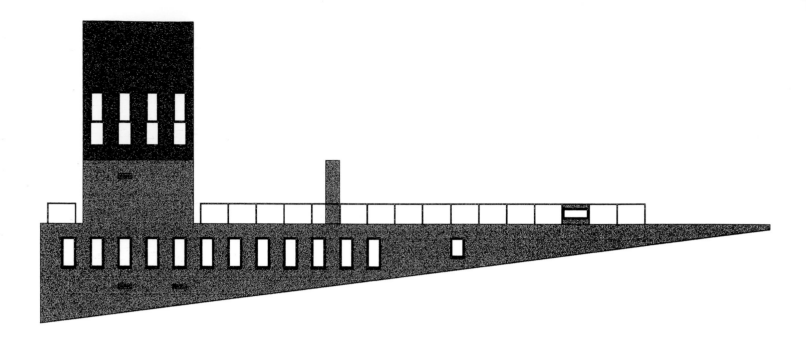

cal, or linguistic classification, drifting between the abstract and the figural, between convention and idiosyncrasy."[7]

Visually arresting, under some angles resembling a fortress or an interconnected web of pre-existing pavilions, the House on Sag Pond was certainly the source of disagreements between the client and the architects. Asked about this, Diana Agrest suggested that the owner had not so much indulged a taste for innovative architecture as he had made a speculative gesture by building a house for himself which he fully intended to resell quickly for a profit. The idea that creative architecture could be an object for speculation, brings such projects all that much closer to contemporary art. As for the suggestion that this house is impractical, as has been written in the press, Diana Agrest replies that it "doesn't have as many leaks as the Villa Savoye."[8]

Perhaps less theoretical and more sculptural in his approach, Simon Ungers has pursued related careers as an installation artist and architect. Tellingly, he compares his T-House (designed with Tom Kinslow) to a sculpture he created with structural steel at Hunter's Point in New York, or with a 1993 work he called "Red Slab in Space." As he says about the latter work, "Red Slab in Space is a monolithic, monochrome construction that integrates the two existing columns of the gallery space and uses them structurally. It is a synthesis of painting, sculpture and architecture and attempts to establish a connection to early modernism, in particular Constructivism, De Stijl and Purism which sought a similar integration. The same could also be said of the T-House."

The house, which is simply named for its shape, is intended to directly express the aspirations of its owner, Lawrence Marcelle. The upper form corresponds to a 14 meter long library, cantilevered over the lower level, which contains a living room, kitchen and bedroom. The intention is apparently to create a symbolic order where the mundane facts of everyday existence support and elevate intellectual pursuits. Despite this functional, indeed programmatic element, Ungers insists on the "seamless, monolithic structure without differentiation of vertical and horizontal surfaces." The first house ever to be built

setzen … Es muß eine neue Architektur entstehen, die sowohl mit transkultureller Kontinuität als auch mit dem poetischen Ausdruck individueller und gemeinschaftlicher Situation vereinbar ist.[5]

Häuser als Kunstwerke

Es scheint, daß die Gesetze der Natur oder zumindest die Gesetze, die die zeitgenössische Architektur beherrschen, gelegentlich außer Kraft gesetzt werden können, falls es sich um Privathäuser in Amerika handelt. Wenn sich der richtige Architekt mit dem richtigen Auftraggeber zusammenfindet, ist fast alles möglich. Das Gemeinschaftsprojekt von Cesar Pelli, Architekt diverser Wolkenkratzer, und einem wohlhabenden, anonymen Kunden im Westen der Vereinigten Staaten wurde bereits erwähnt. Ein weiteres, nahezu mythisches Beispiel – eine Art Ungeheuer von Loch Ness in der Architektur – ist das Haus, das Frank O. Gehry für Peter Lewis, den Inhaber einer Versicherungsgesellschaft in Cleveland, entworfen hat. Falls es jemals gebaut wird, betragen die Baukosten für dieses 3000 m² große Haus mehr als 30 Millionen Dollar. Trotz seiner erklärten Zurückhaltung gegenüber einer solch eklatanten Zurschaustellung von Wohlstand beschreibt Gehry Lewis folgendermaßen:

»Er möchte die Grenzen durchstoßen. Da Lewis umfassende Experimente im Bereich der Bautechnologie finanziert hat, können wir modernste Materialien verwenden; er beauftragte Philip Johnson mit dem Entwurf eines Gästehauses, das wir gemeinsam entwickeln sollen; und er brachte Richard Serra, Larry Bell und andere Künstler ins Spiel.« Und was hat Lewis selbst dazu zu sagen? Er gesteht, daß das Design des Hauses, an dem seit acht Jahren gearbeitet wird, »das offenkundige Trachten nach Unsterblichkeit meinerseits ist. Es könnte ein zweites ›Fallingwater‹ werden«. Paul Goldberger, Chefredakteur für Kultur der »New York Times« erklärt, daß die Wohlhabenden keine Gemälde oder Skulpturen mehr in Auftrag geben, sondern sich statt dessen – zumindest in den Vereinigten Staaten – der Architektur zuwenden. »Häuser«, meint Goldberger, »sind möglicherweise die letzte Form privaten künstlerischen Mäzenatentums.«[6]

Une autre demeure étonnante, mais réalisée celle-là, est la maison sur Sag Pond, à Long Island, dessinée par Diana Agrest et Mario Gandelsonas pour Richard Ekstract. Tous deux nés en Argentine, Agrest et Gandelsonas ont suivi les cours de l'Ecole pratique des Hautes Etudes à Paris, et en particulier l'enseignement de Roland Barthes. Leur approche et sans aucun doute théorique, comme le montre leur description de cette maison qu'ils comparent à «un ensemble d'objets trouvés». Leur travail de «décomposition analytique» de l'architecture, inspiré par le cinéma d'Eisenstein, «résiste à toute classification stylistique, typologique ou linguistique, variant entre abstrait et figuratif, convention et idiosyncrasie».[7]

Arrêtant le regard, faisant penser sous certains angles à une forteresse ou à un enchevêtrement de pavillons pré-existants, la maison sur Sag Pond a certainement provoqué de nombreux désaccords entre le client et ses architectes. Diana Agrest pense que le propriétaire était peut-être moins passionné par l'architecture nouvelle que par la perspective de revendre rapidement la maison avec une belle plus-value. L'idée que l'architecture créative puisse être objet de spéculation rapproche encore davantage ce type de projets de l'art contemporain. A la presse qui fait remarquer que sa maison n'est pas pratique, Diana Agrest répond «qu'elle n'a pas autant de fuites que la Villa Savoye».[8]

Peut-être moins théorique et plus sculptural dans son approche, Simon Ungers poursuit deux carrières parallèles: artiste en installations et architecte. Il est révélateur de l'entendre comparer sa T-House (dessinée avec Tom Kinslow) à une sculpture qu'il a créée avec de l'acier pour le bâtiment de Hunter's Point (New York) ou à une œuvre de 1993 intitulée «Dalle rouge dans l'espace». Il ajoute au sujet de celle-ci: «Dalle rouge dans l'espace est une construction monolithique et monochrome qui intègre structurellement les deux colonnes existantes de l'espace du musée. C'est une synthèse de peinture, de sculpture et d'architecture qui tente d'établir une connexion avec le modernisme primitif – en particulier le constructivisme, De Stijl et le purisme – qui recherchèrent une intégration du même type. On pourrait dire la même chose de T-House.»

Pages 26/27: Simon Ungers and Tom Kinslow, T-House, Wilton, New York, 1988–94.

Seite 26/27: Simon Ungers und Tom Kinslow, T-House, Wilton, New York, 1988–94.

Pages 26/27: Simon Ungers et Tom Kinslow, T-House, Wilton, New York, 1988–94.

Richard Meier, City Hall and Central Library, The Hague, Netherlands, 1986–95. View of the glass facade of the main entrance of the City Hall.

Richard Meier, Rathaus und Zentralbibliothek, Den Haag, Niederlande, 1986–95. Blick auf die verglaste Front des Rathaushaupteinganges.

Richard Meier, hôtel de ville et bibliothèque centrale, La Haye, Pays-Bas, 1986–95. Façade de verre de l'entrée principale de l'hôtel de ville.

entirely with weathering steel, it is easy to take the T-House for a large sculpture.

Modernism with a twist

The large number of experimental forms which seem to be arising from the combined influences of economic and technological change have left some room for interesting variations on the theme of Modernism. Far from being a style of the past, the geometric play of grids created by an architect such as Richard Meier rather assumes a kind of classical purity which can also be appreciated in times of restraint. If Meier in fact needs to answer the criticism which is leveled at him about his ability to do large-scale work, his best answer may be the recently completed City Hall and Library in The Hague.

Clad inside and out with white 85 x 180 cm porcelain-enameled metal panels, this very large group of buildings is located near Centraal Station in The Hague, near the Ministries of Justice and Foreign Affairs on a difficult wedge-shaped site. The alignment of the city streets and of the site inspired Richard Meier to introduce a 12.5° rotation in the two main grids of the structure, corresponding to a 12 story office "slab" and a 10 story block. Between these elements, he has placed the most spectacular feature of the building, a 47 meter high glassed atrium, which is the largest space of its kind in Europe. The City Hall and Public Library building complete the "culture square" of The Hague, which was intended to alleviate the rather sterile atmosphere of neighboring ministries. Theaters by Herman Hertzberger and Rem Koolhaas are very close to the City Hall, on the Turfmarkt and Spui sides, and projects designed by the architects Michael Graves, Cesar Pelli, and KPF are planned for other nearby sites. Three times the size of Meier's Canal+ building in Paris, the City Hall was built with a nearly identical budget. Meier aims here to set a new standard of architectural quality for inexpensive public buildings, surprisingly using computer assisted design for the first time. Despite the massive size of the complex, his work stands out handsomely against the rather bleak modernist background of the area.

Very different, and on a smaller scale, the Banque de

Eine weitere außergewöhnliche Residenz, die allerdings tatsächlich errichtet wurde, ist das House on Sag Pond, Long Island, das Diana Agrest und Mario Gandelsonas für Richard Ekstract entwarfen. Die beiden in Argentinien geborenen Architekten besuchten gemeinsam die Ecole Pratique des Hautes Etudes in Paris und studierten dort bei Roland Barthes. Bei der Beschreibung dieses Hauses zeigt sich deutlich, daß der Ansatz sehr theoretisch ist: Sie vergleichen es mit einer »Anhäufung von Fundstücken«. Von einer »analytischen Dekomposition« der Architektur beeinflußt, die teilweise auf Diana Agrests Studien von Sergei Eisensteins Filmen basiert, widersetzt sich das Haus laut Beschreibung der Architekten »jeder stilistischen, typologischen oder linguistischen Klassifizierung; es treibt zwischen dem Abstrakten und dem Figurativen, zwischen Konvention und Eigenart hin und her.«[7]

Das optisch verblüffende House on Sag Pond, das aus manchem Blickwinkel an eine Festung oder an ein miteinander verbundenes Netz bereits vorhandener Pavillons erinnert, war sicherlich Ursache für die Unstimmigkeiten zwischen Auftraggeber und Architekten. Zu diesen Differenzen befragt, erklärte Diana Agrest, daß der Besitzer weniger seiner Vorliebe für innovative Architektur nachgegeben, als vielmehr ein Spekulationsobjekt gesehen habe, indem er ein Haus für sich bauen ließ, das er mit Gewinn möglichst schnell wieder zu verkaufen gedachte. Die Vorstellung, daß kreative Architektur als Spekulationsobjekt betrachtet wird, läßt diese Projekte in immer größere Nähe zur zeitgenössischen Kunst rücken. Und auf den Vorwurf, daß dieses Haus unpraktisch sei – wie etwa in der Presse behauptet wurde – reagiert Diana Agrest mit den folgenden Worten: »Es weist nicht so viele Mängel auf wie die Villa Savoye.«[8]

Simon Ungers, dessen Ansatz weniger theoretisch als vielmehr skulptural ist, verfolgte bisher zwei eng miteinander verwandte Karrieren: als Installationskünstler und Architekt. Bezeichnenderweise vergleicht er sein T-House (das er zusammen mit Tom Kinslow entwarf) mit einer Skulptur aus Baustahl, die er für den Hunter's Point in New York anfertigte sowie mit einem Werk aus dem Jahre 1993, das er »Red Slab in Space« nannte und folgendermaßen beschrieb: »›Red Slab in Space‹ ist eine monolithische,

La maison, dont le nom évoque la forme, répond aux aspirations de son propriétaire, Lawrence Marcelle. La partie supérieure couvre une bibliothèque de 14 m de long, en porte-à-faux au-dessus du niveau bas qui contient une salle de séjour, une cuisine et une chambre. L'intention semble être de créer un ordre symbolique où les faits banals de l'existence quotidienne soutiennent et élèvent des objectifs intellectuels. Malgré cet élément fonctionnel, répondant au programme, Ungers insiste sur sa réalisation «d'une structure monolithique, lisse, sans différenciation entre les surfaces verticales ou horizontales.» Première maison à être entièrement construite en acier patinable, T-House peut facilement passer pour une grande sculpture.

Le modernisme, mais avec quelque chose en plus

Les nombreuses formes expérimentales neés des influences combinées de la nouvelle donnée économique et de l'évolution technologique semblent laisser peu de place à de vraies variations sur le thème moderniste. Loin d'être un style du passé, le jeu géométrique de plans et de trames d'un architecte comme Richard Meier prétend à une sorte de pureté classique qui peut également être appréciée en termes de mesure. Meier est l'objet de critiques qui lui contestent sa capacité à prendre en charge des œuvres d'envergure. Sa meilleure réponse est sans doute l'hôtel de ville et la bibliothèque de La Haye qu'il vient d'achever.

Plaqué à l'intérieur comme à l'extérieur de panneaux de métal émaillé de 85 x 180 cm, ce très vaste ensemble de bâtiments est situé non loin de la gare centrale de La Haye, près du ministère de la Justice et des Affaires Etrangères, sur un terrain difficile en forme de coin. L'alignement des rues et du site a inspiré à Richard Meier une rotation de 12,5° des deux trames de la construction, qui dégage un bloc de bureaux de 12 niveaux et un second immeuble de 10. Entre ces éléments, il a logé un spectaculaire atrium de verre de 47 m de haut, le plus vaste espace de ce type en Europe. L'hôtel de ville et la bibliothèque publique parachèvent cette «place de la culture» de La Haye, et devraient quelque peu alléger l'atmosphère assez stérilisante qui émane des ministères voisins. Non loin de là se trouvent

Luxembourg headquarters recently completed by Arquitectonica in the tiny capital of European banking is proof that when budgets are sufficient, modern architecture is capable of a level of quality which compares well to buildings from previous periods. Arquitectonica's first European project, this structure is located at the angle of the Boulevard Royal and the Avenue Amélie, in the heart of this 51 square kilometer Grand Duchy, which boasts no less than 230 other banks. This central location, and the choice of Arquitectonica are the doing of Managing Director Robert Reckinger who chose to give architecture "the role of an ambassador carrying our public image... the role of a marketing tool," as he says. Other, more powerful institutions, such as the Deutsche Bank and Hypobank have recently completed buildings in Luxembourg with Gottfried Böhm and Richard Meier as their respective architects, but both of these are located outside the center in the Kirchberg area. The reason for this distinction is that large enough tracts of land are simply not available given the unusual topography of the city center. The Arquitectonica scheme manages to place seven stories of the reinforced concrete structure underground, including four levels of parking, allowing a total floor area of 20000 square meters on a plot of land measuring only 3374 square meters. Beyond the unusual and successful variety of materials and geometries introduced by Arquitectonica principal Bernardo Fort-Brescia, the bank also called on the well-known Antwerp garden designer Jacques Wirtz and on Jean-Michel Wilmotte for the furniture. Wirtz, who is also responsible for part of the new Tuileries garden in Paris, made an interesting effort to relate the very modern main building to the curious historical pastiche called the Villa Amélie at the rear of the complex. Whereas the kind of collaboration imagined here between architects and designers often goes badly wrong, the Banque de Luxembourg has managed the delicate task of blending artistic talent with commercial success. Fort-Brescia, like Meier, has created architectural forms which retain an originality and a quality while satisfying the corporate or municipal client. In both instances the degree of real design innovation may not be great, but architecture is after all meant to serve a purpose more than it is necessarily

monochrome Konstruktion, die die beiden vorhandenen Säulen der Galerie integriert und sie baulich nutzt. Es handelt sich um eine Synthese aus Malerei, Bildhauerei und Architektur, die versucht, eine Verbindung zum frühen Modernismus – insbesondere zum Konstruktivismus, De Stijl und Purismus (die eine ähnliche Integration anstrebten) – herzustellen. Gleiches könnte man auch über das T-House sagen.«

Das einfach nach seiner Form benannte Haus zielt darauf ab, die Ambitionen des Besitzers, Lawrence Marcelle, auszudrücken. Die obere Form entspricht einer 14 Meter langen Bibliothek, die über die untere Ebene vorkragt, auf der sich ein Wohnraum, die Küche und das Schlafzimmer befinden. Offensichtlich soll eine symbolische Ordnung geschaffen werden, bei der die prosaischen Fakten des täglichen Lebens intellektuelle Bestrebungen fördern und unterstützen. Trotz dieser funktionalen, in der Tat programmatischen Elemente besteht Ungers auf einer »fugenlosen, monolithischen Konstruktion ohne Differenzierung von vertikalen und horizontalen Oberflächen.« Das T-House ist das erste Haus, das vollständig aus verwittertem Stahl gefertigt wurde und daher leicht mit einer großen Skulptur verwechselt werden kann.

Modernismus mit einem Dreh

Die große Anzahl experimenteller Formen, die aus wirtschaftlichen und technologischen Veränderungen entstanden zu sein scheinen, haben Raum für interessante Variationen des Modernismus geschaffen. Die von einem Architekten wie Richard Meier entworfenen geometrischen Rasterspiele sind alles andere als ein Stil der Vergangenheit, sondern besitzen eine klassische Klarheit, die auch in Zeiten der Beschränkung ihre Würdigung findet. Falls Meier tatsächlich einmal auf die Kritik reagieren muß, mit der man ihn bezüglich seiner Fähigkeit zur Entwicklung großformatiger Projekte überhäufte, könnte das vor kurzem fertiggestellte Rathaus und die Zentralbibliothek in Den Haag die bestmögliche Antwort darstellen. Diese sehr große Gebäudegruppe liegt in der Nähe des Hauptbahnhofs von Den Haag und in direkter Nachbarschaft des Justiz- und Außenministeriums auf einem schwierigen, keilförmigen Gelände.

les théâtres de Herman Hertzberger et Rem Koolhaas, côté Turfmarkt et Spui, tandis que des projets signés Michael Graves, Cesar Pelli et KPF sont programmés sur des sites voisins. De trois fois la taille de l'immeuble de Canal+ construit à Paris par Meier, l'hôtel de ville a été édifié pour un budget presque identique. Le créateur s'est ici efforcé d'établir un nouveau critère de qualité architecturale applicable à des bâtiments publics économiques, et a utilisé pour cela – et pour la première fois – un ordinateur. Malgré sa masse impressionnante, cet ensemble s'élève avec élégance dans le paysage moderniste assez morne de son voisinage.

Très différent, et à plus petite échelle, le siège de la Banque de Luxembourg récemment achevé par Arquitectonica dans la petite capitale bancaire européenne prouve que, lorsque le budget est suffisant, l'architecture contemporaine peut atteindre un excellent niveau de qualité. Premier projet d'Arquitectonica en Europe, ce bâtiment est situé à l'angle du boulevard Royal et de l'avenue Amélie, au cœur des 51 km² d'un Grand Duché qui ne compte pas moins de 230 banques. Le choix de ce site central et d'Arquitectonica sont à porter au crédit du directeur général de l'établissement, Robert Reckinger, qui a décidé de donner à l'architecture «le rôle d'un ambassadeur chargé de transmettre notre image publique ... le rôle d'un outil de marketing». D'autres institutions plus puissantes, comme la Deutsche Bank et Hypobank, ont récemment fait construire leur siège au Luxembourg, respectivement par Gottfried Böhm et Richard Meier, mais en dehors du centre, dans le quartier de Kirchberg, car il est difficile de trouver des terrains suffisamment vastes dans le centre historique. Arquitectonica a réussi à loger sous terre sept niveaux de sa construction en béton armé, dont quatre de parkings, ce qui donne une surface totale de 20000 m² utiles pour un terrain de 3374 m² seulement. En dehors du recours insolite et réussi à une grande variété de matériaux et de formes dû au principal responsable d'Arquitectonica, Bernardo Fort-Brescia, la banque a également fait appel au célèbre architecte-paysagiste d'Anvers Jacques Wirtz, et à Jean-Michel Wilmotte pour le mobilier. Wirtz, qui a également travaillé à la rénovation des jardins des Tuileries à

Pages 30/31: Arquitectonica, Banque de Luxembourg, Luxembourg, 1989–94. A view of the top floor boardroom and an exterior image showing the way the volumes intersect.

Seite 30/31: Arquitectonica, Banque de Luxembourg, Luxemburg, 1989–94. Ein Blick in den Sitzungssaal im Obergeschoß und eine Außenansicht des Gebäudes veranschaulichen die Durchdringung der Volumina.

Pages 30/31: Arquitectonica, Banque de Luxembourg, Luxembourg, 1989–94. Vue de la salle du conseil au dernier étage, et vue extérieure montrant l'interpénétration des volumes.

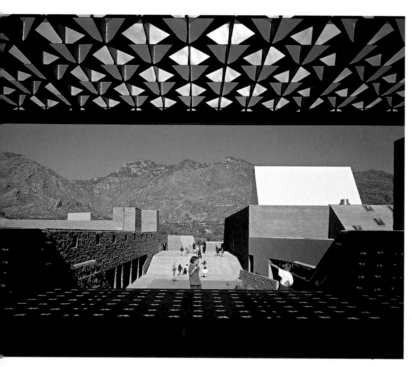

Above: Antoine Predock, Ventata Vista Elementary School, Tucson, Arizona, 1992–94. A view of the central courtyard, with metal screens serving as shades.
Page 33: Antoine Predock, Civic Arts Plaza, Thousand Oaks, California, 1989–94. North-South section through Civic Auditorium and Plaza.

Oben: Antoine Predock, Ventata Vista Elementary School, Tucson, Arizona, 1992–94. Der zentrale Hof mit Metallvorrichtungen, die vor der Sonne schützen.
Seite 33: Antoine Predock, Civic Arts Plaza, Thousand Oaks, Kalifornien, 1989–94. Nord-südlicher Schnitt durch das Auditorium und den Platz.

Ci-dessus: Antoine Predock, Ventata Vista Elementary School, Tucson, Arizona, 1992–94. Vue de la cour centrale. Les écrans métalliques protègent du soleil.
Page 33: Antoine Predock, Civic Arts Plaza, Thousand Oaks, Californie, 1989–94. Section nord-sud, l'auditorium et place.

obliged to be original. The idea of constant invention indeed seems close to the contemporary view of painting or sculpture, with the inherent danger of an excessive tendency to be fashionable.

I.M. Pei's first completed building since the Grand Louvre project is the new Rock and Roll Hall of Fame in Cleveland, Ohio. In explaining the structure, he has spoken of an "explosive energy, as if parts of the building were flying out in all directions." His trademark triangular glazed entrance "tent" certainly gives this new structure the feeling of a Pei building, but its exuberance, which is undoubtedly linked to the Rock and Roll theme is more explicit than in any previous work by this Chinese-born master. Peter Arendt, director of design and construction for the owner of the building called it "an inhabited piece of sculpture." In this respect, the Rock and Roll Hall of Fame can be seen as both an example of the continued vitality of the modernist tradition, and of the trend toward architecture as a work of art in and of itself.

The call of the Southwest

The respected journal of the American Institute of Architects, which is simply called *Architecture*, recently devoted almost an entire issue to Albuquerque based Antoine Predock. Even more unexpected than this regional excursion is the commentary devoted to Predock: "No contemporary American architect has done more to extend architecture's spiritual and symbolic range. Predock listens to the land and detects deep murmurings that his more cloistered academic contemporaries miss. And while his architecture remains consistently spare, planar, and primal, it is richly inflected by ideas and images from freeways, folklore, and cyberspace – the full panoply of contemporary culture."[9] One of Predock's recent projects, the 12000 square meter American Heritage Center in Laramie, Wyoming best symbolizes the reasons for this strong praise. At the center of this complex, a patinated copper cone rises like "an ancient or futuristic war helmet or a UFO," also echoing summits in two nearby mountain groups, the Snowy and Laramie ranges. Predock calls this cone, which houses a research institution for scholars "the volcanic archives." Personable

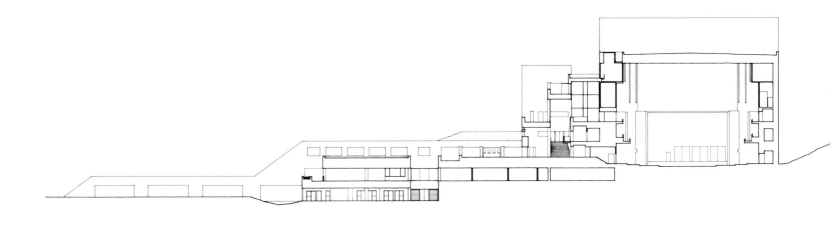

0 5 20 40

Alle Bauten sind innen und außen mit weißen, 85 x 180 cm großen porzellan-emaillierten Metallplatten verkleidet. Der Straßenraster und das Grundstück inspirierten Richard Meier dazu, eine zwölfgeschossige Büroscheibe und einen zehngeschossigen Block um 12,5° gegeneinander zu verschwenken. Dazwischen plazierte er das spektakulärste Element des Komplexes, ein 47 Meter hohes verglastes Atrium, das der größte Raum dieser Art in Europa ist. Rathaus und Bibliothek komplettieren den »Kulturplatz« Den Haags, der die sterile Atmosphäre der benachbarten Ministerien auflockern soll. Ganz in der Nähe, an den Seiten zu Turfmarkt und Spui, befinden sich die Theater von Herman Hertzberger und Rem Koolhaas. Für andere nahegelegene Grundstücke liegen Entwürfe der Architekten Michael Graves, Cesar Pelli und KPF vor. Das Rathaus hat den dreifachen Umfang von Meiers Canal+ Bau in Paris, wurde aber mit einem ungefähr gleich großen Budget durchgeführt. Meier bemühte sich, einen neuen Standard architektonischer Qualität für kostengünstige öffentliche Bauten zu setzen, bei dem er sich überraschenderweise zum ersten Mal eines CAD-Programms bediente. Trotz der massiven Form des Komplexes setzt sich sein Bauwerk auf attraktive Weise von dem eher blassen modernistischen Umfeld dieses Gebietes ab.

Dagegen tritt die vor kurzem von Arquitectonica fertiggestellte Zentrale der Banque de Luxembourg in der winzigen Hauptstadt des europäischen Bankwesens auf völlig unterschiedliche Weise und in einem viel kleineren Maßstab den Beweis an, daß bei einem ausreichenden Budget die moderne Architektur zu einem Qualitätsgrad fähig ist, der sich durchaus mit dem der Bauwerke vorhergehender Epochen vergleichen läßt. Dieses erste europäische Projekt des Architekturbüros Arquitectonica befindet sich auf einem Eckgrundstück am Boulevard Royal und der Avenue Amélie im Zentrum des 51 Quadratkilometer großen Großherzogtums, das 230 Filialen anderer Banken beherbergt. Arquitectonica gelang es, sieben Geschosse ihrer Stahlbetonkonstruktion (einschließlich vier Parkebenen) unterhalb der Erdoberfläche anzulegen und auf diese Weise eine Gesamtnutzfläche von 20000 m² auf einem lediglich 3374 m² großen Gelände zu erreichen. Neben der unge-

Paris, a réussi là une intéressante performance en reliant le très moderne bâtiment principal au curieux pastiche historique appelé Villa Amélie situé en fond de terrain. Alors que les collaborations plus ou moins imposées entre architectes et créateurs se passent souvent mal, la Banque de Luxembourg a remporté le difficile pari de mêler talents artistiques et réussite commerciale. Fort-Brescia, comme Meier, a créé des formes architecturales qui conservent une originalité et une réelle qualité sans se heurter au client, à l'entreprise ou à la municipalité. Dans les deux cas, le degré d'innovation n'est peut-être pas très élevé mais, après tout, le rôle de l'architecture est de remplir une fonction et pas nécessairement de faire preuve d'originalité. L'idée d'invention constante, proche de celle qui règne en peinture ou en sculpture, porte souvent en elle le danger d'une sensibilité excessive aux phénomènes de mode.

Le nouveau Rock and Roll Hall of Fame de Cleveland (Ohio) est le premier chantier important achevé par Pei depuis Pei Grand Louvre. Pour expliquer sa démarche créative, Pei parle «d'une énergie explosive, comme si les parties du bâtiment s'échappaient dans toutes les directions.» Sa «tente» de verre triangulaire, pour l'entrée, est typique de son style, mais son exubérance, indubitablement liée au thème du Rock'n Roll, est plus explicite que dans n'importe laquelle des œuvres précédentes du maître sino-américain. Peter Arendt, responsable du projet pour le propriétaire de l'immeuble, parle «d'une sculpture habitée». Il s'agit en effet là encore d'un exemple de la vitalité permanente de la tradition moderniste et de la tendance de l'architecture à devenir en soi une œuvre d'art.

L'appel du Sud-Ouest
La prestigieuse revue de l'American Institute of Architects, intitulée en toute simplicité «Architecture», a récemment consacré un numéro presque entier à Antoine Predock. Le texte de présentation du dossier est encore plus inattendu encore que cette «excursion» régionale: «Aucun autre architecte américain contemporain n'a développé à ce point la portée symbolique et spirituelle de l'architecture. Predock est à l'écoute de la terre et détecte ses murmures profonds que ses contemporains plus figés dans leurs certi-

and enthusiastic, Predock begins each project with a large collage made with images or objects related to the site. In the case of the Laramie project, the axis is aligned on Medicine Bow Peak and Pilot's Knob, while the rising cone seems at once to reach forward and backward in time. This is a strong form from an architect who has shown his ability to deal well with the budgetary constraints which are part and parcel of most new projects. Although it may not be possible to call forth the kind of geological references visible in Laramie in every project he will undertake, Antoine Predock has apparently tapped into a source of strength which has been conspicuously missing from the great majority of contemporary architecture. As *Architecture* affirms, "He continues to draw inspiration from sources beyond architecture, theory, and history and find ways to include it in his buildings. His walls and roofs vaunt their materiality even as they aspire to higher concepts. Site remains primary, and for Predock, it starts at the center of the earth and reaches out to the cosmos."[10]

A close relationship to geology also marks the new Phoenix Central Library by the architect Will Bruder. Born in 1946, Bruder was self-trained as an architect, but his early apprenticeship under Paolo Soleri and Gunnar Birkerts gives some hint of what he calls his "pursuit of 'architecture as art' married to a hands-on sense of reality." As in the case of Predock's Laramie building, copper is an important element in the cladding of the new Phoenix structure, but here the scale is larger. No less than 40000 kilos of ribbed copper cover the exterior of this 26000 square meter library. Bruder's own description of the building makes clear his intentions : "Arizona's natural beauty provides the poetic metaphor for the library's image. A majestic mesa transplanted from the fantastic landscape of Arizona's Monument Valley... The building's exterior appearance is original rather than traditional, rather like a geological land form or abstract minimalist sculpture." Both Bruder's reference to "architecture as art" and this last comparison to "abstract minimalist sculpture" relate his work to the trends already demonstrated for architects as different as Frank O. Gehry and Steven Holl. Coming from the Southwest where urban growth has been strong and the remarkable landscape is

wöhnlichen und gelungenen Vielfalt an Materialien und geometrischen Formen, die Bernardo Fort-Brescia, der Leiter von Arquitectonica konzipierte, versicherte sich die Bank der Dienste des bekannten Antwerpener Gartenarchitekten Jacques Wirtz und des Designers Jean-Michel Wilmotte für die Innenausstattung. Wirtz, der ebenfalls für einen Teil der neuen Tuilerien in Paris verantwortlich zeichnet, bemühte sich, das sehr moderne Hauptgebäude optisch mit einem kuriosen historischen Pasticcio namens Villa Amélie auf der Rückseite des Komplexes zu verbinden. Während die angestrebte Zusammenarbeit zwischen Architekten und Designern gerade in diesem Punkt häufig fehlschlägt, bewältigte die Banque de Luxembourg die delikate Aufgabe einer Kombination von künstlerischem Talent und kommerziellem Erfolg mit Bravour. Genau wie Meier schuf Fort-Brescia architektonische Formen, die sich ihren Grad an Originalität und Qualität bewahren und zugleich den gewerblichen oder öffentlichen Auftraggeber zufriedenstellen. In beiden Fällen mag es sich nicht um wirklich große Designinnovationen handeln, aber schließlich soll die Architektur einem bestimmten Zweck dienen und muß nicht notwendigerweise originell sein.

Das erste von I.M. Pei nach dem Grand Louvre-Projekt fertiggestellte Gebäude ist die neue Rock and Roll Hall of Fame in Cleveland, Ohio. Bei der Beschreibung dieses Bauwerks sprach Pei von einer »explosiven Energie – als ob die Gebäudeteile in alle Richtungen fliegen würden«. Sein Markenzeichen, ein dreieckiges, verglastes Eingangs-»Zelt« verleiht diesem neuen Komplex charakteristische Züge typischer Pei-Architektur; aber das Gebäude besitzt eine mit dem Rock and Roll-Thema verbundene Überschwenglichkeit, die weit ausgeprägter ist als bei jedem anderen, von diesem in China geborenen Baumeister entworfenen Bauwerk. Peter Arendt, vom Besitzer des Gebäudes beauftragter Direktor für Design und Konstruktion, nannte den Bau »eine bewohnte Skulptur«. In dieser Hinsicht kann die Rock and Roll Hall of Fame nicht nur als exemplarisch für die ungebrochene Vitalität der modernistischen Tradition gesehen werden, sondern auch als Beispiel für einen Trend, der Architektur als eigenständiges Kunstwerk betrachtet.

tudes académiques ne savent entendre. Et si son œuvre reste économe de moyens, d'une simplicité primitive et très appuyée sur un travail sur plan, elle se nourrit abondamment d'idées et d'images d'autoroutes, de folklore et de cyberspace, en fait de toute la panoplie de la culture contemporaine.»[9] L'un des récents projets de Predock, l'American Heritage Center de Laramie (Wyoming, 12000 m²), justifie pleinement ces louanges appuyées. Au centre de cet ensemble, un cône de cuivre patiné s'élève comme «un heaume ancien ou futuriste, ou un objet volant non identifié». Il rappelle également les montagnes proches. Enthousiaste et doté d'une forte personnalité, Predock débute chaque projet par un grand collage d'images ou d'objets liés au site. Pour Laramie, l'axe de la construction est aligné sur Medicine Bow Peak et Pilot's Knob (deux montagnes), tandis que le cône semble plonger simultanément dans le passé et le futur. Nous sommes ici en présence d'une forme puissante, due à un architecte qui a prouvé sa capacité à intégrer les contraintes budgétaires de la plupart de ses projets. Bien qu'il ne soit peut-être pas toujours possible de s'appuyer sur des références géologiques aussi évidentes que dans le projet de Laramie, Antoine Predock puise ses idées dans une source généreuse, à l'évidence absente de la plupart des réalisations de l'architecture contemporaine. Comme l'affirme «Architecture», «il continue à tirer son inspiration de sources qui sont au-delà de l'architecture elle-même, de la théorie ou de l'histoire, et trouve le moyen de les inclure dans ses réalisations. Ses toits et ses murs affichent leur matérialité tout en aspirant à des concepts plus élevés. Le site reste sa préoccupation primordiale. Pour lui, il part du centre de la terre et s'élève jusqu'au cosmos».[10]

Un rapport étroit avec le terrain marque également la nouvelle bibliothèque centrale de Phoenix réalisée par Will Bruder. Né en 1946, Bruder est un architecte autodidacte, mais son apprentissage aux côtés de Paolo Soleri et de Gunnar Birkerts permet de mieux comprendre ce qu'il entend par la «recherche de l'architecture en tant qu'art, mariée à un sens concret des réalités». Comme pour Predock à Laramie, le cuivre joue un rôle important dans la couverture du nouveau bâtiment de Phoenix, mais à une

Will Bruder, Phoenix Central Library, Phoenix, Arizona, 1988–95. Interior view.

Will Bruder, Phoenix Central Library, Phoenix, Arizona, 1988–95. Innenansicht.

Will Bruder, Phoenix Central Library, Phoenix, Arizona, 1988–95. Vue intérieure.

never far removed, Bruder, like Predock calls on a more distant past than any architectural tradition. This search goes back even farther than the "primitivist" exploration of the early modern artists to touch fundamental elements which are still very much part of everyday life in this area of the United States.

How green is my building?
In the fall of 1994, the SITE group from New York was asked by a BBC sponsored television producer, together with three other architects, to develop a proposal for the decommissioning of a nuclear power station in North Wales. Trawsfynydd (pronounced Traus-VEN-ith), is the first major nuclear power plant in Great Britain to be decommissioned, but it is estimated that more than 400 plants worldwide will go out of service within the next twenty years. The owner of the plant, British Nuclear Electric has developed a process called "Early Reduced Height Safestore" which according to the President of SITE, James Wines, amounts to simply closing down production and "leaving the dangerous radioactive core to be removed by the North Wales community in 2136 when it is considered safer to dismantle it." The proposal of SITE, obviously unpopular with British Nuclear Electric because of the high costs involved, would provide for a "rapid" decommissioning using robotics (remote operated vehicles to remove the core materials). They also suggest "a massive greening of the entire area, lake shore, and nuclear electric buildings using moss, ragweed and ivy as a means of removing toxins from soil and water through the bio-chemical reaction of certain natural vegetation to radioactive materials." Finally, SITE proposes the construction on a nearby hillside of a communications center intended to explore the problems of decommissioning and alternative energy sources. Based on a "combination of a Celtic cross and the typical layered mounds of a Neolithic monument," this center, like many of SITE's projects, would be covered with greenery to an extent that it would "become increasingly metamorphic in its physical appearance and less and less visible within its natural context." Another group involved in this hypothetical design project, Arup Associates suggested burying

Der Ruf des Südwestens
Die einfach »Architecture« betitelte, angesehene Zeitschrift des American Institute of Architecture widmete vor kurzem eine gesamte Ausgabe dem in Albuquerque ansässigen Architekten Antoine Predock. Aber noch ungewöhnlicher als dieser regionale Exkurs ist der Predock gewidmete Kommentar: »Kein zeitgenössischer amerikanischer Architekt hat die spirituellen und symbolischen Grenzen der Architektur weiter ausgelotet. Predock hört dem Land zu und entdeckt ein tiefes Murmeln, das seinen weltfremderen akademischen Zeitgenossen entgeht. Und während seine Architektur beständig kärglich, planar und ursprünglich bleibt, ist sie dennoch stark beeinflußt von Ideen und Bildern der Freeways, der Folklore und des Cyberspace – dem gesamten prächtigen Panoptikum zeitgenössischer Kultur.«[9] Eines von Predocks jüngsten Projekten, das 12 000 m² große American Heritage Center in Laramie, Wyoming, symbolisiert am besten die Gründe für dieses Loblied. In der Mitte des Komplexes erhebt sich ein von Patina überzogener Kupferkegel wie »der antike oder futuristische Helm eines Kriegers oder ein UFO«, der aber auch auf die Form der Berggipfel zweier in der Nähe gelegener Gebirgszüge – Snowy Range und Laramie Range – anspielt. Predock nennt diesen Kegel, der eine Forschungseinrichtung für Geisteswissenschaftler beherbergt, die »vulkanischen Archive«. Predock, ein sympathischer und enthusiastischer Mensch, beginnt jedes Projekt mit einer großen Collage aus Bildern oder Objekten, die in einem Zusammenhang mit dem geplanten Baugelände stehen. Bei dem Laramie-Projekt ist die Achse des Zentrums an zwei Berggipfeln ausgerichtet, dem Medicine Bow Peak und dem Pilot's Knob, während der hochaufragende Kegel in die Vergangenheit und in die Zukunft zugleich zu weisen scheint. Hierbei handelt es sich um die aussagekräftige Form eines Architekten, der bewiesen hat, daß er auch mit einem eingeschränkten Budget umzugehen versteht, was heute eine wesentliche Voraussetzung für die meisten neuen Projekte darstellt. Obwohl es wahrscheinlich nicht bei jedem seiner Bauvorhaben möglich ist, solch geologische Assoziationen wie die beim Laramie-Projekt zu erwecken, scheint Antoine Predock aus einem Kraftquell zu schöpfen, der der großen

échelle plus grande. Il n'a pas fallu moins de 40 tonnes de cuivre nervuré pour recouvrir l'extérieur de cette bibliothèque de 26000m². La description qu'en donne Bruder explicite ses intentions: «C'est de la beauté naturelle de l'Arizona que vient la métaphore poétique qui crée l'image de la librairie: une *mesa* majestueuse transplantée dans le paysage fantastique de Monument Valley... L'apparence extérieure du bâtiment est plus originale que traditionnelle, un peu comme une forme géologique ou une sculpture minimaliste abstraite.» Les deux références de Bruder à «l'architecture en tant qu'art» et sa comparaison avec la sculpture minimaliste abstraite inscrivent son travail dans des courants déjà illustrés par des architectes aussi différents que Frank O. Gehry et Steven Holl. Venant du Sud-Ouest, où la croissance urbaine a été particulièrement forte et où les paysages spectaculaires ne sont jamais bien éloignés, Bruder, comme Predock, fait appel à un passé beaucoup plus lointain que n'importe quelle tradition architecturale. Cette recherche va même encore plus loin que l'exploration «primitiviste» des pionniers de l'art moderne pour parvenir à des éléments fondamentaux qui font encore réellement partie de la vie quotidienne de cette région des Etats-Unis.

Mon bâtiment est-il assez «vert»?

A l'automne 1994, un producteur de télévision financé par la BBC demandait au groupe SITE (New York) et à trois autres agences de soumettre leur proposition pour démanteler une centrale nucléaire du nord du Pays de Galles. Trawsfynydd (prononcez Trausvenith) est la première grande centrale atomique a être mise hors service en Grande-Bretagne, mais on estime à 400 dans le monde le nombre de celles qui devraient subir le même sort dans les vingt années à venir. Le propriétaire des installations, British Nuclear Electric, a conçu un programme qui selon le président de SITE, James Wines, consiste simplement à arrêter la production et «à laisser au Pays de Galles le soin d'éliminer les matériaux radioactifs dangereux en 2136, lorsqu'on pourra démanteler la centrale sans prendre de risques». La proposition de SITE, bien entendu très peu appréciée par British Nuclear Electric, ne serait-ce que pour

the plant in waste from nearby slate mines. On these mounds, Arup proposed to plant grass, moss and rings of trees. Because of the capacity of slate to absorb or insulate from radiation this solution does not seem inappropriate, and it too, harkens back to the burial mounds of the earliest phases of western civilization.

Despite the very different location and the fundamentally apocalyptic nature of the problem to be solved, architects have devised schemes for North Wales which in a way call on the very distant, in this case Neolithic past. Built by Sir Basil Spence in 1959, the Trawsfynydd complex was then viewed as an impressive monument to a new era of progress and plenty. It is ironic and significant that 35 years later, this "Brave New World" has become a menacing symbol of the dangers of industrial growth. Herbert Muschamp, in *The New York Times* put it this way : "Today, after decades of increasing public awareness of ecological issues, a visitor is more likely to see the 20-story plant as a monstrous intruder in an Arcadian setting. Nuclear power, so the reasoning went, tapped into the innermost mysteries of nature. Why couldn't it coexist harmoniously with forests and lakes? Today, this kind of thinking is recognized as an integral part of cold war propaganda."[11] It would seem highly unlikely that British Nuclear Electric, or indeed other such similar companies elsewhere in the world would call on qualified outside architects, let alone ecologically oriented groups such as SITE for assistance in decommissioning. Most electrical companies prefer to give the impression that there really is no problem. As the London newspaper The *Independent* has written, however, "by 2010, more than 50 000 megawatts of current nuclear plant (the equivalent of 86 Trawsfynydds) will be made redundant in Britain. Each power station will cost something like £ 600 million to "decommission" and about 135 years to lose its lethal potency."[12] It is difficult to judge if the "phyto-remediation" proposed by SITE really could significantly alter the normal rate of absorption of radioactive elements. This is a matter more for scientists than for architects. It is certain, however, that blind faith in technological progress has led to extremely dangerous situations, and away from the earth-bound wisdom of previous centuries.

Mehrheit zeitgenössischer Architekten völlig fehlt. Die Zeitschrift »Architecture« schrieb: »Er läßt sich von Quellen jenseits der Architektur, der Theorie und der Geschichte inspirieren und findet immer wieder Wege, sie in seine Gebäude zu integrieren. Seine Mauern und Dächer rühmen sich ihrer Stofflichkeit, auch wenn sie nach höheren Zielen streben. Das Gelände bleibt das Wichtigste, und für Predock erstreckt es sich vom Mittelpunkt der Erde bis in den Kosmos.«[10]

Ein enges Verhältnis zur Geologie kennzeichnet auch die neue Phoenix Central Library des Architekten Will Bruder, der 1946 geboren wurde und als Architekt Autodidakt ist. Aber seine frühe Lehrzeit bei Paolo Soleri und Gunnar Birkerts gibt einen Hinweis auf das, was er selbst als seinen »Qualitätsanspruch von Architektur als Kunst, die mit einem praktischen Sinn für Realität verheiratet ist« bezeichnet. Genau wie bei Predocks Bauwerk in Laramie stellt auch bei der Verkleidung des neuen Bibliotheksgebäudes Kupfer ein wichtiges Element dar; allerdings handelt es sich hier um einen größeren Maßstab. Nicht weniger als 40 000 Kilo geripptes Kupfer bedecken die Fassade der 26 000 m² großen Bibliothek. Bruders eigene Beschreibung dieses Gebäudes legt seine Intention offen: »Arizonas natürliche Schönheit liefert die poetische Metapher für das Erscheinungsbild der Bibliothek. Ein majestätisches Tafelland, das von der phantastischen Landschaft des Monument Valley verpflanzt wurde... Das äußere Erscheinungsbild des Gebäudes ist eher originell als traditionell, eher eine geologische Landschaft oder eine abstrakte minimalistische Skulptur.« Sowohl Bruders Anspielung auf die »Architektur als Kunst« als auch dieser Vergleich mit einer »abstrakten minimalistischen Skulptur« setzen seine Arbeit in einen Bezug zu den Trends, die so unterschiedliche Architekten wie Frank O. Gehry und Steven Holl bereits demonstrierten. Der aus dem Südwesten – dort, wo urbanes Wachstum sich kräftig entwickeln konnte und die bemerkenswerte Landschaft niemals weit entfernt ist – stammende Bruder beruft sich (wie Predock) auf eine entfernte Vergangenheit, die weiter zurückliegt als jede architektonische Tradition. Diese Suche geht sogar noch weiter zurück als die »primitivistische« Erkundung der Künstler der

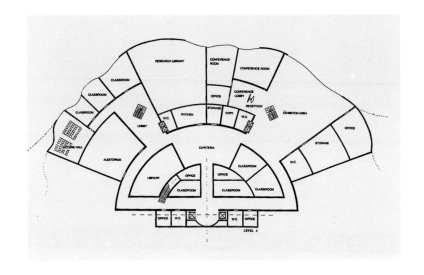

son coût, permettrait une mise en sécurité «rapide» grâce à
la robotique (des véhicules téléguidés prélevant les matériaux radioactifs). SITE suggère également de «traiter par la
végétation l'ensemble de la zone, des rives du lac et des
bâtiments de la centrale avec de la mousse, des mauvaises
herbes et du lierre pour diminuer la radioactivité du sol et
de l'eau, grâce à une réaction biochimique de certains
végétaux face aux matières radioactives». SITE propose
enfin de construire, sur une colline proche, un centre
d'information qui devrait étudier les problèmes de démantèlement nucléaire et les sources d'énergie alternatives.
Fondé sur une «combinaison de la croix celtique et des
tumulus néolithiques», ce centre, comme de nombreux
projets SITE, serait recouvert de verdure au point qu'il
«deviendrait de plus en plus métaphorique dans son apparence physique, et de moins en moins visible dans son
milieu naturel». Un autre participant à ces projets hypothé-
tiques, Arup Associates, a suggéré d'enterrer la centrale
sous les déchets des anciennes ardoisières de la région.
L'ardoise ayant la capacité d'absorber ou d'isoler des radiations cette solution semble appropriée et fait, elle aussi,
retour aux grands monuments funéraires du passé.

Il est intéressant de noter que les architectes qui ont travaillé sur Trawsfynydd ont aussi réfléchi à des schémas qui
rappellent un peu le passé néolithique du Pays de Galles.
Construite par Sir Basil Spence en 1959, cette centrale
nucléaire était considérée à l'époque comme un majes-
tueux monument à une nouvelle ère de progrès et d'abon-
dance. L'ironie de l'histoire est que, 35 ans plus tard,
ce «meilleur des mondes» est devenu le symbole mena-
çant des dangers de la croissance industrielle. Herbert
Muschamp l'analyse ainsi dans «The New York Times»:
«Maintenant, après des décennies de prise de conscience
de plus en plus forte des enjeux écologiques par le grand
public, un visiteur perçoit plutôt cette centrale haute de 20
étages comme une monstrueuse intrusion dans un paysage
bucolique. L'énergie nucléaire, pensait-on, exploite les mys-
tères les plus profonds de la nature. Pourquoi ne coexiste-
rait-elle pas harmonieusement avec les forêts et les lacs?
Aujourd'hui, ce type de pensée est considéré comme rele-
vant de la propagande de la guerre froide.»[11] Il semble a

SITE, Tennessee Aquarium Imax Building,
project, Chattanooga, Tennessee. Plan and
Watercolor drawing by James Wines.

SITE, Tennessee Aquarium Imax Building,
Projekt, Chattanooga, Tennessee.
Grundriß und Aquarellzeichnung von James
Wines.

SITE, Tennessee Aquarium Imax Building,
projet, Chattanooga, Tennessee.
Plan et dessin à l'aquarelle de James Wines.

Solutions for a new era

James Wines and his colleagues see hope for the regeneration of architecture, and indeed of society through an ecological approach. The end of the economic boom of the 1980s certainly has played a role in the renewed public perception of ecology as an area of interest. Resources of all types are clearly available only in finite quantities, populations everywhere are increasing, and some of the cornerstones of "modern" society and its use of power have been more and more openly questioned. James Wines, by training a sculptor, has looked carefully into numerous scientific solutions which may permit architecture to be more respectful of its environment, but he has not, unlike many other architects, sought out the benefits in terms of design innovation to be derived from active use of computers.

In times when the very reasoning at the base of architecture is called into play by numerous factors, design seems to be taking several different paths, which are nonetheless related. In a society which sees art as the highest form of human achievement, and indeed venerates artists as being somehow above the ordinary, there is a natural desire on the part of some architects to want to be artists. Calling on the contemporary wizardry of the computer, Frank O. Gehry is the foremost of the American "artist-architects," and his notoriety confirms that status goes hand-in-hand with his sculptural achievement. A much younger architect, Simon Ungers also created an art form with his T-House, albeit one less inclined to the lyrical billowing of Gehry's present style.

A second approach to change in contemporary architecture is more rigorously theoretical. This is architects' architecture, a form which is in many ways introspective. Peter Eisenman is probably the most readily acknowledged master of architecture as theory, fully harnessing philosophy in the past, and computer technology today to make his points. This tactic is not, however, universally appreciated. Eisenman was the object of a blistering attack in a recent issue of the professional magazine *Progressive Architecture*. In an article entitled "Eisenman's Bogus avant-garde," Diane Ghiradro wrote, "The divorce of architecture from the contamination of the real world has been a constant in

frühen Moderne, geleitet von dem Wunsch, mit fundamentalen Elementen in Berührung zu kommen, die in dieser Region der Vereinigten Staaten noch immer zum täglichen Leben gehören.

Grüne Architektur

Im Herbst 1994 trat ein von der BBC gesponsorter Fernsehproduzent an das Architekturbüro SITE und drei weitere Architekten mit der Bitte heran, einen Entwurf für die Stillegung eines 1959 gebauten Atomkraftwerks in Nordwales zu entwickeln. Trawsfynydd (Trahs-ven-ith ausgesprochen) ist das erste größere Atomkraftwerk Großbritanniens, das vom Netz genommen werden soll, aber man nimmt an, daß in den kommenden zwanzig Jahren weltweit mehr als 400 weitere Atomkraftwerke außer Betrieb gesetzt werden müssen. Die Eigentümerin dieses Kraftwerks, British Nuclear Electric, hat ein Verfahren namens »Early Reduced Height Safestore« entwickelt, das laut des Leiters von SITE, James Wines, auf eine einfache Schließung des Kraftwerks hinausläuft, wobei »der gefährliche radioaktive Kern bis zum Jahre 2136 bestehen bliebe, um dann – wenn ein Abbau als gefahrlos eingestuft wird – von der Gemeinde Nordwales entsorgt zu werden.« Der Vorschlag von SITE stieß bei der British Nuclear Electric aufgrund der hohen Kosten bei einer »schnellen« Demontage mit Hilfe von Robotern (ferngesteuerte Fahrzeuge, die den Brennkern abtransportieren) natürlich nicht auf große Gegenliebe. Darüber hinaus empfahl SITE eine »massive Bepflanzung des gesamten Gebietes, des Uferbereichs und der Reaktorgebäude, um mit Moosen, Kreuzkraut und Efeu den Boden und das Grundwasser von Giftstoffen zu befreien. Das Ganze basiert auf biochemischen Reaktionen, die einige Pflanzen gegenüber radioaktiven Materialien zeigen.« Und schließlich schlägt SITE die Errichtung eines Kommunikationszentrums auf einem nahegelegenen Hügel vor, das der Erforschung von Demontage-Arbeiten und alternativen Energiequellen dienen soll. Beim Design des Study Center handelt es sich um die »Kombination eines keltischen Kreuzes und den auf typische Weise aufgehäuften Erdhügeln neolithischer Monumente«, und das gesamte Gebäude würde – wie viele SITE-Projekte – derart von Vegetation

priori improbable que British Nuclear Electric, ou toute
autre compagnie de ce genre, quelle que soit sa nationalité,
veuille faire appel à des architectes extérieurs, et de plus
«écologisants», comme SITE, pour démanteler ses centrales. La plupart des producteurs d'électricité préfèrent
donner l'impression qu'il n'y a aucun problème. Comme
l'écrit cependant le quotidien londonien «The Independent»: «En 2010, les installations de production de plus
50000 mégawatts d'origine nucléaire seront devenues
obsolètes rien qu'en Grande-Bretagne (l'équivalent de 86
Trawsfynydd). Le démantèlement de chaque centrale coû-
tera quelque 600 millions de £, et il faudra 135 ans pour
qu'elles perdent leur caractère dangereux.»[12] Il est encore
un peu tôt pour savoir si le phyto-traitement proposé par
SITE peut réellement modifier le taux normal d'absorption
des éléments radioactifs. La question est davantage posée
aux scientifiques qu'aux architectes.

Solutions pour une ère nouvelle
James Wines et ses confrères ont foi en la régénération de
l'architecture, et du même coup en celle de la société grâce
à l'écologisme. La fin de la croissance économique des
années 80 a certainement joué un rôle dans le retour en
grâce de l'écologie. Les ressources ne sont pas illimitées,
la population mondiale augmente, et certains fondements
de la société «moderne», comme l'utilisation de l'énergie,
sont remis en question. James Wines, sculpteur de forma-
tion, a étudié avec beaucoup d'attention les nombreuses
solutions scientifiques qui pourraient permettre à l'architecture de respecter davantage l'environnement mais, à la différence de beaucoup d'autres architectes, il ne s'est pas
penché que les bénéfices créatifs que pourrait lui apporter
l'informatique.

A l'heure où la base même du raisonnement architectural
est mise en jeu par de nombreux facteurs, la conception de
l'architecture semble s'engager dans plusieurs voies différentes, bien que liées. Dans une société qui considère l'art
comme la forme la plus élevée de l'activité humaine et
accorde aux artistes une place hors du commun, certains
architectes ont naturellement envie devenir à leur tour des
artistes. S'appuyant sur la magie de l'ordinateur, Frank O.

Eisenman's work, the precondition for his self-creation as a cultural figure of international repute."[13] Although excessive in its aggressivity toward Peter Eisenman, this article does effectively point out the distance which separates the theoretical from the numerous problems of construction and everyday existence. Another theoretically oriented project of spectacular visual appearance is the House on Sag Pond by Agrest and Gandelsonas.

Far less theoretical, but more visual and practical, architects such as Richard Meier and Arquitectonica continue to create very interesting buildings which serve their purpose well. They have naturally evolved with the increasing possibilities offered by contemporary technology, both in terms of design, and of construction methods or choice of materials. It may be legitimate to ask if anyone is really demanding more than this of architecture. The soaring space of Meier's Hague City Hall atrium is a testimony to the power and capacity to amaze of modern architecture, and despite his veiled reference to De Stijl or other art and architecture movements, this is a style and a work which may well mark the times more than ephemeral speculation about the past and the future.

Steven Holl is an example of an architect who has taken yet another approach, attempting to create a synthesis between the upheavals of high technology and local conflicts. Thoughtful and capable of almost revolutionary forms like the Storefront for Art and Architecture, Holl seems to be driven by the desire to make his work live and evolve in the world as it is today, and as it will become tomorrow. These are hallmarks of an important figure whose influence will undoubtedly be substantial, particularly if he can continue to make the difficult transition from the written word to the completed building. Often, seductive rhetoric in architecture leads to disappointing buildings, but Holl seems to be one of the few figures capable of going beyond a simple desire to be original, or worse still, famous. His attempt to place architecture in question would appear to be more profound and timely than many of his colleagues would care to admit.

Modern architecture, like much of the art it is intrinsically related to, somewhere veered away from the age-old wis-

überwuchert werden, daß es »in seinem physischen Erscheinungsbild in zunehmendem Maße metamorph, und in seiner natürlichen Umgebung immer weniger sichtbar würde«. Eine weitere, an diesem hypothetischen Projekt beteiligte Architektengruppe, Arup Associates, entwickelte den Vorschlag, das Kraftwerk unter dem Abraum der nahegelegenen Schiefersteinbrüche zu begraben. Diese künstlichen Hügel könnten dann mit Gras, Moos und Bäumen bepflanzt werden. Da Schiefer die Fähigkeit besitzt, radioaktive Strahlung zu absorbieren bzw. zu isolieren, scheint dieser Lösungsvorschlag nicht ungeeignet; außerdem spielt man damit wieder auf die Grabhügel der frühesten westlichen Zivilisationen an.

Interessanterweise haben beide Architekten – trotz des völlig unterschiedlichen Standorts und des grundsätzlich apokalyptischen Charakters dieses zur Debatte stehenden Problems – Pläne für Nordwales entworfen, die auf eine weit zurückliegende Vergangenheit, in diesem Fall auf das Neolithikum, zurückgreifen. Der 1959 von Sir Basil Spence errichtete Trawsfynydd-Komplex galt damals als imposantes Monument eines neuen Zeitalters des Fortschritts und des Wohlstandes. Es ist eine Ironie des Schicksals, daß diese »schöne neue Welt« 35 Jahre später zum bedrohlichen Symbol für die Gefahren des industriellen Wachstums wurde. Herbert Muschamp schrieb in der »New York Times«: »Heutzutage – nach Jahrzehnten eines wachsenden öffentlichen Bewußtseins für ökologische Themen – würde ein Besucher das 20-geschossige Kernkraftwerk wahrscheinlich eher als monströsen Störenfried in einer idyllischen Landschaft betrachten. Die Atomkraft – so lautete damals die Argumentation – schöpfe aus den geheimsten Mysterien der Natur. Warum könnte sie nicht in einer harmonischen Koexistenz mit Wäldern und Seen bestehen? Heute ist diese Denkweise als ein integraler Bestandteil der Propaganda des Kalten Kriegs entlarvt.«[11] Es scheint sehr unwahrscheinlich, daß British Nuclear Electric oder vergleichbare Firmen qualifizierte, unabhängige Architekten, geschweige denn umweltbewußte Gruppen wie SITE bei der Demontage eines Kernkraftwerks um Unterstützung bitten würden. Die meisten Energiegesellschaften vermitteln lieber den Eindruck, daß es eigentlich überhaupt kein

Gehry est le plus en vue de ces «artistes-architectes» américains, et sa notoriété confirme que ce statut va de pair avec sa réussite de «sculpteur». Simon Ungers, un créateur bien plus jeune, a également créé une forme artistique avec sa T-House, même s'il est moins porté sur l'emphase lyrique qui caractérise le style actuel de Gehry.

La seconde approche favorable au changement dans l'architecture contemporaine est plus rigoureusement théorique. C'est l'architecture d'architecte, une forme à bien des égards introvertie. Peter Eisenman, le maître le plus connu et reconnu de l'architecture théorique, s'appuie sur la philosophie du passé et les technologies informatiques d'aujourd'hui. Mais il a été vivement critiqué dans un récent numéro de «Progressive Architecture». Dans un article intitulé «Eisenman: la fausse avant-garde», Diane Ghiradro écrit: «Le rejet par l'architecture de la contamination du monde réel est constant dans le travail d'Eisenman; c'est la condition de départ de son auto-proclamation de figure culturelle de réputation internationale.»[13] Bien qu'excessif dans son agressivité envers Eisenman, cet article dénonce fort bien le hiatus entre théorie architecturale et construction au quotidien. L'autre grand projet à orientation théorique et spectaculaire est la maison sur Sag Pond d'Agrest et Gandelsonas.

Beaucoup moins théoriques, mais plus visuels et pratiques Richard Meier et Arquitectonica continuent à créer des bâtiments intéressants qui répondent parfaitement à leur objet. Ils ont tout naturellement évolué avec les possibilités grandissantes offertes par les technologies contemporaines, que ce soit en termes de dessin, de méthodes de construction ou de choix de matériaux. L'espace aérien de Meier pour l'atrium de l'hôtel de ville de La Haye est un témoignage de la puissance et de la capacité d'innovation de l'architecture actuelle, et malgré sa référence voilée au groupe De Stijl et à d'autres mouvements artistiques architecturaux, nous sommes là face à un style et une œuvre qui marqueront peut-être plus leur époque que les spéculations éphémères sur le passé et le futur.

Steven Holl est l'exemple de l'architecte qui a choisi une approche assez différente, tentant de créer une synthèse entre les bouleversements de la haute technologie et les

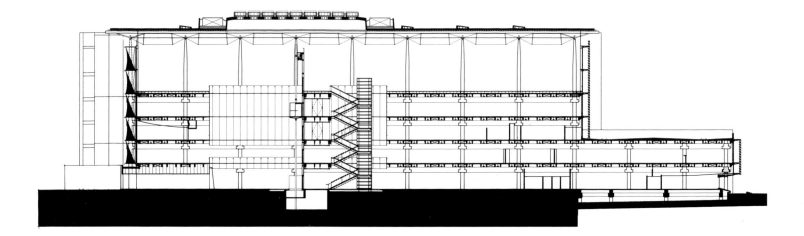

dom expressed by Vitruvius and others. A building which enters the collective conscience as a symbol not of its time, but of human achievement must be profoundly related to its location, to history, and indeed to the human body. The economics of construction and mass-production drove architecture as much as any theory toward geometric standardization. Straight beams and square windows do cost much less to make, or did at least until a very recent date, than anything more exotic. This machine-esthetic was resolved into a virtue by critics and the architects themselves, and it did have the advantage of permitting the creation of vast numbers of housing units or offices in record time. But mechanical forms correspond little to human anatomy and today are ceding their place to other types of environment, created for example by the computer. Cyberspace is the name given to the virtual domain of interconnected computers. Here, words and shapes appear and are mutated at an astonishing rate, often in totally unexpected ways. Communication, in its various guises, or the media as some, since the time of Marshall McLuhan's seminal 1964 essay *Understanding Media: The Extensions of Man*, have said, is changing the face of civilization. McLuhan's words, viewed in retrospect, seem truly prophetic : "Literate man, once having accepted an analytic technology of fragmentation is not nearly so accessible to cosmic patterns as tribal man. He prefers separateness and comparimented spaces, rather than the open cosmos. He becomes less inclined to accept his body as a model of the universe, or to see his house – or any other of the media of communication, for that matter – as a ritual extension of his body. Once men have adopted the visual dynamic of the phonetic alphabet, they begin to lose the tribal man's obsession with cosmic order and ritual as recurrent in the physical organs and their social extension. Indifference to the cosmic, however, fosters intense concentration on minute segments and specialist tasks, which is the unique strength of Western man. For the specialist is one who never makes small mistakes while moving toward the grand fallacy."[14] Inspiration rising from and reaction against the growing importance of the sphere of communications will be an integral part of architecture for the foreseeable future. The direc-

Problem gibt. Die Londoner Zeitschrift »The Independent« schrieb allerdings: »Im Jahre 2010 werden allein in Großbritannien über 50000 Megawatt Atomenergie (das entspricht etwa 86 Trawsfynydds) freigestellt. Bei jedem Kernkraftwerk belaufen sich die Kosten für Stillegung und Demontage auf etwa 600 Millionen Pfund, und es dauert ca. 135 Jahre, bis sich seine tödliche Strahlungswirkung verliert.«[12] Ob die von SITE vorgeschlagene »Phyto-Remediation« die normale Zerfallsrate radioaktiver Elemente tatsächlich bedeutend verändern kann, ist schwierig zu beurteilen. Mit dieser Frage sollte sich eher die Wissenschaft als die Architektur befassen. Eines steht jedoch fest: Der blinde Glaube an den technischen Fortschritt hat uns in extrem gefährliche Situationen geleitet und von der erdverbundenen Weisheit vorheriger Jahrhunderte fortgeführt.

Lösungen für eine neue Zeit
James Wines und seine Kollegen sehen in einem ökologischen Ansatz neue Hoffnung für eine Regeneration der Architektur und der Gesellschaft. Das Ende des Wirtschaftsbooms der 80er Jahre hat zweifellos dazu beigetragen, daß die Ökologie im öffentlichen Bewußtsein einen anderen Stellenwert einnehmen konnte. Bodenschätze jeglicher Art stehen eindeutig nur in begrenzter Menge zur Verfügung, die Bevölkerungszahlen steigen weltweit, und einige der Eckpfeiler unserer »modernen« Gesellschaft – wie etwa der Energieverbrauch – werden immer häufiger in Frage gestellt. Der gelernte Bildhauer James Wines hat sich sorgfältig mit zahlreichen wissenschaftlichen Lösungsvorschlägen beschäftigt, die es der Architektur gestatten, mehr Respekt gegenüber der Umwelt zu zeigen; aber im Gegensatz zu vielen seiner Architektenkollegen hat er die Vorteile einer aktiven Nutzung des Computers zur Innovation des Designs noch nicht erforscht.

In einer Zeit, in der die bloße Argumentation über die Grundlagen der Architektur von zahllosen Faktoren in Gang gebracht wird, scheint das Design verschiedene unterschiedliche Wege zu gehen, die nichtsdestotrotz miteinander verwandt sind. Und in einer Gesellschaft, die die Kunst als höchste Form menschlicher Errungenschaften betrachtet und die ihre Künstler als Persönlichkeiten weit über das

conflits locaux. Réfléchi et capable de créations formelles
presque révolutionnaires, comme le Storefront for Art and
Architecture, Holl semble poussé par le désir de faire
vivre et évoluer son œuvre dans le monde tel qu'il est
aujourd'hui, et tel qu'il deviendra demain. Ce sont les
marques d'une personnalité importante dont l'influence
sera certainement substantielle, en particulier s'il peut
continuer à réussir la difficile transition de l'écrit à la réalisation achevée. Holl semble être l'un des rares créateurs
capables d'aller au-delà d'un simple désir d'originalité, ou
pire, de célébrité.

L'architecture moderne, comme beaucoup de formes
artistiques qui lui sont liées, s'est d'une certaine façon
écartée de l'ancienne sagesse exprimée par Vitruve et
quelques autres. Un bâtiment qui marque la conscience collective, qui reste un symbole non de son époque, mais de
l'accomplissement de l'homme, doit rester en liaison pro-
fonde avec son site, avec l'histoire, et bien entendu avec le
corps humain. Au moins autant que n'importe quelle théorie, c'est la conjoncture économique qui a poussé l'architecture vers la standardisation géométrique. Les poutres
droites et les fenêtres carrées étaient moins coûteuses à
fabriquer que n'importe quelle solution plus créative. Cette
esthétique mécaniste fut transformée en vertu par les critiques et les architectes eux-mêmes, et elle avait en effet
l'avantage de permettre la construction d'un grand nombre
d'unités d'habitation ou de bureaux en un temps record.
Mais les formes mécaniques correspondent assez peu à
l'anatomie humaine, et cèdent aujourd'hui la place à
d'autres types d'environnements, créés par exemple par
ordinateur. Le cyberspace est le nom donné à l'univers
virtuel des ordinateurs en réseau. Ici, les mots et les
formes apparaissent et sont modifiés à une vitesse étonnante, souvent de façon totalement inattendue. Comme
l'avait annoncé Marshall McLuhan dans «Pour comprendre
les médias» (1964), la communication en général, et les
médias en particulier, ouvre une ère nouvelle pour l'huma-
nité. Rétrospectivement, les intuitions de McLuhan
semblent prophétiques: «Dès lors qu'il a fait sienne une
technologie analytique de fragmentation, l'homme ‹typogra-
phique› se ferme à l'univers perceptif global de l'homme

tions this inspiration may take depend not only on the evolution of the technology, but naturally on the reactions of the still essential human operators of the design computer.

For some ecologically oriented architects, and certainly for the new figures of the Southwest, Antoine Predock and Will Bruder, a reference to cosmic, or at least geological order, long neglected by modern architecture is a natural outgrowth of the physical settings they are building in, but also, undoubtedly of the metaphysical poverty of architectural form and thought. With the obvious failure of certain technological systems like nuclear power, people are quite simply reminded that beneath the man-made world lies another much more profound and durable order. Contemporary construction has undoubtedly proved capable of damaging or destroying some aspects of that order, but nature takes its revenge, as Southern Californians have discovered in recent years through what one local joke calls their "four seasons:" earthquake, flood, drought and fire.

Technology can naturally be turned toward an analysis of the most efficient means to use building materials or toward systems of heating and cooling which are not fundamentally destructive of the environment. With expanding populations and limited resources, "green" architecture looks set to become increasingly popular. An architecture which is responsive to its environment and yet is designed in an attractive, livable way, an architecture which places some of its most fundamental ideas in question may well be the net result of the economic and political turmoil which has stirred the world since the late 1980s. If that is the case, optimism about the future may again be possible.

Maß gewöhnlicher Sterblicher erhebt, entsteht bei einigen Architekten der natürliche Wunsch, ein Künstler sein zu wollen. In bezug auf die zeitgenössische Computerzauberei stellt Frank O. Gehry den führenden amerikanischen »Künstler-Architekten« dar, und sein Ruf bestätigt, daß dieser Status Hand in Hand mit seinem skulpturalen Werk geht. Ein erheblich jüngerer Architekt, Simon Ungers, schuf mit seinem T-House ebenfalls eine Kunstform, die allerdings weniger zu den lyrischen Nebelschwaden neigt, die Gehrys momentanen Stil kennzeichnen.

Durch ihren rigorosen theoretischen Ansatz zeichnet sich eine zweite Strömung innerhalb der zeitgenössischen Architektur aus. Dabei handelt es sich um die Architektur der Architekten, eine in vielerlei Hinsicht introspektive Form. Peter Eisenman ist wahrscheinlich der anerkannteste Meister der Architektur als Theorie, der für seine Argumentation früher die Philosophie und heute die Computertechnologie einspannt. Allerdings erfreut sich diese Taktik nicht überall gleich großer Beliebtheit. Vor kurzem wurde Eisenman in einer Ausgabe der Fachzeitschrift »Progressive Architecture« heftig angegriffen. In ihrem Artikel »Eisenman's Bogus avant-garde« schrieb Diane Ghiradro: »Die Trennung der Architektur von der Verseuchung der realen Welt ist eine Konstante in Eisenmans Œuvre, die Voraussetzung für seine Selbsternennung zur Kultfigur von internationalem Ruf.«[13] Obwohl der Artikel von unangemessen starker Aggressivität gegenüber Peter Eisenman geprägt ist, legt er die Distanz zwischen der Theorie und den zahllosen Problemen im Bauwesen und im täglichen Leben offen dar. Auch das von Agrest und Gandelsonas entworfene House on Sag Pond bildet ein theoretisch konzipiertes Projekt mit einem spektakulären optischen Erscheinungsbild.

Dagegen erschaffen erheblich weniger theoretische als vielmehr visuell und praktisch orientierte Architekten wie Richard Meier und Arquitectonica sehr interessante Gebäude, die ihren Zweck durchaus erfüllen. Sie haben sich sowohl in bezug auf das Design als auch hinsichtlich ihrer Konstruktionsmethoden oder Baumaterialien langsam und natürlich mit den wachsenden Möglichkeiten der heutigen Technologie weiterentwickelt. In diesem Zusammenhang sollte die Frage gestattet sein, ob man wirklich mehr von

tribal. Il préfère le morcellement et les espaces cloisonnés à l'infinité du cosmos. Il est moins enclin à voir dans son corps le modèle de l'univers, et à considérer sa maison (ou tout autre vecteur de communication, en l'occurrence) comme une extension rituelle de son corps. Une fois qu'ils obéissent à la dynamique visuelle de l'alphabet phonétique, les hommes commencent à ne plus percevoir l'ordre et le rituel cosmiques récurrents dans les organes physiques et leurs extensions sociales. Mais cette indifférence au cosmos se traduit par une concentration intense sur des espaces parcellaires et sur les tâches spécialisées, et cette faculté est l'apanage de l'homme occidental. Car le spécialiste est celui qui ne fait jamais de petites erreurs, tout en marchant vers la grande faute.»[14] L'inspiration née de l'importance croissante de la communication (ou en réaction contre elle) sera bientôt un élément intrinsèque de l'architecture. Les directions que pourra prendre cette inspiration ne dépendront peut-être pas seulement de l'évolution de la technologie, mais naturellement des réactions de ces êtres encore essentiellement humains qui contrôlent les ordinateurs d'aide à la création.

Pour certains architectes séduits par les idées écologistes – et c'est certainement le cas des nouvelles grandes figures du Sud-Ouest comme Antoine Predock et Will Bruder – la référence au cosmos, ou du moins à l'ordre géologique, longtemps négligée par l'architecture moderne, est le produit naturel du site physique sur lequel ils construisent, mais également, de la pauvreté métaphysique de la pensée et de la forme architecturale. Face à l'échec évident de certaines technologies comme l'énergie nucléaire, on devine sous le monde construit par l'homme un ordre beaucoup plus profond et naturel. La construction contemporaine a prouvé qu'elle était capable de saper ou de détruire certains aspects de cet ordre, mais la nature prend toujours sa revanche, comme les Californies l'ont redécouvert ces dernières années à travers ce que certains nomment en plaisantant leurs quatre saisons tremblement de terre, inondation, sécheresse et incendie.

La technologie peut naturellement s'orienter vers la recherche de matériaux et de systèmes de régulation thermique plus respectueux de l'environnement. L'Architec-

Notes · Anmerkungen

[1] Goldberger, Paul. "The Masterpieces They Call Home." *The New York Times Magazine*, March 12, 1995.

[2] Fisher, Thomas. "Art as Architecture." *Progressive Architecture*, May 1995.

[3] Dixon, John Morris. "The Santa Monica School. What's Its Lasting Contribution?" *Progressive Architecture*, May 1995.

[4] Interview of Peter Eisenman, Peter Eisenman, Architects, 40 West 25th Street, New York, NY, May 15, 1995.

[5] Noever, Peter, ed. *The End of Architecture?* Munich: Prestel, 1993.

[6] Goldberger, Paul. "The Masterpieces They Call Home." *The New York Times Magazine*, March 12, 1995.

[7] *Agrest and Gandelsonas, Works.* Introduction by Anthony Vidler. New York: Princeton Architectural Press, 1995.

[8] Telephone conversation with Diana Agrest, June 26, 1995.

[9] "Antoine Predock, American Visionary." *Architecture*, March, 1995.

[10] Ibid.

[11] Muschamp, Herbert. "Building on the Ruins of Temples to Nuclear Power." *The New York Times*, April 2, 1995.

[12] Glancey, Jonathan. "Ideas beyond the nuclear station." *The Independant*, April, 12, 1995.

[13] Ghiradro, Diane. "Eisenman's Bogus Avant-Garde." *Progressive Architecture*, November 1994.

[14] McLuhan, Marshall. *Understanding Media: The Extensions of Man.* New York: McGraw-Hill, 1963.

der Architektur verlangen kann. Die lichte Höhe des Atriums in Meiers Rathaus in Den Haag ist der Beweis für die Kraft moderner Architektur und für ihre Fähigkeit, zu verblüffen. Trotz seiner verschleierten Anspielungen auf De Stijl und andere Kunst- und Architekturströmungen handelt es sich bei Meiers Gebäude um einen Stil und ein Werk, die vermutlich nachhaltigere Spuren hinterlassen als alle vergängliche Spekulationen über Vergangenheit und Zukunft.

Steven Holl ist ein Beispiel für einen Architekten mit einem völlig anderen Ansatz. Er strebt eine Synthese zwischen den Umwälzungen der Hochtechnologie und den örtlichen Kontroversen an. Holl – ein nachdenklicher und zu fast allen revolutionären Formen fähiger Architekt (wie im Falle der Storefront for Art and Architecture) – scheint von dem Wunsch beseelt, seine Werke in der heutigen Welt zum Leben zu erwecken, sie weiterzuentwickeln und in die Welt von morgen zu überführen. Dies sind die Kennzeichen einer wichtigen Persönlichkeit, deren Einfluß zweifellos von Dauer sein wird, insbesondere wenn Holl weiterhin der schwierige Schritt vom geschriebenen Wort zum fertiggestellten Gebäude gelingt. Häufig führt eine verführerische Rhetorik in der Architektur zu enttäuschenden Gebäuden, aber Holl scheint zu den wenigen Architekten zu zählen, die in der Lage sind, sich über den simplen Wunsch hinwegzusetzen, originell oder – schlimmer noch – berühmt sein zu wollen. Sein Versuch, die Architektur in Frage zu stellen, erscheint profunder und angebrachter, als viele seiner Kollegen zugeben mögen.

Genau wie die Kunst, mit der sie im Grunde eng verbunden ist, entfernte sich die moderne Architektur von den jahrhundertealten Weisheiten, die in den Werken Vitruvs und anderer zum Ausdruck kommen. Ein Gebäude, das in das kollektive Bewußtsein eingeht und nicht ein Symbol seiner Zeit, sondern der menschlichen Errungenschaften an sich darstellt, muß in einem engen Bezug zum Standort, zur Geschichte und zum menschlichen Körper stehen. Die Bauökonomie und die Vorteile der Massenproduktion trieben die Architektur wie jede andere Theorie in Richtung einer geometrischen Standardisierung. Die Fertigung von geraden Balken und quadratischen Fenstern ist – oder war zumindest bis vor kurzem – erheblich kostengünstiger als

ture «verte» va probablement connaître de plus en plus de succès. Une architecture en harmonie avec son environnement et offrant un cadre de vie agréable, une architecture qui remet en question certaines de ses bases les plus fondamentales: voilà peut-être l'apport de cette crise économique et politique qui secoue le monde depuis la fin des années 80. Si tel est le cas, l'optimisme est à nouveau permis.

jedes exotischere Modell. Diese Maschinenästhetik wurde von den Kritikern und den Architekten selbst in eine Tugend verwandelt, und sie besaß den Vorteil, daß große Mengen von Wohneinheiten oder Büroräumen in Rekordzeit fertiggestellt werden konnten. Aber erstens passen mechanische Formen kaum zur menschlichen Anatomie, und zweitens treten sie heute ihren Platz an andere, zum Beispiel vom Computer geschaffene Formen ab. Cyberspace ist der Name für eine virtuelle Welt miteinander vernetzter Computer. Hier erscheinen Worte, Formen und Veränderungen in überraschender Geschwindigkeit und häufig auch auf völlig unerwartete Art und Weise. Wie schon Marshall McLuhans zukunftsweisendes Essay »Understanding Media: The Extension of Man« aus dem Jahre 1964 besagt, verändert Kommunikation mit ihren zahlreichen Erscheinungsformen – oder die Medien als eine dieser Formen – das Antlitz der Gesellschaft. Rückschauend betrachtet erscheinen McLuhans Worte wahrhaft prophetisch: »Der gebildete Mensch, der einmal eine analytische Technik der Fragmentation akzeptiert hat, ist für kosmische Muster nicht annähernd so offen wie der Stammesmensch. Er bevorzugt Abgeschiedenheit und aufgeteilte Räume gegenüber dem offenen Kosmos. Er neigt weniger dazu, seinen Körper als ein Modell des Universums zu betrachten oder sein Haus – oder irgendein anderes Kommunikationsmedium – als eine rituelle Erweiterung seines Körpers. Sobald die Menschen einmal die optische Dynamik des phonetischen Alphabets übernommen haben, verlieren sie die Obsession des Stammesmenschen für Rituale und eine kosmische Ordnung, die in den physischen Organen und ihren sozialen Verlängerungen periodisch wiederkehren. Gleichgültigkeit gegenüber dem Kosmos fördert allerdings eine enorme Konzentration auf winzige Segmente und spezialisierte Aufgaben, der einzigartigen Stärke des westlichen Menschen. Denn der Spezialist ist ein Mensch, der niemals kleine Fehler macht, während er gleichzeitig einem großen Trugschluß erliegt.«[14] In absehbarer Zukunft wird die Inspiration, die aus der wachsenden Bedeutung einer Welt der Kommunikation und aus der Antihaltung gegenüber dieser Welt entsteht, einen integralen Bestandteil der Architektur bilden. Die Richtung, die diese Inspiration möglicherweise ein-

schlägt, hängt nicht nur von der Entwicklung der Technologie ab, sondern natürlich auch von den Reaktionen des noch unentbehrlichen menschlichen Bedieners des Designcomputers.

Für einige umweltbewußte Architekten und sicherlich für die neuen Architekturpersönlichkeiten des Südwestens, Antoine Predock und Will Bruder, ist der Bezug zum Kosmos oder zumindest zu einer geologischen Ordnung, die von der modernen Architektur lange Zeit vernachlässigt wurde, eine natürliche Folge des physischen Rahmens, in dem sie ihre Gebäude errichten, aber zweifellos auch der metaphysischen Armut architektonischer Form und Theorie. Dank des offensichtlichen Versagens bestimmter Technologiesysteme wie der Kernkraft wird die Menschheit auf recht einfache Weise daran erinnert, daß sich unter der von Menschen geschaffenen Welt eine viel profundere und beständigere Ordnung befindet. Das moderne Bauwesen hat zweifellos seine Fähigkeit unter Beweis gestellt, einige Aspekte dieser Ordnung zu schädigen oder zu zerstören, aber die Natur schlägt zurück, wie die Menschen in Südkalifornien in den vergangenen Jahren feststellen mußten. Dort benannte ein geflügeltes Wort die »vier Jahreszeiten« bereits um – in Erdbeben, Flut, Dürre und Feuer.

Natürlich kann die Technik auch für eine Analyse der effizientesten Mittel zur Verwendung von Baumaterialien verwendet werden oder für Heiz- bzw. Kühlsysteme, die nicht notwendigerweise die Umwelt zerstören. Aufgrund der wachsenden Bevölkerungszahl und der nur begrenzten Menge an Rohstoffen wird sich die »grüne« Architektur mit ihren unterschiedlichsten Erscheinungsformen wahrscheinlich immer größerer Beliebtheit erfreuen. Eine Architektur, die auf ihre Umwelt eingeht und sich gleichzeitig durch ein attraktives, lebendiges Design auszeichnet, eine Architektur, die einige ihrer grundlegendsten Ideen in Frage stellt, bildet möglicherweise das Endergebnis der wirtschaftlichen und politischen Unruhen, die die Welt seit Ende der 80er Jahre bewegen. Sollte dies der Fall sein, scheint ein optimistischer Blick in die Zukunft wieder möglich.

Agrest and Gandelsonas

Diana Agrest and Mario Gandelsonas

House on Sag Pond, Sagaponack, Long Island, New York, 1990–94. View of the gazebo from the south garden.

House on Sag Pond, Sagaponack, Long Island, New York, 1990–94. Ansicht des Sommerhauses vom südlichen Bereich des Gartens aus.

House on Sag Pond, Sagaponack, Long Island, New York, 1990–94. Le belvédère, vu du jardin sud.

Diana Agrest and her partner Mario Gandelsonas were both born in Argentina. They studied in Buenos Aires, then attended the Ecole Pratique des Hautes Etudes under Roland Barthes in Paris, which may have influenced their theoretical approach to architecture. Both teach and write actively, Gandelsonas as a professor of architecture at Princeton since 1991. Their firm Agrest and Gandelsonas was founded in 1980. They completed their own summer house at Easthampton in 1985. Diana Agrest has written about an "analytical decomposition" of architecture partially based on film theory. According to the architects, the House on Sag Pond published here "resists stylistic, typological, or linguistic classification, drifting between the abstract and the figural, between convention and idiosyncrasy." Despite its coded language, this description suits the unusual forms imagined by these conceptual designers.

Diana Agrest und Mario Gandelsonas stammen aus Argentinien. Nach dem Studium in Buenos Aires besuchten sie die Ecole Pratique des Hautes Etudes in Paris und studierten dort bei Roland Barthes, dessen Einfluß in ihrem sehr theoretischen Architekturansatz spürbar ist. Beide sind als Dozenten und Autoren tätig; Gandelsonas lehrt seit 1991 in Princeton. 1985 stellten sie ihr eigenes Sommerhaus in Easthampton fertig. Diana Agrest veröffentlichte eine Arbeit über die »analytische Dekomposition« der Architektur, die auf Filmtheorien basiert. Das House on Sag Pond widersetzt sich laut der Architekten »jeder stilistischen, typologischen oder linguistischen Klassifizierung; es treibt zwischen dem Abstrakten und dem Figurativen, zwischen Konvention und Eigenart hin und her«. Diese Aussage paßt zu den ungewöhnlichen Formen, die diese beiden Konzeptualisten anstreben.

Diana Agrest et son associé Mario Gandelsonas sont tous deux nés en Argentine. Après des études à Buenos Aires, ils suivent les cours de Roland Barthes à Paris, ce qui a peut-être exercé une influence sur leur approche assez théorique de l'architecture. Tous deux enseignent et écrivent beaucoup. Gandelsonas est professeur d'architecture à Princeton depuis 1991. L'agence Agrest and Gandelsonas a été fondée en 1980. Les deux architectes ont construit leur résidence d'été à Easthampton en 1985. Diana Agrest s'intéresse à une «décomposition analytique» de l'architecture en partie basée sur la théorie cinématographique. La maison sur Sag Pond reproduite ici «résiste à toute classification stylistique, typologique ou linguistique, allant de l'abstrait à la figuration, de la convention à l'idiosyncrasie». La description s'applique parfaitement aux formes insolites imaginées par ces deux intellectuels.

House on Sag Pond, Sagaponack, Long Island, New York 1990–94

This "cluster of found objects" is located on a 3 hectare lot facing Sagaponack Pond and surrounded by fields. A central 33 meter long vault enclosing living spaces is surrounded by six towers connected by bridges. On the upper floor separate areas for the master bedroom to the south and guest rooms to the north are provided with independent access. The glass "silo" contains a study. The total built area of the complex, including the pool house and the garage is about 800 square meters. Despite its unusual configuration, Diana Agrest points out that the cost of building this house was $ 185 per square foot, as opposed to standard construction costs of $ 200 per square foot. In reference to other work, Agrest and Gandelsonas have spoken of "architecture between memory and amnesia." This house, whose spatial sequencing is apparently influenced by an "analytical decomposition" of architecture as related to the film maker Eisenstein's concept, where "the spectator moves through a series of carefully disposed phenomena which he observes in order with his visual sense," is certainly innovative. The client, Richard Ekstract claims that he told the architects that he "wanted a traditional country house." It seems that he may have gotten more than he bargained for.

Diese »Gruppe von ›objets trouvés‹« liegt auf einem 3 Hektar großen Gelände am Rande des Sagaponack Pond. Um das zentrale 33 Meter lange Gewölbe, das die Wohnräume beherbergt, gruppieren sich sechs Türme, die durch Brücken miteinander verbunden sind. Der nach Süden ausgerichtete Schlafraum des Hausherrn im Obergeschoß sowie die nach Norden weisenden Gästezimmer auf der gleichen Etage besitzen jeweils separate Eingänge; das Arbeitszimmer ist in einem gläsernen »Silo« untergebracht. Der gesamte Gebäudekomplex, einschließlich des Poolgebäudes und der Garage, umfaßt eine Nutzfläche von etwa 800 m². Diana Agrest betont, daß die Baukosten für dieses Haus – trotz seiner ungewöhnlichen Konfiguration – nur 1991 Dollar pro Quadratmeter betrugen, während bei herkömmlichen Konstruktionen die Baukosten bei etwa 2152 Dollar pro Quadratmeter liegen. Im Zusammenhang mit anderen Projekten sprachen Agrest und Gandelsonas einmal von einer »Architektur zwischen Erinnerung und Vergessen«. Die räumliche Gliederung dieses Hauses ist von einer »analytischen Dekomposition« der Architektur beeinflußt – ein Konzept vergleichbar dem des Filmemachers Eisenstein, dessen »Zuschauer durch eine Reihe sorgfältig präsentierter Phänomene geleitet wird, die er in Übereinstimmung mit seinem Gesichtssinn wahrnimmt«. Der Bauherr Richard Ekstract hatte den Architekten seinen Wunsch nach »einem traditionellen Landhaus« mitgeteilt; offenbar hat er mehr bekommen, als er erwartet hatte.

Cette «grappe d'objets trouvés» a été construite sur un terrain de 3 hectares au bord du lac de Sagaponack, au milieu des champs. Une voûte centrale de 33 m de long entourée de six tours reliées par des passerelles recouvre l'espace habitable. Au niveau supérieur, les zones réservées à la chambre principale, face au sud, et aux chambres d'invités, au nord, disposent d'un accès indépendant. Le «silo» de verre contient un bureau. La surface totale construite de l'ensemble, y compris du pavillon de piscine et le garage est d'environ 800 m². Malgré la configuration insolite de cette demeure, Diana Agrest fait remarquer que son coût de construction ne s'est élevé qu'à 1991 dollars le m² au lieu des classiques 2152 dollars. Agrest et Gandelsonas se situent dans une «architecture entre mémoire et amnésie». La séquence spatiale de cette maison résolument innovatrice est apparemment influencée par une «décomposition analytique» de l'architecture qui rappelle le cinéma selon Eisenstein: «le spectateur avance à travers une série de phénomènes articulés avec soin qu'il observe dans l'ordre grâce à son sens visuel.» Le client, Richard Ekstract, prétend qu'il avait demandé «une maison de campagne traditionnelle». Ce n'est pas tout à fait ce qu'il a eu...

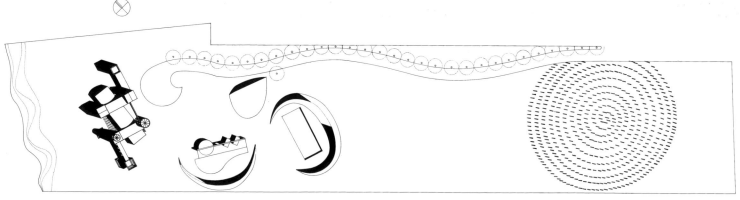

SITE PLAN

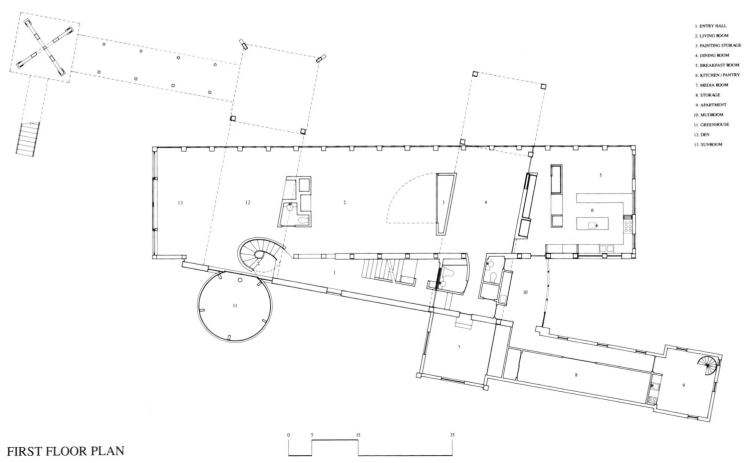

1. ENTRY HALL
2. LIVING ROOM
3. PAINTING STORAGE
4. DINING ROOM
5. BREAKFAST ROOM
6. KITCHEN / PANTRY
7. MEDIA ROOM
8. STORAGE
9. APARTMENT
10. MUDROOM
11. GREENHOUSE
12. DEN
13. SUNROOM

FIRST FLOOR PLAN

0   5   15   35

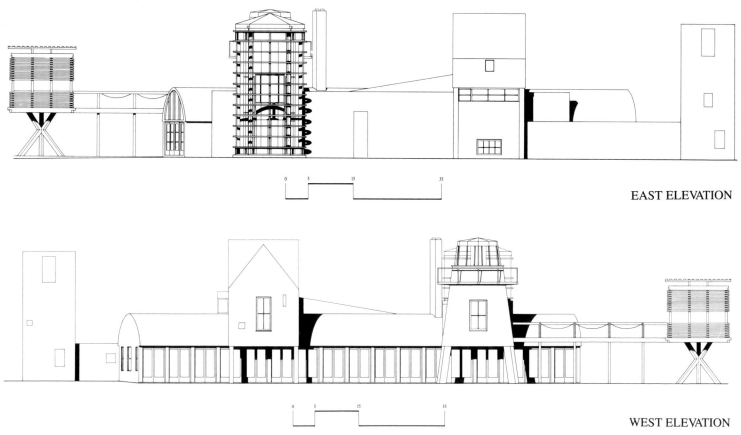

EAST ELEVATION

WEST ELEVATION

Pages 52–57: Plans, elevations and photographs of the House on Sag Pond emphasize its articulation as a "cluster of found objects" connected together to give the owner or the visitor a series of different visual and spatial impressions.

Seite 52–57: Pläne, Aufrisse und Fotografien des House on Sag Pond unterstreichen seine Konzeption als »Gruppe von ›objets trouvés‹«, die miteinander verbunden sind und so für den Betrachter einen Eindruck optisch und räumlich unterschiedlicher Komponenten erzeugen.

Pages 52–57: Plans, Elévations et vues de la maison sur Sag Pond montrant l'articulation de cette «grappe d'objets trouvés», réuni et de façon à offrir au propriétaire ou au visiteur une multitude d'impressions spatiales et visuelles.

Arquitectonica

Bernardo Fort-Brescia and
Laurinda Spear

Banque de Luxembourg,
Luxembourg, 1989–94.
A 43 ton raw Normandy granite
block marks the entrance.

Banque de Luxembourg,
Luxemburg, 1989–94.
Der 43 Tonnen schwere Monolith
aus normannischem Granit vor dem
Eingang zur Bank.

Banque de Luxembourg,
Luxembourg, 1989–94.
A l'entrée de la banque, bloc de 43
tonnes de granit brut de Normandie.

Although the rather flashy projects in Miami which brought Arquitectonica to international attention in the late 1970s and early 1980s did not necessarily presage a long and fruitful career, the couple Bernardo Fort-Brescia/Laurinda Spear have succeeded in establishing themselves as much more than flamboyant local architects. In fact the shift of architectural fashion away from the Post-Modernism of the 1970s has placed their own brand of spectacular Modernism firmly in the mainstream. This position was confirmed when the firm was chosen to build its first European project in Luxembourg, and its first major building in New York, in both instances by powerful figures in the banking and corporate sectors. Although it remains to be seen if the Times Square project will indeed live up to the "crashing comet" image which presided over its conception, the Luxembourg bank shows that within a set of rigorous formal and technical constraints, Arquitectonica is able to inject a considerable note of innovation.

Bernardo Fort-Brescia und Laurinda Spear ist es gelungen, sich international zu etablieren und den Status regional bekannter, extravaganter Architekten hinter sich zu lassen. Die Abkehr der Architekturströmungen weg von der Postmoderne der 70er Jahre hat dafür gesorgt, daß Arquitectonicas persönliche Spielart eines spektakulären Modernismus heute fest im Mainstream verankert ist. Ihre Position wurde zusätzlich gefestigt, als man die Gruppe bat, ein Großprojekt in New York und ihr erstes Projekt auf europäischem Boden (in Luxemburg) zu bauen, wobei es sich in beiden Fällen um bedeutende Auftraggeber aus dem Finanz- bzw. Firmensektor handelt. Obwohl abzuwarten bleibt, inwieweit das Projekt am Times Square wirklich dem bei seiner Konzeption bestimmenden Bild eines »explodierenden Meteoriten« entsprechen wird, beweist das Hauptgebäude der Banque de Luxembourg, daß Arquitectonica auch inmitten einer Welt rigoroser formaler und technischer Beschränkungen in der Lage ist, seinen Entwürfen innovativen Charakter zu verleihen.

Même si l'immeuble un peu voyant de Miami qui attira l'attention internationale sur Arquitectonica à la fin des années 70 et au début des années 80 ne laissait pas forcément présager une carrière longue et fructueuse, Bernardo Fort-Brescia et Laurinda Spear ont réussi à dépasser leur image de flamboyants architectes locaux. En fait, la fin de la mode du post-modernisme des années 70 a propulsé leur style moderniste spectaculaire sur le devant de la scène. Cette position est confirmée par la commande d'un important programme à Luxembourg, et d'un premier grand immeuble à New York, dans les deux cas par des personnalités du monde économique. Bien qu'il faille encore attendre pour voir si le projet de Times Square traduira réellement l'idée de «chute de comète» qui a présidé à sa conception, la banque de Luxembourg montre que, même dans le cadre de rigoureuses contraintes formelles et techniques, Arquitectonica est capable de faire preuve d'un remarquable esprit d'innovation.

Banque de Luxembourg, Luxembourg
1989–94

The first European project of Arquitectonica, this structure is located on an angle of the Boulevard Royal in the city center. As design principal Bernardo Fort-Brescia says "we needed to express that, in spite of the bank's long history, it is a progressive institution." This aim was achieved using several different forms: a cantilevered stone box clad in Chassagne stone with flush square amber glass windows aligns with the Boulevard, while a pie-wedge shaped tower of tinted green glass echoes the curve of the street. Connecting these two volumes is a parallelogram of polished black granite. An 43 ton raw Normandy granite boulder marks the entrance. Seven stories of the reinforced concrete structure are underground, including four levels of parking, a total of two-thirds of the building's 20000m². The 3374m² lot is also occupied by gardens designed by the Belgian Jacques Wirtz. Their form echoes the radiating lines and curves of main building. Signs and furniture for the bank headquarters were designed by the Parisian Jean-Michel Wilmotte. One unusual feature of the project is the so-called "Villa Amélie" to the rear of the main building. Principally housing executive dining rooms, this structure intentionally imitates the exterior form of the neighboring French embassy.

Dieses erste europäische Projekt des Architekturbüros Arquitectonica befindet sich auf einem Eckgrundstück am Boulevard Royal im Stadtzentrum Luxemburgs. Der für den Entwurf verantwortliche Leiter, Bernardo Fort-Brescia, erklärte: »Wir wollten zum Ausdruck bringen, daß es sich bei dieser Bank trotz ihrer langen Tradition um eine zukunftsorientierte Institution handelt.« Dieses Ziel wurde durch die Verwendung unterschiedlicher Bauformen erreicht: ein vorkragender Steinkasten mit einer Verkleidung aus Chassagne-Stein, dessen bündig abschließende, quadratische Braunglasfenster eine Linie mit dem Boulevard bilden, während ein keilförmiger Turm aus grüngetöntem Glas die Krümmung der Straße widerspiegelt. Als Bindeglied dieser beiden Baukörper dient ein Parallelogramm aus poliertem schwarzem Granit. Den Eingang markiert ein 43 Tonnen schwerer, unbehauener Monolith aus normannischem Granit. Sieben Geschosse dieser Stahlbetonkonstruktion (einschließlich vier Parkebenen) liegen unterhalb der Erdoberfläche und umfassen insgesamt zwei Drittel der gesamten Nutzfläche von 20000m². Auf dem 3374m² großen Gelände befinden sich außerdem verschiedene Gartenanlagen, die von dem belgischen Gartenarchitekten Jacques Wirtz entworfen wurden und deren Konturen das strahlenförmige Linienspiel des Hauptgebäudes noch einmal aufnehmen. Für die Wegweiser und die Innenausstattung der Zentrale der Banque de Luxembourg zeichnet der Pariser Architekt und Designer Jean-Michel Wilmotte verantwortlich. Ein ungewöhnlicher Bestandteil dieses Projekts ist die sogenannte »Villa Amélie« auf der Rückseite des Hauptgebäudes, die die Speisesäle der leitenden Angestellten beherbergt und deren Konstruktionsweise gezielt das äußere Erscheinungsbild der angrenzenden französischen Botschaft imitiert.

Premier projet d'Arquitectonica pour l'Europe, cet immeuble est situé à un angle du boulevard Royal, en plein centre-ville. Comme le précise Bernardo Fort-Brescia, qui l'a dessiné: «Nous voulions dire qu'en dépit de sa longue histoire, la banque était bien une institution de progrès.» Cet objectif a été atteint à travers diverses formes architecturales: une «boîte» en pierre de Chassagne en porte-à-faux et à grandes fenêtres carrées en verre ambré s'aligne sur le boulevard, tandis qu'une tour recouverte de glace verte suit la courbe de la rue. Ces deux volumes sont reliés par un parallélogramme de granit noir poli, et un bloc de granit brut de Normandie pesant 43 tonnes marque l'entrée. Sept niveaux de cette construction en béton renforcé sont souterrains, dont quatre pour les parkings. Ils représentent les deux tiers des 20000m² de l'immeuble. Le terrain de 3374m² est également occupé par un jardin dessiné par le paysagiste belge Jacques Wirtz, dont le plan rappelle les radiales et les courbes du bâtiment principal. La signalétique et le mobilier sont l'œuvre du designer parisien Jean-Michel Wilmotte. Une des surprises de ce projet est la «Villa Amélie», petit hôtel particulier à l'arrière du bâtiment principal. Elle abrite essentiellement les salles à manger de direction, et s'inspire des façades de l'ambassade de France toute proche.

Page 61 top: A view of the Bank from the Boulevard Royal. Bottom left: The building at the rear, showing the garden by Jacques Wirtz. Bottom right: The "Villa Amélie."

Seite 61 oben: Ansicht der Bank vom Boulevard Royal aus. Unten links: Der von Jacques Wirtz entworfene Garten auf der Rückseite. Unten rechts: Die »Villa Amélie«.

Page 61 en haut: La banque vue du Boulevard Royal. En bas à gauche: Le jardin à l'arrière, dessiné par Jacques Wirtz. En bas à droite: La «Villa Amélie».

Bottom: Watercolor plan of the site and garden by Jacques Wirtz. Right: The oval elevator descending from ground level.
Page 63: The lower level banking hall.

Unten: Aquarellstudie des Geländes und des Gartens von Jacques Wirtz. Rechts: Der ovale Lift, vom Erdgeschoß auf dem Weg nach unten.
Seite 63: Die Schalterhalle im Untergeschoß.

En bas: Plan aquarellé du site et du jardin, par Jacques Wirtz. A droite: L'ascenseur ovale.
Page 63: Le niveau inférieur du hall de la banque.

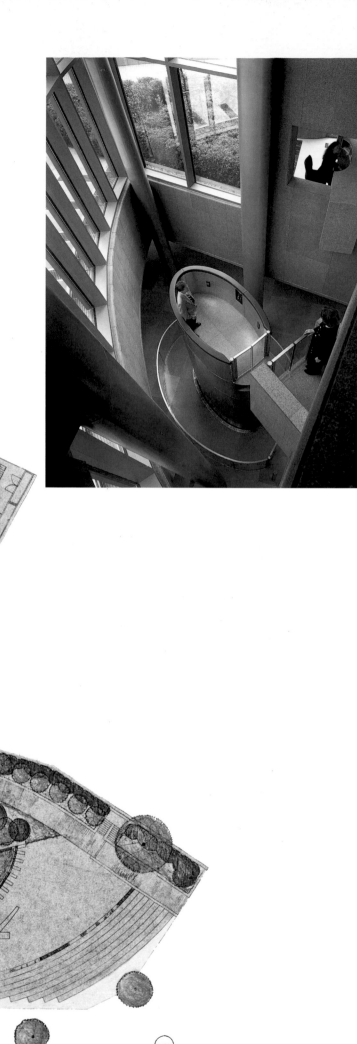

42nd Street Project, New York, New York 1995 (project)

A cooperative venture of the Disney Corporation and the Tishman Urban Development Corporation, this multi-building complex, meant to symbolize the rebirth of Times Square is scheduled to open on January 1, 2000. Located at the corner of Eighth Avenue and 42nd Street, the building is designed to look like a crashing comet. Arquitectonica, who won this project in a competition over Michael Graves and Zaha Hadid will design a 47 story tower for a 680 room hotel sheathed in colored glass, like the curving tail of the comet. A retail and entertainment complex closer to ground level will be covered with "supersigns," and a tower of video monitors will mark the entrance of the hotel on the corner of Eighth Avenuc. The New York Times called this project "an apocalypse with room service," but it seems evident that the animation desired by the clients for this difficult site has been achieved by Arquitectonica. The apparently chaotic appearance of the lower levels was designed by the architects as an echo of the highly commercial and occasionally dangerous surrounding streets. With this project, if it is successfully completed, Arquitectonica will not only prove its ability to work in the very particular environment of Manhattan with major corporate clients, but also, hopefully, show that intriguing modern architecture can have a beneficial impact on urban blight.

Bei diesem, zahlreiche Bauten umfassenden Gebäudekomplex handelt es sich um ein Gemeinschaftsprojekt der Disney Corporation und der Tishman Urban Development Corporation, das bei seiner geplanten Eröffnung am 1. Januar 2000 die Wiedergeburt des Times Square symbolisieren soll. Das Design des auf einem Eckgelände an der Eighth Avenue und 42nd Street gelegenen Gebäudes soll an einen explodierenden Meteor erinnern. Das Architekturbüro Arquitectonica, das sich bei der Ausschreibung gegen Michael Graves und Zaha Hadid durchsetzen konnte, wird einen 47-geschossigen, buntglasverkleideten Hotelturm mit 680 Zimmern entwerfen, der dem gebogenen Schweif des Meteors ähneln soll. Ein Ladengeschäfts- und Unterhaltungsbereich in der Nähe des Erdgeschosses wird hinter »Supersigns« versteckt sein, während ein Turm aus Videomonitoren den Eingangsbereich zum Hotel an der Ecke zur Eighth Avenue markiert. Die »New York Times« bezeichnete dieses Projekt als »eine Apokalypse mit Zimmerservice«, aber es scheint klar ersichtlich, daß der von den Bauherren geäußerte Wunsch nach einer Belebung dieses schwierigen Geländes von Arquitectonica erfüllt wurde. Das offensichtlich chaotische Erscheinungsbild der unteren Geschosse entwarfen die Architekten als Spiegelbild der hochkommerziellen und gelegentlich gefährlichen umliegenden Straßenzüge. Mit diesem Projekt – sollte es denn erfolgreich fertiggestellt werden – wird Arquitectonica nicht nur beweisen, daß das Büro in der Lage ist, im sehr schwierigen Umfeld Manhattans mit Kunden aus der Großindustrie zusammenzuarbeiten, sondern auch hoffentlich dokumentieren, daß faszinierende moderne Architektur einen wohltuenden Einfluß auf verwahrloste Wohngegenden und Stadtlandschaften haben kann.

Réalisation commune de Disney Corporation et Tishman Urban Development Corporation, cet ensemble de plusieurs bâtiments destiné à symboliser la renaissance de Times Square devrait être inauguré le 1er janvier 2000. Arquitectonica a remporté le concours en compétition contre Michael Graves et Zaha Hadid. Situé à l'angle de la 8ème avenue et de la 42ème rue, le projet évoque un explosion de météore. Il comprend une tour de 47 étages pour un hôtel de 680 chambres gainé de verre teinté, et incurvé comme la queue d'une comète. Un complexe de commerces et de salles de spectacles sera recouvert de «supersigns» (enseignes et panneaux publicitaires géants) et une tour de moniteurs vidéo marquera l'entrée de l'hôtel à l'angle de la 8ème avenue. «The New York Times» a qualifié ce projet d'«apocalypse avec service à la chambre», mais il semble certain que l'animation souhaitée par les clients pour ce site difficile et très en vue sera atteinte. Aux yeux des architectes, l'apparence visuellement chaotique des niveaux inférieurs fait écho au caractère hautement commercial et accessoirement dangereux des rues avoisinantes. Avec ce projet, s'il est mené à bien, Arquitectonica aura non seulement prouvé sa capacité à travailler pour des clients prestigieux dans l'environnement très particulier de Manhattan, mais également, espérons-le, montré qu'une architecture moderne surprenante peut avoir un effet bénéfique sur la décrépitude urbaine.

Page 65: The shape of the 42nd Street tower is intended to resemble a comet crashing into Times Square. Shops at street level retain the animated atmosphere typical of this part of Manhattan.

Seite 65: Die Form des 42nd Street-Turms soll an einen auf dem Times Square einschlagenden Meteor erinnern. Die Ladengeschäfte im Erdgeschoß sorgen für eine belebte Atmosphäre, die typisch ist für diesen Teil Manhattans.

Page 65: La forme de la tour élevée sur 42nd Street veut évoquer une comète s'écrasant sur Times Square. Les magasins au niveau de la rue conserveront l'atmosphère animée caractéristique de ce quartier de Manhattan.

Will **Bruder**

Will Bruder

Phoenix Central Library, Phoenix, Arizona, 1988–95. The main reading room on the upper level of the library.

Phoenix Central Library, Phoenix, Arizona, 1988–95. Der große Lesesaal im Obergeschoß der Bibliothek.

Phoenix Central Library, Phoenix, Arizona, 1988–95. La grande salle de lecture, au niveau supérieur de la bibliothèque.

Although he is only now coming to national and even international attention, Will Bruder has already been working for 28 years on a total of 350 commissions. His style can be situated between the Modern and the Organic style which flourished in the southwestern United States with such masters as Frank Lloyd Wright and Bruce Goff. The fact that he is self-trained as an architect and that he pointedly refers to his own "quality pursuit of architecture as art married to a hands-on sense of reality" does not contribute to his being seen as a mainstream figure. Cultivating his image of a "rebel with long hair" Bruder sought out not only Goff but other unusual figures of the architecture world such as Paolo Soleri under whom he participated in a summer workshop in 1967 at Arcosanti, and the California architect John Lautner. More recent influences have included Carlo Scarpa, whose work he encountered during a stay at the American Academy in Rome in 1987, and Antoine Predock, the other key figure in the current rise of southwestern architecture.

Will Bruder ist bereits seit 28 Jahren als Architekt tätig und hat in dieser Zeit etwa 350 Projekte fertiggestellt. Sein Stil kann zwischen Moderne und organischem Stil eingeordnet werden, der im Südwesten der USA von Meistern wie Frank Lloyd Wright und Bruce Goff populär gemacht wurde. Bruder ist als Architekt Autodidakt und spricht anzüglich von seinem eigenen »Qualitätsanspruch von Architektur als Kunst, die mit einem praktischen Sinn für Realität verheiratet ist« – beide Punkte machen es schwer, ihn als typischen Architekten des Mainstream zu sehen. Darüber hinaus kultivierte Bruder sein Image des »langhaarigen Rebellen«, indem er bei Goff und einigen anderen ungewöhnlichen Größen der Architekturwelt lernte. Dazu gehörten auch Paolo Soleri, bei dem er 1967 in Arcosanti an einem Sommer-Workshop teilnahm, sowie der kalifornische Architekt John Lautner. Zu seinen neueren Einflüssen zählen Carlo Scarpa sowie Antoine Predock, eine weitere Schlüsselfigur im gegenwärtigen Boom der Architektur des amerikanischen Südwestens.

Bien qu'il vienne tout juste d'accéder à la reconnaissance nationale et même internationale, Will Bruder travaille déjà depuis 28 ans et est intervenu sur 350 chantiers. Son style se situait entre le modernisme et l'architecture organique qui a fleuri dans les Etats du sud-ouest américain avec des maîtres comme Frank Lloyd Wright et Bruce Goff. Le fait qu'il soit architecte autodidacte et qu'il revendique sa «poursuite qualitative de l'architecture en tant qu'art associée à un sens concret des réalités», en font un personnage à part. Cultivant son image de «rebelle aux cheveux longs», il s'est inspiré de Goff mais aussi d'autres grandes figures du monde de l'architecture comme Paolo Soleri, qui dirigeait un séminaire auquel il participait à Arcosanti en 1967, et l'architecte californien John Lautner. Parmi ses influences plus récentes, citons l'œuvre de Carlo Scarpa, qu'il découvrit lors d'un séjour à l'Académie américaine de Rome, en 1987, et Antoine Predock, autre figure-clé de la montée en puissance actuelle de l'architecture du sud-ouest.

Phoenix Central Library, Phoenix, Arizona
1988–95

This 25000 square meter structure is intended to serve as the central library of Phoenix until at least 2040, presently containing over one million volumes. A prominent feature is the ribbed copper cladding used to cover a good part of the exterior, especially on the east and west facades. The southern elevation is entirely glass covered. Inside, the ground floor combines current fiction, audio, video, computing, a children's reading room, a theater, and a café. The library's services are spread on five floors with copper-clad mechanical and service "saddlebags" which protect the interior from the extremely hot desert sun. The most spectacular interior space is the fifth floor 4000 square meter reading room, housing the entire collection of circulating non-fiction books. Arrival to this "great room" is via glass elevators or a grand sculptural staircase of steel, concrete and translucent glass. At the center of the building, there is a five story atrium/light well which Bruder has dubbed the "Crystal Canyon." According to the architect, the cost per square foot was $97.60 – within the $100 budget – and half the price of libraries built recently in Chicago, Los Angeles and San Francisco.

Dieses 25000m² große Gebäude soll der Stadt Phoenix mindestens bis zum Jahre 2040 als Räumlichkeit für die Zentralbibliothek dienen, die zur Zeit bereits mehr als 1 Million Bände umfaßt. Zu den herausragenden Kennzeichen dieses Komplexes gehört die Kupferrippenverkleidung, die einen Großteil der Fassade und insbesondere die östlichen und westlichen Bereiche bedeckt. Die Südseite ist dagegen vollständig verglast. Im Erdgeschoß befinden sich die Abteilungen Belletristik, Audio, Video und Computer sowie ein Kinderlesesaal, ein Theater und ein Café. Die eigentliche Bibliothek umfaßt fünf Stockwerke, deren kupferverkleidete »Satteltaschen« (hinter denen sich die Technik und die Versorgungsleitungen verbergen) die Innenräume vor der extrem heißen Wüstensonne schützen. Der aufsehenerregendste Raum ist der 4000m² große Lesesaal im fünften Stock, der die gesamte ausleihbare Sachbuch-Sammlung enthält. Diesen »großen Saal« erreicht man über gläserne Aufzüge oder durch ein imposantes skulpturales Treppenhaus aus Stahl, Beton und Milchglas. In der Mitte des Gebäudes erstreckt sich ein Atrium/Lichtschacht über alle fünf Geschosse – von Bruder als »Crystal Canyon« bezeichnet. Laut Aussage des Architekten beliefen sich die Baukosten pro Quadratmeter auf 1050 Dollar und blieben damit innerhalb des vorgegebenen Budgets von 1076 Dollar pro Quadratmeter; dies entspricht der Hälfte der Baukosten für die in letzter Zeit fertiggestellten Bibliotheken in Chicago, Los Angeles und San Francisco.

Contenant déjà plus d'un million de volumes, ce bâtiment de 25000 m² devrait servir de bibliothèque centrale de la ville de Phoenix jusqu'en 2040. Il se signale de loin par une couverture en cuivre nervuré sur une bonne partie des surfaces extérieures, en particulier les façades est et ouest. La façade sud est entièrement vitrée. A l'intérieur, le rez-de-chaussée accueille la littérature, les sections audio, vidéo et informatique ainsi qu'une salle de lecture pour enfants, un auditorium et un café. Les services de la bibliothèque sont répartis sur cinq niveaux avec des espaces techniques en forme de «saddlebags» (sacoches de selle) plaqués de cuivre, et protégeant leur contenu du soleil brûlant du désert. L'espace intérieur le plus spectaculaire est la salle de lecture de 4000 m², qui, au cinquième niveau, abrite toute la collection de livres de prêt non littéraires. L'arrivée sur cette vaste salle se fait par des ascenseurs en verre ou un grand escalier sculptural en acier, béton et verre translucide. Au centre du bâtiment s'ouvre, sur cinq niveaux, un puits-atrium que Bruder appelle «le canyon de cristal». Selon l'architecte, le coût au mètre carré de ce programme a été inférieur aux 1050 dollars le m² prévus, soit la moitié du prix des bibliothèques actuellement édifiées à Chicago, Los Angeles et San Francisco.

Page 69: The Phoenix Central Library in Phoenix. The fifth floor plan shows the 4000 square meter main reading room, as well as the technical areas called "saddlebags" by Bruder on each side.

Seite 69: Die Phoenix Central Library in Phoenix. Der Grundriß des fünften Stocks zeigt den 4000 m² großen Lesesaal sowie die »Satteltaschen« (wie Bruder sie bezeichnet), in denen Versorgungsleitungen und technische Einrichtungen untergebracht sind.

Page 69: The Phoenix Central Library à Phoenix. Plan du cinquième étage montrant la grande salle de lecture (4000 m²) et, de chaque côté, les zones techniques appelées «saddle bags» (sacoches de selle) par Bruder.

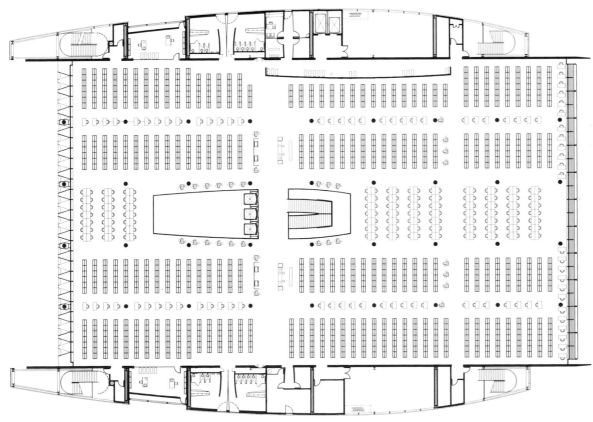

Pages 72/73: A system of stretched sails over the glass covered southern facade of the building shields the interior from the intense local sunlight.

Seite 72/73: Ein System von gespannten Segeln über der glasverkleideten Südfassade des Gebäudes schützt die Innenräume vor dem intensiven Sonnenlicht dieser Gegend.

Pages 72/73: Un système de voiles tendues sur la façade sud vitrée protège l'intérieur de l'intensité du soleil de la région.

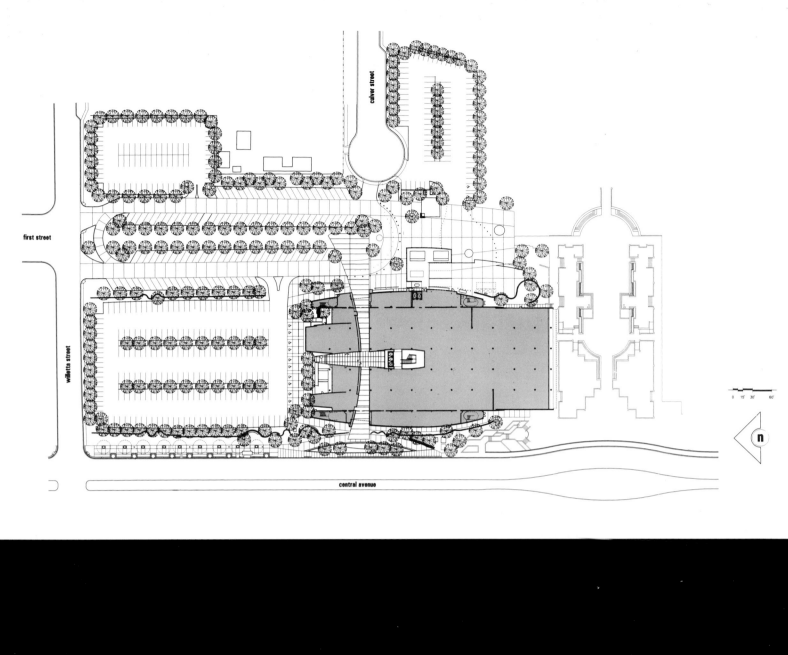

first street

willetta street

culver street

central avenue

0 15' 30' 60'

n

Peter **Eisenman**

Peter Eisenman

A model of the Max Reinhardt Haus shows how much higher it would be than surrounding buildings.

Das Modell des Max Reinhardt Hauses zeigt deutlich, daß es die umliegenden Gebäude bei weitem überragen würde.

Maquette de la Max Reinhardt Haus montrant à quel point l'immeuble dominera les constructions avoisinantes.

Peter Eisenman remains one of the more controversial figures in the American architecture world, and it would seem that that is precisely the status he cultivates. Having recently moved to less spacious offices on 25th Street in New York, Peter Eisenman remains philosophical. "I'm not a rebel," he says, "I just go with my flow. I manage to continue to build. I build one out of 20 projects I design, but I would rather do that than endlessly repeat the things I've done before." Intent on redefining architecture itself, Eisenman continues, "I am looking for ways of conceptualizing space that will place the subject in a displaced relationship because they will have no iconographic references to traditional forms of organisation. That is what I have always been trying to do – to displace the subject – to oblige the subject to reconceptualize architecture." Although his Max Reinhardt Haus project poses numerous problems which may not allow it to be built, his Arnoff Center for Design and Art in Cincinnati, Ohio is nearing completion.

Peter Eisenman zählt zu den umstrittensten Figuren der amerikanischen Architekturwelt, und allem Anschein nach ist dies genau der Status, den er anstrebt. Trotz seines Umzugs in weniger großzügige Räume auf der 25th Street in New York bleibt Eisenman philosophisch. »Ich bin kein Rebell«, sagt er, »ich gehe einfach meiner Arbeit nach. Ich bin in der glücklichen Lage, ständig bauen zu können. Ich baue zwar nur eines von 20 Projekten, die ich entwerfe, aber dies ist mir lieber als eine endlose Wiederholung der Dinge, die ich schon einmal getan habe«. »Ich suche nach Wegen, Räume in Begriffe zu fassen, die ein Objekt in verschobene Zusammenhänge stellen, weil sie keinerlei ikonographische Bezüge zu traditionellen Organisationsformen mehr aufweisen. Das ist es, was ich immer versucht habe – das Objekt zu verschieben und es zu zwingen, der Architektur eine neue Begrifflichkeit zu geben.« Sein Projekt des Max Reinhardt Hauses gelangt vielleicht nicht zur Ausführung, während sich sein Arnoff Center for Design and Art in Cincinnati, Ohio, der Vollendung nähert.

Peter Eisenman reste l'une des figures les plus controversées de l'architecture américaine, et il semble bien qu'il cultive ce statut. Récemment installé dans des bureaux moins spacieux de la 25ème rue, à New York, il reste philosophe: «Je ne suis pas un rebelle, j'obéis à mon propre rythme. Je fais en sorte de continuer à construire. Je construis un sur vingt des projets que je dessine, mais je préfère cette solution plutôt que de répéter sans fin ce que j'ai fait auparavant.» Tout entier à redéfinir l'architecture elle-même, il poursuit: «Je recherche des façons de conceptualiser l'espace qui va mettre le sujet dans une relation déplacée parce qu'il ne trouvera pas de référence iconographiques aux formes traditionnelles d'organisation. C'est ce que j'ai toujours essayé de faire, de déplacer le sujet—d'obliger le sujet à reconceptualiser l'architecture.» Si les deux tours de sa Max Reinhardt Haus posent tellement de problèmes qu'elles ne seront peut-être jamais construites, son Arnoff Center for Design et Art à Cincinnati, Ohio, est en passe d'être achevé.

Max Reinhardt Haus, Berlin, Germany
1994 (project)

Located at the major intersection formed by Unter den Linden (east-west) and Friedrichstrasse (north-south), the site of this project was recognized as pivotal, according to Peter Eisenman, and chosen as a location for potential landmarks such as the project for the first glass "skyscraper" designed by Mies van der Rohe shortly after World War I. Named for a famous German theatrical entrepreneur, it would be built in the same place as his Schauspielhaus designed by Hans Poelzig. Designed in obvious violation of Berlin height restrictions, one reason that it has not yet been built, the double tower is the result of computer "morphing" of a Möbius strip. According to Eisenman, it would have a "prismatic" character, folding into itself, but also opening itself out to an infinite, always fragmentary, and constantly changing array of metropolitan references and relationships." Eisenman goes on to say, "it will become a truly prophetic building. Such a structure amounts to a singularity in the city itself, acquiring the capacity to represent on one site that which is of many places."

Die Lage dieses an einer der größten Berliner Straßenkreuzungen geplanten Projekts – Unter den Linden (Ost-West-Richtung) und Friedrichstraße (Nord-Süd-Richtung) – wurde nach Aussage des Architekten Peter Eisenman als geeigneter Standort für ein potentielles Wahrzeichen der Stadt ausgewählt (vergleichbar dem ersten, von Mies van der Rohe kurz nach dem Ersten Weltkrieg entworfenen Glas-Wolkenkratzer). Das nach dem berühmten deutschen Theaterregisseur benannte Gebäude soll auf dem gleichen Gelände entstehen wie das von Hans Poelzig entworfene Schauspielhaus. Für das offensichtlich in krassem Widerspruch zu Berlins Bauhöhenvorschriften geplante Gebäude – ein Grund dafür, daß es bisher nicht gebaut wurde – ist ein Doppelturm vorgesehen, der das Ergebnis eines computergesteuerten »Morphing« eines Moebiusschen Bandes ist. Laut Eisenman würde das Gebäude »einen prismatischen Charakter aufweisen: es klappt nicht nur in sich selbst zusammen, sondern öffnet sich auch einer unendlichen, stets fragmentarischen und beständig wechselnden Phalanx metropolitischer Bezüge und Beziehungen«. Der Architekt fährt fort: »Es wird ein wahrhaft prophetisches Bauwerk werden. Eine solche Konstruktion summiert sich zu etwas Einzigartigem mitten in der Stadt, und sie besitzt die Fähigkeit, auf einem einzigen Gelände das zu repräsentieren, was sonst über viele Orte verteilt ist.«

Situé à un grand carrefour entre Unter den Linden (est-ouest) et Friedrich-strasse (nord-sud), l'emplacement de ce projet est stratégique et, selon Peter Eisenman, destiné à des réalisations monumentales comme celle du premier «gratte-ciel» de verre de Mies van der Rohe, qui y avait été prévu, peu après la première guerre mondiale. Nommé en hommage à un célèbre producteur de théâtre allemand, cet immeuble devrait être construit au même endroit que sa «Schauspiel-haus» dessinée par Hans Poelzig. Ses plans qui violent ouvertement le code d'urbanisme local, d'où le refus de permis de construire des autorités berlinoises résultent d'un traitement par ordinateur d'un ruban de Möbius. Pour Eisenman, la Max Reinhardt Haus devrait offrir un caractère «prismatique», se repliant sur elle-même tout en s'ouvrant sur une multiplicité infinie, toujours fragmentaire et constamment changeante de références et de relations à la ville. «Ce sera un immeuble réellement prophétique. Avec sa capacité de représenter en un seul site ce qui appartient à de multiples lieux, une telle construction marquera de sa singularité le cœur de la cité elle-même.»

Page 77: This tower which Eisenman has described as "bi-sexual," would in his mind also be a reminder, through its form, of such events as the "Kristallnacht."

Seite 77: Dieser von Eisenman als »bisexuell« bezeichnete Turm erinnert den Architekten aufgrund seiner Form an historische Ereignisse wie die »Reichskristallnacht«.

Page 77: Cette tour décrite par Eisenman comme «bi-sexuelle», devrait aussi rappeler par sa forme des événements comme «la Nuit de cristal».

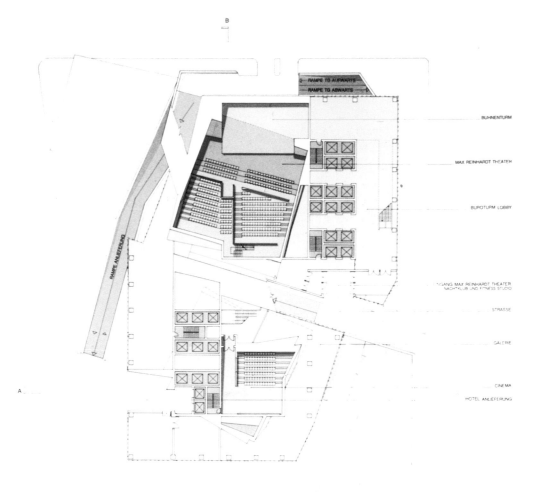

EBENE 0   MAX REINHARDT THEATER UND BURO TURM LOBBY

Peter **Forbes**

Peter Forbes

House on Mount Desert Island, Maine, 1991–93. A view of the facade emphasizes the extremely simple design of the house.

House on Mount Desert Island, Maine, 1991–93. Die Ansicht der Fassade betont das extrem schlichte Design des Hauses.

Maison sur Mount Desert Island, Maine, 1991–93. Vue de la façade mettant en valeur la simplicité extrême du dessin de la maison.

After working with the large firm of Skidmore, Owings and Merrill in Chicago (1965–66), Peter Forbes began his career in Boston as an associate partner with PARD Team, Inc., Architects and Planners. President of Forbes Hailey Jeas Erneman from 1972 to 1980, he created Peter Forbes and Associates in Boston and Southwest Harbor, Maine in 1980. Aside from numerous private houses in Massachusetts, New York or Maine, he built the Public Library in Southwest Harbor, and a church in Sacco, ME (1990) and has designed numerous retail outlets for Origins Natural Resources. His house on Mount Desert Island, ME, published here represents an interesting effort to build for a client with chemical sensitivities and environmental concerns. This required that all of the materials used in the construction be environmentally inert. The steel, aluminum and glass used are recycled, and the wood used (maple and cedar) is not an endangered species. Plywood, polyurethane varnishes, PVC piping and other frequently used building materials were not employed for environmental reasons.

Nachdem er 1965–66 für das bekannte Architekturbüro Skidmore, Owings & Merrill in Chicago gearbeitet hatte, begann Peter Forbes seine Laufbahn in Boston als Teilhaber von PARD Team, Inc., Architects and Planners. Von 1972 bis 1980 war er Präsident von Forbes Hailey Jeas Erneman, 1980 gründete er Peter Forbes and Associates mit Niederlassungen in Boston und Maine. Neben Privathäusern in Massachusetts, New York und Maine entwarf er die öffentliche Bibliothek von Southwest Harbor, eine Kirche in Sacco, Maine (1990) sowie Einzelhandelsgeschäfte für Origins Natural Resources. Sein Haus auf Mount Desert Island, Maine, stellt einen interessanten Versuch dar, umweltbewußt und weitestgehend frei von chemischen Substanzen zu bauen. Deshalb mußten alle beim Bau verwendeten Materialien umweltverträglich sein. Forbes benutzte recycelten Stahl, Aluminium und Glas sowie Ahorn- und Zedernholz, die nicht zu bedrohten Pflanzenarten zählen. Dagegen verzichtete er auf Sperrholz, Polyurethanlacke, Rohrleitungen aus PVC und andere häufig verwendete Baumaterialien.

Après avoir travaillé pour Skidmore, Owings & Merrill à Chicago (1965–66), Peter Forbes a commencé sa carrière comme associé de PARD Team Inc. Architects and Planners, Boston. Président de Forbes Hailey Jeas Erneman de 1972 à 1980, il crée Peter Forbes & Associates à Boston et Southwest Harbor (Maine) en 1980. Professeur invité à Harvard (1989, 1991, 1994), et University of Michigan (1987), il a été président de l'Association des Architectes de Boston (1988–89). On lui doit la bibliothèque de Southwest Harbor, une église à Sacco, Maine (1990), et nombreuses boutiques pour Origins Natural Resources. Sa maison de Mount Desert Island répond aux attentes d'un client soucieux d'écologie. L'acier, l'aluminium et le verre sont des matériaux recyclés, et l'érable utilisé appartient à une espèce abondante. Le contreplaqué, les vernis au polyuréthane et les tuyauteries en plastique, et autres matériaux courants ont été bannis pour des raisons écologiques.

House on Mount Desert Island, Maine 1991–93

This small house of about 150 square meters is situated on a 2 hectare lot. The owner wished to be able to have a good view of the changing seasons in the surrounding mountainous, wooded landscape. Although large glass surfaces are not generally considered to be the most ecologically efficient form of wall, the steel, glass, maple and cedarwood used here are all strictly untreated and non allergenic both for health reasons and to meet the client's ecological requirements. Designed around a tubular steel framework, the house provides spectacular unobstructed space, with an open sleeping area on the ground floor. The strong, simple designs of Peter Forbes, who began his career as a project designer at Skidmore, Owings and Merrill in Chicago, and created his own firm in 1980 have led him to receive numerous commissions for private houses in Massachusetts, Maine, and New York, as well as stores he has designed for Origins Natural Resources in New York, Connecticut, California and Maine.

Dieses kleine, etwa 150 m² umfassende Haus liegt auf einem 2 Hektar großen Gelände. Der Besitzer wünschte sich eine gute Aussicht, die es ihm erlaubte, den Wechsel der Jahreszeiten in der umliegenden gebirgigen und bewaldeten Landschaft zu beobachten. Obwohl große Glasflächen im allgemeinen nicht als besonders umweltfreundliche Wandformen gelten, wurden die hier verwendeten Materialen – Stahl, Glas, Ahorn- und Zedernholz – aufgrund der vom Bauherrn gewünschten Umweltverträglichkeit sowie aus gesundheitlichen Gründen unter anti-allergischen Gesichtspunkten ausgewählt und bewußt nicht chemisch behandelt. Das um eine röhrenförmige Stahlskelettkonstruktion entworfene Haus bietet diverse aufsehenerregende, großzügige Räume wie etwa den offenen Schlafbereich im Erdgeschoß. Aufgrund seiner aussagekräftigen, einfachen Entwürfe erhielt der Architekt Peter Forbes – der seine Karriere als Projektdesigner bei Skidmore, Owings & Merrill in Chicago begann und 1980 seine eigene Firma gründete – zahlreiche Aufträge für Privathäuser in Massachusetts, Maine und New York sowie für mehrere Ladenlokale, die er für Origins Natural Resources in New York, Connecticut, Kalifornien und Maine gestaltete.

Cette petite maison de 150 m² environ est édifiée sur un terrain de 2 hectares. Son propriétaire souhaitait bénéficier d'une vue dégagée pour mieux profiter des changements de saisons particulièrement spectaculaires dans ce paysage boisé et montagneux. Certes, les murs largement vitrés ne sont généralement pas propices aux économies d'énergie, mais, l'acier, le verre, l'érable et le cèdre utilisés ici sont tous strictement non traités et anallergéniques, pour des raisons de santé et pour répondre au souci d'écologie du client. Dessinée autour d'une structure d'acier tubulaire, la maison offre un volume spectaculairement libre avec un espace ouvert pour dormir au rez-de-chaussée. Le style simple et puissant de Peter Forbes, qui a commencé sa carrière comme dessinateur de projet chez Skidmore, Owings and Merrill et a créé sa propre agence en 1980, lui a valu de nombreuses commandes de résidences privées dans le Massachusetts, le Maine et l'Etat de New York, ou de magasins comme ceux de Origins Natural Resources à New York, dans le Connecticut, le Maine et en Californie.

Page 81: Located on Mount Desert Island, the largest island off the coast of Maine, this wedge-shaped house offers spectacular views of the surrounding landscape through its large glazed sides.

Seite 81: Dieses keilförmige, auf Mount Desert Island – der größten Insel vor der Küste von Maine – gelegene Haus bietet durch seine großen Glasflächen an den Seiten eine spektakuläre Aussicht auf die umliegende Landschaft.

Page 81: Située sur Mount Desert Island, la plus grande des îles au large du Maine, cette maison en coin offre, avec ses vastes baies, une vue spectaculaire sur le paysage environnant.

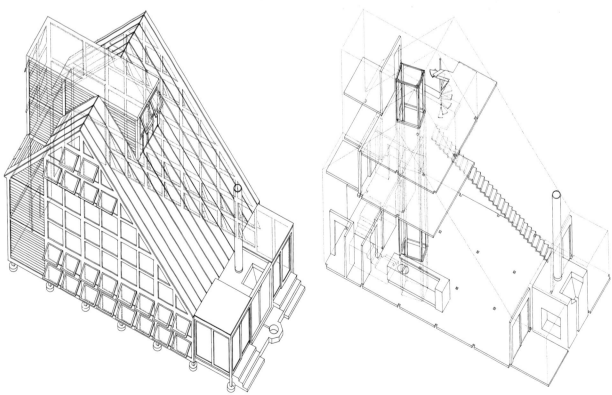

Page 82: The main stairway, running parallel to the sloping roof.
Page 83: The site plan and a photo show how the house is surrounded by trees.

Seite 82: Das Haupttreppenhaus, das parallel zur Dachschräge verläuft.
Seite 83: Der Geländeplan und die Fotografie zeigen, daß das Haus von zahlreichen Bäumen umgeben ist.

Page 82: L'escalier principal, parallèle au toit en pente.
Page 83: Le plan de situation et la photo montrent l'environnement arboré de la maison.

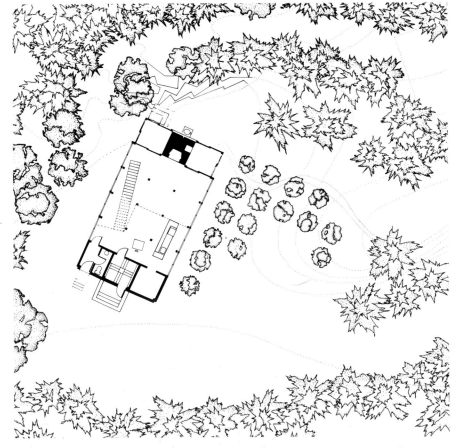

Frank O. Gehry

Frank O. Gehry

Vitra Headquarters, Basel, Switzerland, 1988/92–94. Painted stucco and zinc panels mark the exuberant exterior forms of the Vitra Headquarters.

Vitra Headquarters, Basel, Schweiz, 1988/92–94. Gestrichener Putz und Zinkblechpaneele kennzeichnen die geschwungenen Formen der Vitra-Hauptverwaltung.

Siège social de Vitra, Bâle, Suisse, 1988/92–94. Les enduits peints et les panneaux en zinc soulignent l'exubérance du bâtiment.

Born in Toronto, Canada in 1929, Frank O. Gehry is one of the more influential architects working today. Not only has he successfully called into question the forms which modern architecture has taken for granted, but he has done the same for materials of construction. It is not that steel and concrete are absent from his work, but rather that chain link, corrugated aluminum, or utility grade construction board are present. Gehry seems to be as much at ease building a giant fish (Fishdance Restaurant, Kobe, Japan, 1984), as he is with an office building whose facade incorporates a huge pair of binoculars (designed by Claes Oldenburg for Chiat/Day, Venice, California, 1989). His largest project to date, the Disney Concert Hall in Los Angeles has been halted for the moment for lack of fundraising and budgetary reasons. Ongoing work includes: the Guggenheim Museum, Bilbao, Spain; the Samsung Museum, Seoul, Korea; commercial projects in Prague, Czech Republic, Düsseldorf, Hannover, Germany; the Mighty Ducks Rink, L. A., and an administration building for Disneyland in California.

Der 1929 in Toronto, Kanada geborene Frank O. Gehry ist einer der einflußreichsten Architekten der heutigen Zeit. Er stellt nicht nur die Formen, sondern auch die Baumaterialien in Frage, die die moderne Architektur als selbstverständlich voraussetzte. Er baut zwar nicht ohne Stahl und Beton, aber im Vordergrund seiner Arbeiten stehen Wellblech und Fertigbauteile. Darüber hinaus scheint er ein ebenso großes Vergnügen daran zu haben, einen gewaltigen Fisch zu bauen (Fishdance Restaurant, Kobe, Japan, 1984) wie die Fassade eines Bürogebäudes mit einem riesigen Fernglas zu krönen (Entwurf Claes Oldenburg für Chiat/ Day, Venice, Kalifornien, 1989). Bei seinem bisher größten Projekt, der Disney Concert Hall in Los Angeles, erfolgte ein budgetbedingter Baustopp mangels Fundraising. Zu Gehrys derzeitigen Arbeiten zählen das Guggenheim Museum, Bilbao, Spanien, das Samsung Museum, Seoul, gewerbliche Projekte in Prag, Düsseldorf und Hannover und das Eisstadion der Mighty Ducks in Los Angeles und ein Verwaltungsgebäude für Disneyland, Kalifornien.

Né à Toronto (Canada), en 1929, Frank O. Gehry a non seulement remis brillamment en question des formes que l'architecture moderne tenait pour acquises, mais il a fait de même avec les matériaux. Il utilise bien sûr l'acier et le béton, mais ne se prive pas de faire appel au treillage métallique, à l'aluminium ondulé ou aux planches en bois de construction. Il semble aussi à l'aise pour dessiner un poisson géant (Fishdance Restaurant, Kobé, Japon, 1984) qu'un immeuble de bureaux dont la façade s'orne de jumelles géantes (créées par Claes Oldenburg, pour l'agence de publicité Chiat/Day, Venice, Californie, 1989). Son plus important projet à ce jour, le Disney Concert Hall (Los Angeles) est pour l'instant arrêté pour des raisons budgétaires, et à cause de l'insuffisance des fonds recueillis. Parmi ses autres projets en cours: Le Guggenheim Museum (Bilbao, Espagne), le musée Samsung à Séoul, des projets d'immeubles commerciaux à Prague, Düsseldorf et Hanovre, le Mighty Ducks Rink (Los Angeles) et le bâtiment administratif de Disneyland en Californie.

Vitra Headquarters, Basel, Switzerland
1988/1992–94

This project is the first phase of a planned development for the same German furniture manufacturer who has already called on Frank O. Gehry for the design of a museum in Weil am Rhein, just across the border from Basel. The museum is of course on the same site as factory buildings by Nicholas Grimshaw and Alvaro Siza, a conference center by Tadao Ando and a fire station by Zaha Hadid. The headquarters, located in Birsfelden, outside Basel, is a 6000 square meter building designed so that the offices can become showrooms. Zoning in the area required a building less than ten meters high, and the Swiss energy code did not allow air-conditioning in offices, so natural ventilation was provided for through windows and the southern wall shaded by a large canopy. The main entrance and reception area is located centrally to permit its use in the case of possible future expansion. Plans for the building make clear that the richer, sculpted space is concentrated around the entrance, ceding to much more rectilinear design elsewhere. The concrete and masonry structure is covered with a combination of painted stucco, and zinc metal panels.

Dieses Projekt bildet die erste Phase eines geplanten Bauvorhabens für einen deutschen Möbelfabrikanten, der Frank O. Gehry bereits mit der Gestaltung des Vitra-Museums in Weil am Rhein, direkt an der deutsch-schweizerischen Grenze, beauftragte. Das Museum liegt natürlich auf dem gleichen Gelände wie die Fabrikgebäude von Nicholas Grimshaw und Alvaro Siza, das Konferenzzentrum von Tadao Ando und die Feuerwache von Zaha Hadid. Die in Birsfelden, außerhalb von Basel, gelegene und 6000 m² umfassende Zentrale wurde so entworfen, daß die Büroräume zu Ausstellungsflächen umgewandelt werden können. Der örtliche Flächennutzungsplan verlangte ein maximal zehn Meter hohes Gebäude, und da die schweizerischen Energiesparbestimmungen keine Klimaanlagen in Bürogebäuden gestatten, mußte mit Hilfe der Fenster eine natürliche Be- und Entlüftung gewährleistet und die Südwand mit einem großen Vordach versehen werden. Der Haupteingang und der Empfangsbereich liegen zentral, um eine weitere Verwendung bei einem eventuellen späteren Anbau zu ermöglichen. Die Baupläne des Gebäudes zeigen deutlich, daß die aufweniger gestalteten Räume um den Eingangsbereich zentriert sind; im Anschluß folgen die erheblich gradlinigeren Räume in den übrigen Gebäudebereichen. Die eigentliche Beton- und Mauerwerkkonstruktion verbirgt sich hinter einer Kombination aus gestrichenem Putz und Zinkblechpaneelen.

Ce projet est la première phase de réalisation des nouvelles installations d'un fabricant de meubles allemand qui avait déjà fait appel à Frank O. Gehry pour dessiner un musée du design à Weil am Rhein, en Allemagne, face à Bâle, sur le même site que des bâtiments industriels signés Nicholas Grimshaw et Alvaro Siza, un centre de conférences de Tadao Ando et un poste d'incendie de Zaha Hadid. Ce nouveau siège social de Birsfelden, à la périphérie de Bâle, est un bâtiment de 6000 m² dont les bureaux peuvent servir de salles d'exposition commerciale. La réglementation de cette zone interdisait de dépasser une hauteur de 10 m, et le code suisse de l'énergie prohibe l'air conditionné dans les bureaux. Il a donc fallu prévoir une ventilation naturelle par les fenêtres, et le mur sud a été protégé par un immense dais. L'entrée principale et l'aire d'accueil sont au centre, pour faciliter une extension éventuelle du bâtiment. Les plans montrent que l'espace le plus riche, le plus «sculpté», se concentre autour de l'entrée, et cède la place plus loin à une conception plus rectiligne. La structure en béton et en maçonnerie est recouverte d'un mélange d'enduits peints et de panneaux en zinc.

Pages 87–89: The complex architectural forms of the Vitra Headquarters are concentrated in the entrance area, situated so that it can also serve for future expansions. The unusual exteriors of Frank O. Gehry's buildings translate into a sculptural approach to the light and volume of the interiors.

Seite 87–89: Die komplexen architektonischen Formen der Vitra-Hauptverwaltung konzentrieren sich um den Eingangsbereich, der so konzipiert ist, daß weitere Anbauten noch möglich sind. Die ungewöhnlichen Fassaden von Frank O. Gehrys Gebäuden korrespondieren mit einem skulpturalen Ansatz hinsichtlich Licht und Ausdehnung der Innenräume.

Pages 87–89: La complexité architecturale de l'immeuble Vitra est concentrée sur l'entrée, située de manière à s'adapter à de futures extensions. Les insolites façades des bâtiments de Gehry permettent d'intéressants jeux de volumes et de lumière intérieurs.

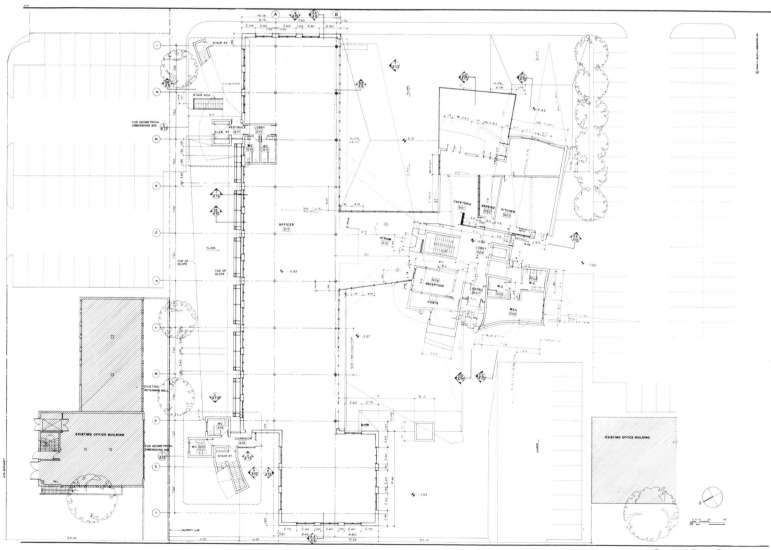

Ground Floor Plan

Guggenheim Museum, Bilbao, Spain
1991–97

Located in the center of the cultural district formed by the Museo de Bellas Artes, the University de Deusto, and the Opera House on a 32700m² site formerly occupied by a factory and parking lot, the new Guggenheim Museum is scheduled to open in the summer of 1997. Three firms participated in an invited competition, Gehry, Arata Isozaki and Coop Himmelblau, and the groundbreaking took place on October 22, 1993. Designed in a co-operative arrangement with New York's Guggenheim, the museum will have 10500m² of galleries, 2500m² of public space, with a 50 meter high atrium, an auditorium, a museum store, a restaurant, and a café. Project costs for the 24000m² building are estimated at $100 million. A sculptural metallic roof form reminiscent of a "metallic flower," designed with the assistance of the CATIA three dimensional aerospace computer modeling program, unifies the project into a single architectural composition. Building materials are titanium, limestone, and glass. The museum's largest space will be a large boat-shaped gallery completely free of structural columns and measuring 130m by 30m. Most gallery ceiling heights will be six meters or more which together with the spectacular atrium, should give a very generous feeling of space to the whole.

Das neue Bilbao Museum, das in der Mitte eines durch das Museo de Bellas Artes, die Universidad de Deusto und das Opernhaus stark kulturell geprägten Viertels auf einem 32700m² großen Gelände entsteht (auf dem früher eine Fabrik und ein Parkplatz lagen), soll voraussichtlich im Sommer 1997 eröffnet werden. Zu dem Wettbewerb wurden drei Architekturbüros – Gehry, Arata Isozaki und Coop Himmelblau – eingeladen; der erste Spatenstich fand am 22. Oktober 1993 statt. Dem in einem Gemeinschaftsprojekt mit dem New Yorker Guggenheim entworfenen Museum werden 10500m² für Ausstellungsflächen sowie 2500m² für öffentliche Räume zur Verfügung stehen – unter anderem ein 50 Meter hohes Atrium, ein Auditorium, ein Museumsgeschäft, ein Restaurant und ein Café. Die geschätzten Baukosten für das 24000m² umfassende Gebäude belaufen sich auf 100 Millionen Dollar. Ein skulpturales Metalldach, dessen Form an eine »Metallblüte« erinnert und das mit Unterstützung von CATIA (einem dreidimensionalen Flugzeugbau-Computerprogramm) entworfen wurde, vereinigt das Projekt zu einer einheitlichen architektonischen Komposition. Als Baumaterialien dienten Titan, Kalkstein und Glas. Den größten Raum des zukünftigen Museums bildet eine 130x30 Meter große, schiffsförmige Galerie, die ohne jegliche Stützen auskommen wird. Die lichte Deckenhöhe der meisten Ausstellungsräume von mindestens 6 Metern in Kombination mit dem außergewöhnlichen Atrium werden dem Gebäude einen großzügigen, weiträumigen Eindruck verleihen.

Implanté au centre du quartier culturel formé par le Museo de Bellas Artes, l'université de Deusto et l'opéra, sur un terrain de 32700m² précédemment occupé par une usine et un parking, le nouveau musée de Bilbao devrait ouvrir à l'été 1997. Trois architectes avaient été invités à soumettre leur projet: Gehry, Arata Isozaki et Coop Himmelblau. Le creusement des fondations a débuté le 22 octobre 1993. Réalisé en collaboration avec le Guggenheim (New York), le musée offrira 10500m² de galeries, 2500m² d'espaces publics, un atrium de 50m de haut, un auditorium, une boutique, un restaurant et un café. Le coût de ses 24000m² est estimé à 100 millions de dollars. Un toit métallique sculptural évoquant une «fleur de métal», conçu avec l'assistance du logiciel de conception en trois dimensions CATIA, mis au point par Dassault, unifie la vaste composition du projet. Les matériaux de construction sont le titane, le calcaire et le verre. Le plus grand espace du musée sera une galerie de 130x30 m, en forme de nef, libre de toute colonne. La plupart des galeries mesureront 6 m de hauteur ou plus, ce qui, avec l'énorme atrium, devrait donner à l'ensemble un généreux sentiment d'espace.

Page 91: No method other than sophisticated computer modeling could have permitted Frank O. Gehry to successfully design such complex forms. In this instance, computer assisted design also assures that the structure can in fact be built.

Seite 91: Nur mit Hilfe modernster Computertechnik gelang es Frank O. Gehry, eine solch komplexe Form zu entwerfen. Darüber hinaus gewährleistet das CAD-Programm, daß die Konstruktion auch tatsächlich errichtet werden kann.

Page 91: L'assistance de l'ordinateur a joué un rôle essentiel dans l'obtention de formes aussi complexes. Dans cet exemple, la CAO permet aussi de vérifier la faisabilité de la construction.

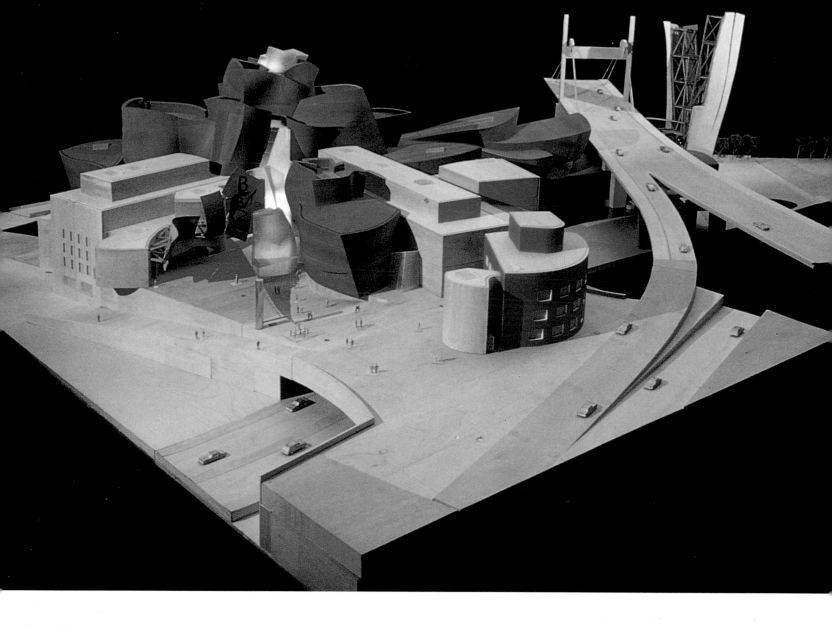

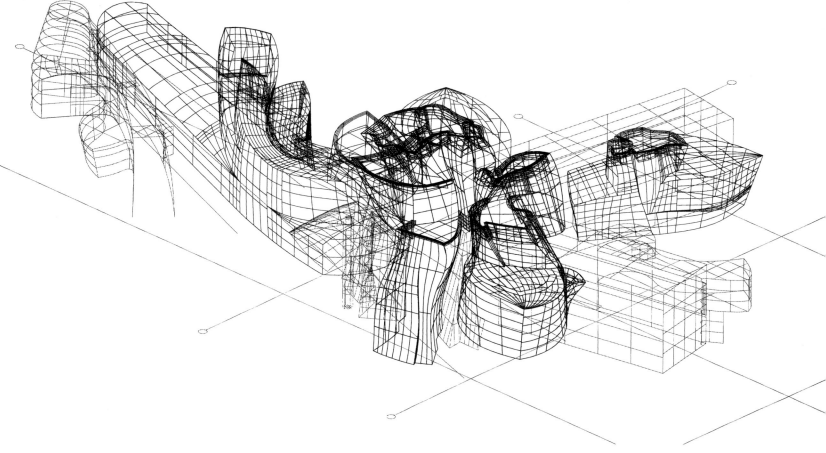

Frank O. Gehry 91

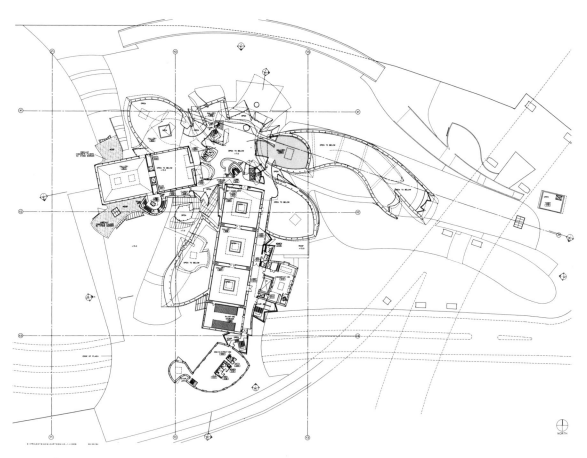

92 Guggenheim Museum

Pages 92/93: Both a plan and model views make it obvious that the Guggenheim Museum will resemble no large building ever built before. It seems closer to large-scale sculpture than to most other architectural forms.

Seite 92/93: Sowohl der Grundriß als auch das Modell veranschaulichen, daß das Guggenheim Museum keinem bisher gebauten großen Bauwerk ähneln wird. Tatsächlich erinnert es eher an eine großformatige Skulptur als an architektonische Formen.

Pages 92/93: Le plan et la maquette montrent l'originalité absolue du futur musée de Bilbao. Il ressemble plus à une énorme sculpture qu'à une architecture.

Steven Holl

Steven Holl

Table designed by Steven Holl in the offices of D.E. Shaw and Company in New York.

Ein von Steven Holl entworfener Tisch in den Büroräumen von D.E. Shaw and Company, New York.

Table dessinée par Steven Holl pour les bureaux de D.E. Shaw & Company, New York.

"A new architecture must be formed that is simultaneously aligned with transcultural continuity and with the poetic expression of individual situations and communities," writes Steven Holl, one of the more promising young architects working in the United States. Although his approach is often unexpected, as in the singularly open facade of the Storefront for Art and Architecture published here, Holl's theoretical stance seems to be coherent with a reevaluation of what architecture is all about in a time of intense political and technological change. This attitude is certainly refreshing in a profession where economic expediency is more often than not the guiding force. Personally reserved, Steven Holl has not cultivated the media personality associated with architects such as Peter Eisenman, but it may be that his approach is fundamentally even more radical than that of some more visible figures.

»Eine neue Architektur muß geformt werden, die sich sowohl an transkultureller Kontinuität als auch am poetischen Ausdruck individueller Situationen und Gemeinschaften ausrichtet«, schreibt Steven Holl, einer der vielversprechendsten jungen Architekten der Vereinigten Staaten. Obwohl sein Ansatz häufig als sehr radikal zu bezeichnen ist – wie im Falle der hier vorgestellten, offenen Fassade der Storefront for Art and Architecture – scheint Holls theoretische Einstellung mit einer Neubewertung dessen übereinzustimmen, was Architektur in einer Zeit immenser politischer und technologischer Veränderungen ausmacht. Diese Haltung ist sicherlich erfrischend – vor allem in einem Berufszweig, in dem ökonomische Zweckdienlichkeit meist die treibende Kraft darstellt. Zwar hat der eher zurückhaltende Holl nicht die Art einer Medienpersönlichkeit kultiviert, die man mit Architekten wie Peter Eisenman verbindet, aber es ist durchaus denkbar, daß sein architektonischer Ansatz im Grunde deutlich radikaler ausfällt als der einiger wesentlich bekannterer Kollegen.

«Il faut que se crée une nouvelle architecture, simultanément alignée sur la continuité transculturelle et l'expression poétique des situations individuelles et des groupes humains», écrit Steven Holl, l'un des plus prometteurs jeunes architectes américains. Bien que son approche soit souvent inattendue, comme pour la façade curieusement ouverte de Storefront for Art and Architecture illustrée ici, la position théorique de Holl semble en cohérence avec une réévaluation de l'objet même de l'architecture, à une époque d'évolution politique et technologique accélérée. Cette attitude est rafraîchissante dans une profession guidée plus souvent qu'il n'est nécessaire par l'opportunité économique. Holl est un homme réservé. Contrairement à certains de ses confrères (et Peter Eisenman en particulier), il n'a pas d'image médiatique, mais son approche est peut-être plus profondément radicale que celle d'architectes plus en vue.

D. E. Shaw and Company Office, New York, New York
1991–92

Located on the top two floors of a skyscraper on 45th Street between 6th and 7th Avenues these are offices for a company which makes extensive use of computers for trading, pausing only in the one and a half hour period when the Tokyo exchange has closed and the London exchange has not yet opened. Steven Holl's design, which received a 1992 National Honor Award from the American Institute of Architects explores color reflection or "projected color." According to Holl's description, "The metal framing and sheet-rock with skim-coat plaster was carved and notched at precise points around the central 31 foot cube of space at the entry. Color was applied to the backs of surfaces, invisible to the viewer within the space. Natural and artificial lights project this color back into the space around walls and fissures. As the phenomenon greatly reduces the intensity of the color being reflected, a range of fluorescent colors could be utilized on the unseen surfaces, creating a mysterious calm glow." Completed within a $500000 budget, this project was intended as part of an ongoing expansion.

Die in den beiden obersten Geschossen eines Wolkenkratzers an der 45th Street (zwischen der 6th und 7th Avenue) gelegenen Räume dienen als Büro für eine Börsenmaklerfirma, die einen Großteil ihrer Arbeit mit Hilfe von Computern erledigt und nur während der eineinhalbstündigen Pause zwischen der Schließung der Tokioter Börse und der Eröffnung der Londoner Börse geschlossen hat. Steven Holls Entwurf, der mit dem 1992 National Honor Award des American Institute of Architects ausgezeichnet wurde, erkundet Farbreflexionen oder »projizierte Farben«. Laut Holls Beschreibung wurden »der Metallrahmen und die Steinplatten mit dem Feinputz an exakt vermessenen Stellen rund um den zentralen, gut 9 m hohen Kubus im Eingangsbereich ausgemeißelt und eingekerbt. Dann trug man Farbe auf die Rückseite der Oberflächen auf, die für den Betrachter innerhalb des Raumes unsichtbar sind. Natürliches und künstliches Licht projizieren diese Farbe zurück in den Raum auf Wände und Spalten. Da diese Erscheinung die Intensität der reflektierten Farbe erheblich reduziert, konnten auf den nicht sichtbaren Oberflächen eine Reihe von fluoreszierenden Farben verwendet werden, die ein geheimnisvolles Leuchten erzeugen.« Dieses Projekt, das innerhalb des festgelegten Budgets von 500000 Dollar fertiggestellt wurde, war als Teil eines größeren Erweiterungsbauvorhabens geplant.

Située aux deux derniers étages d'un gratte-ciel de la 45ème rue, entre les 6ème et 7ème avenues, cette salle de marchés ne s'arrête de travailler qu'une heure et demie par jour – entre la réfraction de la bourse de Tokyo et l'ouverture de celle de Londres. Les plans de Steven Holl, distingués par un National Honor Award de l'American Institute of Architects en 1992 explorent la réfraction de la couleur, ou «couleur projetée». Selon la description de Holl, «le cadre métallique tendu de placoplâtre a été creusé et découpé a certains endroits précis autour de l'espace cubique central de l'entrée. La couleur a été appliquée au dos des surfaces, si bien que le spectateur qui se trouve dans cet espace ne la voit pas. Des sources lumineuses naturelles et artificielles projettent cette couleur dans l'espace autour des murs et des découpes. Comme le phénomène diminue de beaucoup l'intensité de la couleur réfléchie, des couleurs fluorescentes pourraient être utilisées, créant un halos, mystérieux.» Réalisé dans les limites d'un budget de 500000 dollars, ce projet fait partie d'un programme d'agrandissements en cours.

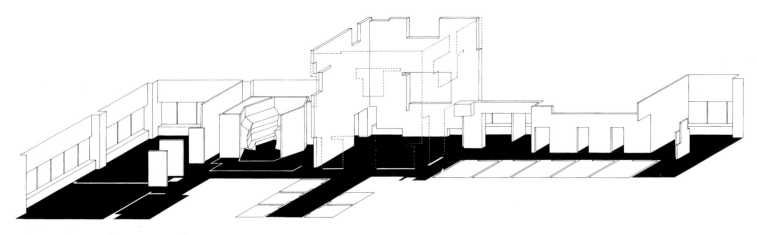

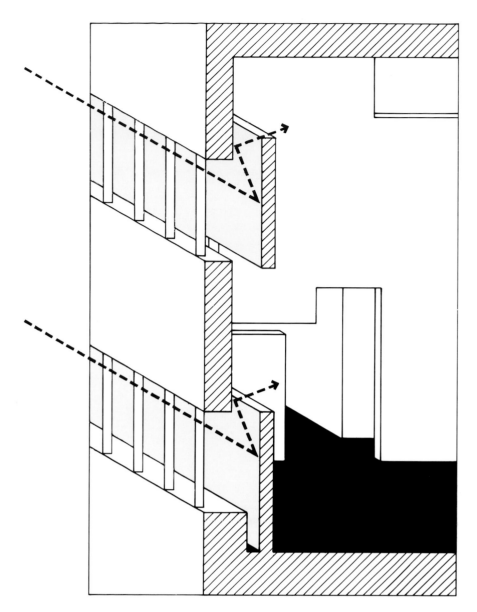

Page 96: The plan of the offices with the central cubic entrance, over 9 meters with its "projected color" effects.
Pages 97–99: The "projected color" system used in the D.E. Shaw and Company offices by Steven Holl uses saturated colors on surfaces which are not directly visible to infuse space with less intense hues.

Seite 96: Der Grundriß der Büroräume mit dem zentralen, kubusartigen, 9 Meter hohen Eingangsbereich und seinem »projizierten Farbsystem«.
Seite 97–99: Das von Steven Holl entworfene »projizierte Farbsystem« in den Büroräumen von D.E. Shaw and Company verwendet satte Farben, die jedoch nicht direkt sichtbar sind und so den Raum in weniger intensive Farbtöne tauchen.

Page 96: Plan des bureaux et du cube central de l'entrée (de plus de 9 m de côté) aux effets de «couleur projetée».
Pages 97–99: Le système de «couleur projetée» imaginé par Steven Holl pour les bureaux de D.E. Shaw & Company utilise des couleurs saturées appliquées sur des surfaces non directement visibles et qui projettent une sorte de halo lumineux.

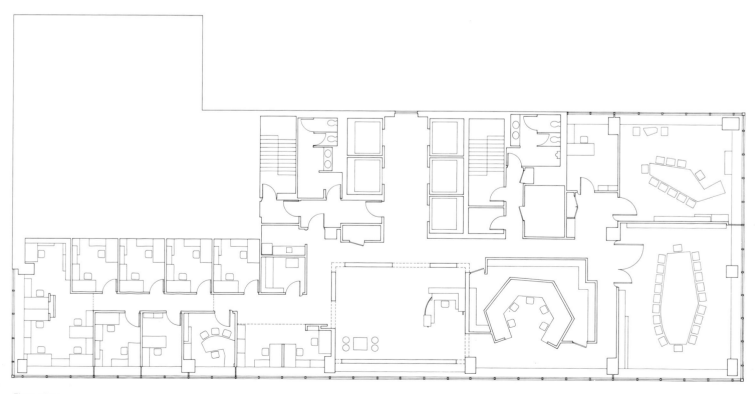

Floor plan

Storefront for Art and Architecture, New York, New York 1994

Located on Kenmare Street, at the eastern extremity of the Soho gallery area in Manhattan, this tiny wedge-shaped space was redesigned by Steven Holl and the artist Vito Acconci. Pivoting concrete-and-wood fiber panels replace the old storefront. Cut into differently sized geometric shapes, the panels open completely towards the street, with the interior of the space being left much as it was, aside from a small office cubicle. The Storefront is a well-known New York location for rather politically-oriented exhibitions, and the director of the space, Kyong Park, hopes to commission a redesign of the gallery every two years. Although this may not in fact be the immediate fate of Steven Holl's design the point that much contemporary architecture and design is fundamentally ephemeral has been made. The Pace Collection Showroom designed by Holl at the corner of 72nd Street and Madison Avenue (1985–86), for example has already replaced by a Ralph Lauren clothing store. Since the Storefront has neither windows nor doors in the traditional sense, its practicality is almost a moot point. This is radical design for a new, unsettled era.

Das an der Kenmare Street im äußersten Osten von Sohos Galerienbereich in Manhattan gelegene, winzige keilförmige Gebäude wurde von Steven Holl und dem Künstler Vito Acconci umgebaut. Die alte Ladenfront ersetzen schwenkbare, in unterschiedliche geometrische Formen geschnittene Beton-Holzfaser-Platten, die sich zur Straße hin vollständig öffnen, so daß der Innenraum – bis auf einen winzigen Büroraum – fast völlig unverändert bleiben konnte. Die Storefront ist eine in New York wohlbekannte Veranstaltungsstätte für eher politisch orientierte Ausstellungen, und der Direktor des Gebäudes, Kyong Park, hofft, daß er alle zwei Jahre eine Neugestaltung der Galerie in Auftrag geben kann. Obwohl dies wahrscheinlich nicht das unmittelbare Schicksal von Steven Holls Entwurf bedeutet, brachte er damit die Ansicht zum Ausdruck, daß zeitgenössische Architektur und Design grundsätzlich vergänglich sind. So wurde beispielsweise der von Holl auf der Ecke der 72nd Street und Madison Avenue errichtete Pace Collection Showroom (1985–86) bereits durch ein Ralph Lauren-Bekleidungsgeschäft ersetzt. Da die Storefront weder Fenster noch Türen im traditionellen Sinne besitzt, ließe sich über seine Zweckmäßigkeit fast schon debattieren. Dieses Bauwerk zeigt ein radikales Design für eine neue, ungewisse Ära.

Située sur Kenmare Street à l'extrémité est du quartier des galeries de Soho, à Manhattan, ce petit espace en coin a été redessiné par Steven Holl et l'artiste Vito Acconci. Des panneaux pivotants en béton et fibre de bois remplacent l'ancienne façade de magasin. Découpés en diverses formes géométriques, il s'ouvrent complètement vers la rue, l'intérieur de l'espace ayant été laissé plus ou moins comme il était, à l'exception d'un petit bureau. Le Storefront est un lieu connu à New York pour ses expositions assez politisées, et son directeur Kyong Park espère réaménager l'espace de la galerie tous les deux ans. Ce n'est pas le cas dans l'immédiat du projet de Steven Holl, s'il ne semble pas menacé de disparition dans l'immédiat, le projet de Holl n'en revendique pas moins le caractère foncièrement éphémère de l'architecture et du design contemporains. Le Pace Collection Showroom, également de Holl, au coin de 72nd Street et de Madison Avenue (1985–86) a déjà été remplacé par une boutique de vêtements Ralph Lauren. Comme il ne possède à proprement parler ni portes ni fenêtres, le Storefront n'est guère fonctionnel. Mais c'est un projet radical bien en phase avec des temps nouveaux et incertains.

Page 101: The entire facade of the Storefront for Art and Architecture pivots, providing sculptural openings into the small interior space. The lack of glass of course makes it difficult to fully open the facade in winter.

Seite 101: Die gesamte Fassade der Storefront for Art and Architecture ist schwenkbar und bietet damit skulpturale Öffnungen zu den kleinen Innenräumen. Die fehlenden Glasscheiben machen es im Winter jedoch schwierig, die Fassade vollständig zu öffnen.

Page 101: La totalité des éléments de la façade de Storefront for Art and Architecture pivote en découpant des ouvertures sculpturales sur le petit espace intérieur. L'absence de vitre pose des problèmes pour l'utilisation de la façade ouverte en hiver.

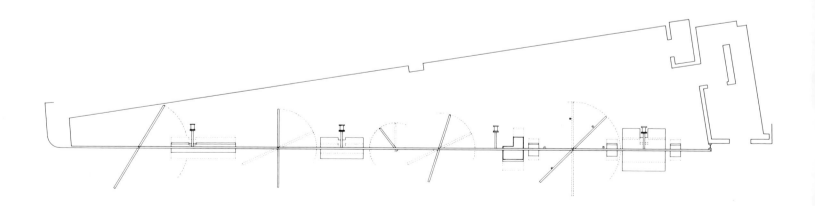

Pages 102/103: Located on a street corner some-
what removed from the Soho gallery area, the
Storefront's radical architectural concept fits well
with its challenging and sometimes controversial
exhibitions.

Seite 102/103: Die an einer Straßenecke in der
Nähe von Sohos Galerienbereich gelegene
Storefront zeichnet sich durch ein radikales
architektonisches Konzept aus, das gut zu den
provozierenden und manchmal umstrittenen
Ausstellungen paßt.

Pages 102/103: Situé à un angle de rue légèrement éloigné du quartier des galeries de Soho, le
Storefront est bien adapté aux expositions décoif-
fantes et parfois controversées qui s'y tiennent.

June
1986 – January
1995

Richard **Meier**

Richard Meier

Richard Meier's signature style is omnipresent in the vast spaces of The Hague City Hall and Library.

Richard Meiers Handschrift ist in den riesigen Räumen des Rathauses und der Zentralbibliothek von Den Haag allgegenwärtig.

La signature stylistique de Richard Meier est omniprésente dans les vastes espaces de l'hôtel de ville et de la bibliothèque de La Haye.

A member of the "New York Five", Richard Meier has been an architect whose consistent, some would even say obsessional use of Modernist white forms has become a universally recognizable signature style. Influenced by Le Corbusier, Meier has proven that a gridded, geometrical vocabulary is capable of an astonishing variety of types of expression. Initially on a small scale, for numerous private residences, and later in progessively larger commissions, office buildings, museums or housing, he has evolved toward more complex floor plans, and a shifting of axes which has come to be considered typical of much contemporary architecture. The Hague City Hall marks a first for him in terms of scale and public visibility in a major European city. It remains to be seen if the largest project of his career, the new Getty Center, scheduled for completion in 1996 in Los Angeles will confirm his reputation as one of the most outstanding architects of his generation.

Die konsequente, von einigen auch als »besessen« bezeichnete Verwendung weißer Baukörper gilt als das Markenzeichen Richard Meiers, einem Mitglied der »New York Five«. Der von Le Corbusier beeinflußte Architekt hat bewiesen, daß auch auf einem Raster basierende geometrische Formen vielfältige Ausdrucksmöglichkeiten bieten. Meier begann in kleinem Rahmen mit zahlreichen Privathäusern und entwickelte später bei größeren Aufträgen für Verwaltungsgebäude, Museen oder Wohnanlagen immer kompliziertere Grundrisse und Achsenverschiebungen, die heute als typisch für einen Teil zeitgenössischer Architektur angesehen werden können. Das Den Haager Rathaus ist sein erstes großes, öffentlichkeitswirksames Bauwerk in einer europäischen Großstadt. Es bleibt abzuwarten, ob das bisher größte Projekt seiner Karriere, das neue Getty Center in Los Angeles, dessen Fertigstellung für 1996 geplant ist, seinen Ruf als einer der wichtigsten Architekten unserer Zeit bestätigen wird.

Membre des «New York Five», Richard Meier, adepte fervent (certains disent obsessionnel) des formes modernistes et du blanc, possède une signature stylistique qui le fait reconnaître dans le monde entier. Influencé par Le Corbusier, Meier a prouvé qu'un vocabulaire esthétique à base de trames géométriques permet une étonnante richesse d'expression. A travers des résidences privées, dans un premier temps, puis plus tard et progressivement, des commandes de plus en plus importantes d'immeubles d'habitation ou de bureaux et de musées, il a évolué vers une complexité de plus en plus grande des plans de masse, et vers les glissements d'axes qui sont devenus la marque de beaucoup de réalisations architecturales contemporaines. L'hôtel de ville de La Haye représente pour lui une étape, tant par la taille du bâtiment que par son importance pour une grande ville européenne. Reste à voir si le plus grand projet de sa carrière, le nouveau Getty Center, qui devrait être achevé en 1996 à Los Angeles, confirmera sa réputation d'un des plus brillants architectes de sa génération.

City Hall and Central Library, The Hague, Netherlands 1986–95

Clad inside and out with white 85×180 cm porcelain-enameled metal panels, this large group of buildings is located near Centraal Station in The Hague, near the Ministries of Justice and Foreign Affairs on a difficult wedge-shaped site. The alignment of the city streets and of the site inspired Richard Meier to introduce a 12.5° rotation in the two main grids of the structure, corresponding to a 12-story office "slab" and a 10-story block. Between these elements, he has placed the most spectacular feature of the building, a 47 meter high glassed atrium, which is the largest space of its kind in Europe. Though well ordered, in the style of Meier, this atrium does have Piranesian connotations with its two banks of internal bridges. The City Hall and Public Library building complete the "culture square" of The Hague, which was conceived to alleviate the sterile atmosphere of neighboring ministries. Theaters by Herman Hertzberger and Rem Koolhaas are close to the City Hall, on the Turfmarkt and Spui sides, and projects designed by architects Michael Graves, Cesar Pelli, and KPF are planned for other nearby sites. The choice of Richard Meier was the result of a limited competition between contractors. The client is technically not the city, but the ABP pension funds which have leased the site on a long-term basis from the Dutch government. Three times the size of the Canal+ building in Paris, the City Hall was built with a nearly identical budget, and is Meier's first computer designed project.

Diese sehr große Gebäudegruppe liegt in der Nähe des Hauptbahnhofs von Den Haag und in direkter Nachbarschaft des Justiz- und Außenministeriums auf einem schwierigen, keilförmigen Gelände. Alle Bauten sind innen und außen mit weißen, 85 x 180 cm großen porzellan-emaillierten Metallplatten verkleidet. Die Ausrichtung von Straßenführung und Grundstück zueinander inspirierte Richard Meier dazu, eine zwölfgeschossige Büroscheibe und einen zehngeschossigen Block um 12,5° gegeneinander zu verschwenken. Dazwischen plazierte er das spektakulärste Element des Komplexes, ein 47 Meter hohes verglastes Atrium, der größte Raum dieser Art in Europa. Trotz des durchdachten, für Meier charakteristischen Stils spielt der Architekt bei diesem Atrium mit seinen zwei, frei in den Raum gestellten Brückenkonstruktionen auf Entwürfe von G.B. Piranesi an. Rathaus und Bibliothek komplettieren den »Kulturplatz« Den Haags, der die sterile Atmosphäre der benachbarten Ministerien auflockern soll. Ganz in der Nähe, an den Seiten zu Turfmarkt und Spui, befinden sich die Theater von Herman Hertzberger und Rem Koolhaas. Für andere nahegelegene Grundstücke liegen Entwürfe der Architekten Michael Graves, Cesar Pelli und KPF vor. Die Wahl Richard Meiers war im Grunde das Ergebnis eines begrenzten Wettbewerbs unter den Baufirmen. Bauherr im technischen Sinne ist nicht die Stadt, sondern der ABP-Pensionsfonds, der das Grundstück langfristig vom Staat gepachtet hat. Das Rathaus hat den dreifachen Umfang von Canal+ in Paris, wurde aber mit einem ungefähr gleich großen Budget durchgeführt und stellt Meiers erstes am Computer entworfenes Projekt dar.

Recouvert à l'intérieur comme à l'extérieur de panneaux métalliques émaillés de 85 x 180 cm, ce très vaste ensemble de bâtiments est situé près de la gare centrale de La Haye, non loin des ministères de la Justice et des Affaires Etrangères, sur un terrain triangulaire difficile. L'alignement des rues et le site ont donné à Richard Meier l'idée de faire pivoter de 12,5° les deux trames principales de la construction, ce qui donne une «tranche» de 12 étages de bureaux et un bloc de 10 étages. Entre ces éléments, il a inscrit un spectaculaire atrium de verre de 47 m de haut, le plus vaste espace de ce type en Europe. Bien que soigneusement ordonnancé, et dans le style de Meier bien sûr, il évoque, avec ses deux volées de passerelles intérieures, un univers piranèsien. Cet ensemble complète la «place culturelle» de La Haye, conçue pour alléger l'atmosphère austère des bâtiments ministériels voisins. Les théâtres d'Herman Hertzberger et Rem Koolhaas sont proches de l'hôtel de ville – côté Tufmarkt et Spui – et des projets signés Michael Graves, Cesar Pelli et KPF sont prévus sur des terrains avoisinants. Le choix s'est porté sur Richard Meier à l'issue d'un concours restreint. Théoriquement, ce n'est pas la ville de La Haye qui est le client, mais un fonds de pension, ABP, qui a signé un bail de longue durée avec l'Etat néerlandais. De trois fois la taille de l'immeuble de Canal+ (Paris), l'hôtel de ville a été construit pour un budget similaire. C'est le premier projet de Meier conçu à l'aide de l'ordinateur.

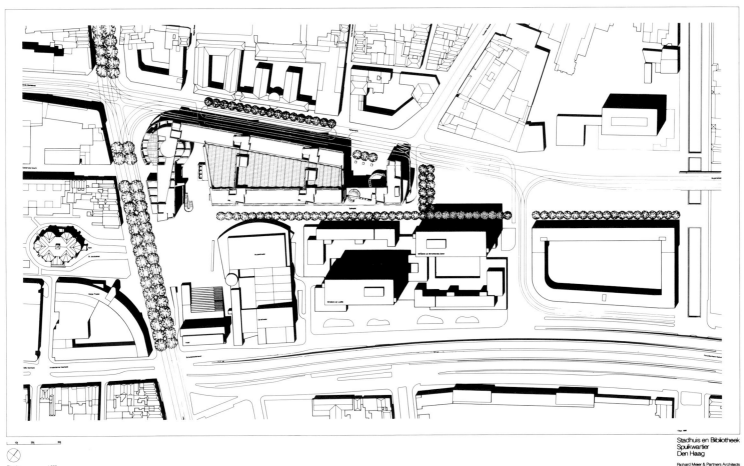

Stadhuis en Bibliotheek
Spuikwarter
Den Haag

Richard Meier & Partners Architects

Situatie 1:500

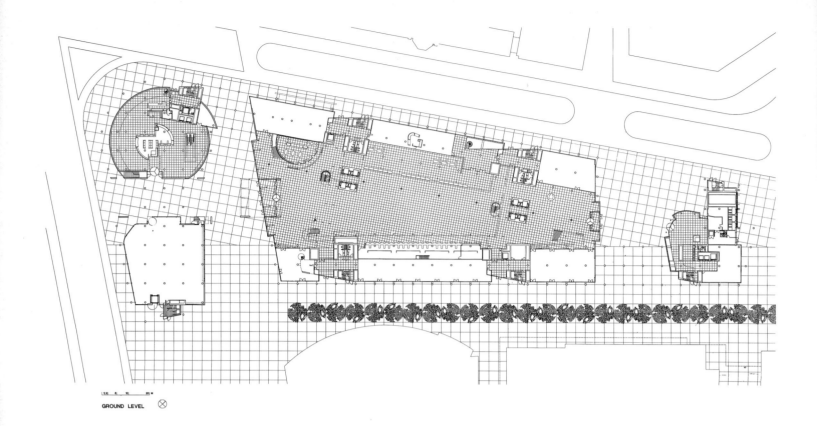

GROUND LEVEL ⊗

Page 107: The rounded volume on the Spui
facade is the Central Library, a passage to its right
leading into the City Hall atrium.
Pages 108/109: The enormous 47 meter high
atrium formed by the 12.5° rotation of the two
grids employed by Meier is crossed by two banks
of suspended bridges.

Seite 107: Der gerundete Baukörper auf der Spui-
Seite ist die Zentralbibliothek, auf deren rechter
Seite eine Passage zum Rathaus-Atrium führt.
Seite 108/109: Das gewaltige, 47 Meter hohe
Atrium entstand aus der Verschwenkung zweier
Raster um 12,5 Grad. Es wird von zwei frei in den
Raum gestellten Brückenkonstruktionen durch-
quert.

Page 107: Le volume arrondi – façade côté Spui –
contient la bibliothèque centrale; à sa droite, un
passage mène à l'atrium de l'hôtel de ville.
Pages 108/109: L'énorme atrium de 47 m de haut
est formé par le pivotement sur 12,5° des deux
grilles utilisées par Meier. Il est traversé par deux
rangées de passerelles suspendues.

Eric Owen Moss

Eric Owen Moss

Ince Theater, Culver City, California, 1994, (project). The site of the future Ince Theater is a parking lot in Culver City, California.

Ince Theater, Culver City, Kalifornien, 1994, (Projekt). Das zukünftige Ince Theater soll auf einem ehemaligen Parkplatz in Culver City, Kalifornien, stehen.

Ince Theater, Culver City, Californie 1994, (projet). Le site du futur Ince Theater, parking de Culver City, en Californie.

The architect Philip Johnson has called Eric Owen Moss, born in Los Angeles in 1943 "a jeweler of junk." In his work built to date, this young California architect has placed an emphasis on unusual materials. Old chains, broken trusses and other incongruous elements take their place in his buildings, much as they might participate in a modern sculpture. The visual arts have acquired a freedom which seemed forbidden to architecture because of the constraints of practicality and building codes, but also because of peoples' expectations. Like the Austrian Wolf Prix, principal of the Coop Himmelblau firm who praises his work, Eric Owen Moss is in the process of exploring the ways in which architecture can be deconstructed. His own particularity, as evidenced in the buildings he has completed in Culver City, California remains his extensive, and unexpected experimentation with materials and forms.

Der Architekt Philip Johnson bezeichnete den 1943 in Los Angeles geborenen Eric Owen Moss als »Juwelier des Schrotts«. Dieser junge kalifornische Architekt legte in seinen bisherigen Bauten den Schwerpunkt vor allem auf ungewöhnliche Materialien. In seinen Entwürfen finden sich alte Ketten, gebrochene Balken und andere scheinbar deplazierte Elemente, die genauso auch zu einer modernen Skulptur passen könnten. Die bildenden Künste haben eine Freiheit erworben, die für die Architektur sowohl aufgrund der Durchführbarkeit und der Baubestimmungen als auch aufgrund der Erwartungen ihrer Klientel undenkbar schien. Eric Owen Moss sucht ebenso nach neuen Wegen, auf denen die Architektur dekonstruiert werden kann, wie der Österreicher Wolf Prix von Coop Himmelblau, der von Moss' Arbeiten begeistert ist. Sein Kennzeichen ist der intensive und experimentelle Umgang mit Materialien und Formen, wie man es in seinen Bauten in Culver City, Kalifornien, feststellen kann.

L'architecte Philip Johnson a pu dire d'Eric Owen Moss, né à Los Angeles en 1943, qu'il était «un joaillier de la ferraille». Dans ses travaux réalisés jusqu'ici, ce jeune architecte californien a mis l'accent sur des matériaux inhabituels: vieilles chaînes, poutres brisées et autres éléments incongrus trouvent leur place dans ses constructions, un peu comme dans une sculpture contemporaine. Les arts plastiques ont acquis une liberté qui semblait interdite à l'architecture pour des contraintes pratiques évidentes, dont le code du bâtiment et les attentes des clients. Comme l'Autrichien Wolf Prix, associé principal de Coop Himmelblau, qui apprécie son travail, Eric Owen Moss explore actuellement les possibilités de déconstruction de l'architecture. Son style propre réside, comme le montrent les immeubles achevés à Culver City, Californie, dans l'emploi de matériaux et de formes insolites.

Ince Theater, Culver City, California
1994 (project)

The project for a 450 seat theater is to be located in the present parking lot between the Gary Group-Paramount Laundry-Lindblade Tower complex. Though not yet under construction, another part of this series of buildings, now called Metafor (formerly GEM) is being completed. Intended for live performance or movies, the Ince Theater's unusual form is a computer-generated interaction between three spheres. Whereas the other Gary Group buildings were largely conversions from existing warehouse space, the Ince Theater further explores the possibilities of spatial innovation which Moss proved himself to be capable of in the Lawson-Westen House (Brentwood, 1989–93). The apparent complexity of the structure as seen in computer drawings, resolves itself into an unusual and elegant solution to the age-old problems of theater design. According to the original plans, a pedestrian bridge would link the theater to the as yet unbuilt Sony building across the street. The presence of Sony, would make the idea of a theater in this otherwise rather forlorn section of Los Angeles more viable. Exterior and interior stairs would make it possible to climb onto the roof. This is a dynamic form, and as Eric Owen Moss has said, "if a building itself can include oppositions, so that it is about movement or the movement of ideas, then it might be more durable."

Das 450 Sitze umfassende Theater ist auf einem Gelände innerhalb des Gary Group-Paramount Laundry-Lindblade Tower-Komplexes geplant, auf dem sich zur Zeit noch ein Parkplatz befindet. Obwohl noch nicht mit den Bauarbeiten für das Theater begonnen wurde, konnte ein anderer Teil aus dieser Gebäudereihe, das Metafor (das ehemalige GEM), fertiggestellt werden. Die ungewöhnliche Form des für Livedarbietungen und Filmvorführungen geplanten Ince Theater basiert auf einer computererzeugten Interaktion zwischen drei Kugeln. Während es sich bei den anderen Gary Group-Gebäuden größtenteils um Umbauten bestehender Lagerräumlichkeiten handelt, erkundet das Ince Theater die Möglichkeiten räumlicher Innovation – ein Schritt, zu dem sich Moss bereits bei seinem Lawson-Westen House (Brentwood, 1989–93) als fähig erwiesen hatte. Die offensichtliche Komplexität der Konstruktion, die sich in den Computerentwürfen zeigt, verwandelt sich selbst zu einer außergewöhnlichen und eleganten Lösung für die Probleme, die das Theaterdesign seit Jahrhunderten aufwirft. Gemäß den Originalplänen wird eine Fußgängerbrücke das Theater mit dem noch zu errichtenden Sony-Gebäude auf der gegenüberliegenden Straßenseite verbinden. Die Anwesenheit der Firma Sony ließ die Vorstellung eines Theaters in dieser eher verlassenen Gegend der Stadt Los Angeles denkbar erscheinen. Außen- und Innentreppen ermöglichen einen direkten Zugang zum Dach, welches sich durch eine dynamische Form auszeichnet, die Eric Owen Moss folgenderweise kommentierte: »Wenn ein Gebäude Gegensätze in sich vereinen kann und von Bewegung oder der Bewegung von Ideen handelt, ist es möglicherweise beständiger.«

Ce futur théâtre de 450 places devrait être édifié sur un parking au milieu des bâtiments du Gary Group-Paramount Laundry-Lindblade Tower. Bien que sa construction n'ait pas encore débuté, une autre partie de cet ensemble baptisé Metafor (anciennement GEM) est en cours d'achèvement. La forme inhabituelle de cette salle de spectacle et de cinéma résulte d'un jeu entre trois sphères, généré par ordinateur. Alors que les autres locaux du Gary Group étaient essentiellement des entrepôts reconvertis, l'Ince Theater explore beaucoup plus avant les possibilités d'innovation spatiale dont Moss s'était déjà montré capable dans la Lawson-Westen House (Brentwood, 1989–93). L'apparente complexité du bâtiment, qui transparaît sur les plans par ordinateur, s'efface d'elle-même dans une solution nouvelle et élégante aux problèmes classiques de la conception d'un théâtre. Selon les plans originaux, une passerelle pour piétons relierait le théâtre à l'immeuble Sony situé de l'autre côté de la rue, mais non encore construit. La présence de Sony pourrait rendre plus viable l'implantation d'une telle salle dans ce quartier un peu perdu de Los Angeles. Les escaliers intérieurs et extérieurs permettront de monter sur le toit. Cette forme est dynamique, et comme le déclare Eric Owen Moss, «si un bâtiment peut intégrer des contrastes, qui font de lui un commentaire sur le mouvement, ou le mouvement des idées, il a plus de chances de durer».

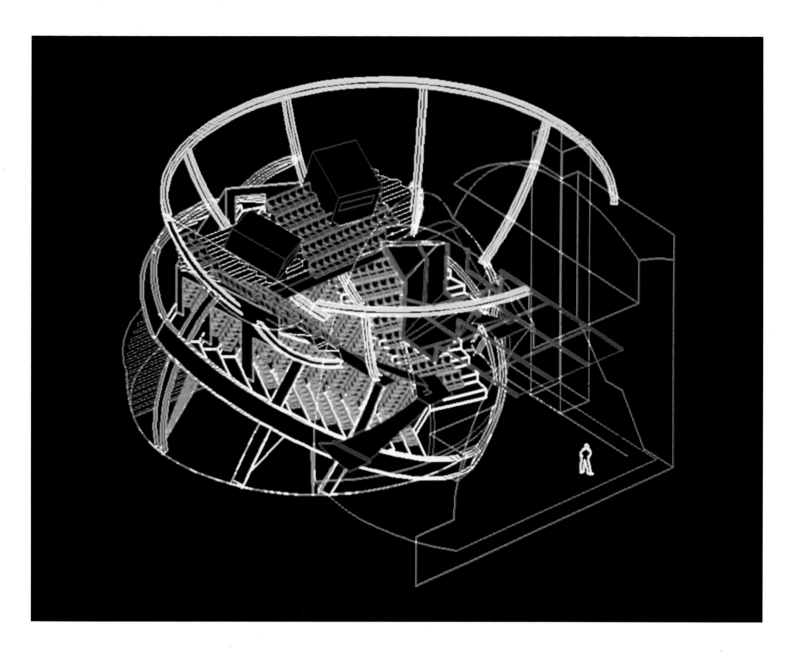

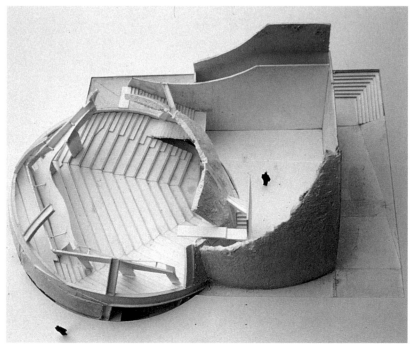

As in his Lawson-Westen House, Eric Owen Moss experiments here with a renewal of the usual geometry of modern architecture. Using a computer, he twists and turns the space of the theater, while retaining a readily functional interior design.

Genau wie bei seinem Lawson-Westen House erprobt Eric Owen Moss auch hier eine Erneuerung der üblichen geometrischen Formen in der modernen Architektur. Mit Hilfe eines Computers drehte und wendete er die Räumlichkeiten des Theaters, ohne dabei auf eine funktionale Innenausstattung verzichten zu müssen.

Comme pour sa Lawson-Westen House, Eric Owen Moss tente ici de renouveler la géométrie classique de l'architecture moderne. A l'aide d'un ordinateur, il tord l'espace du théâtre, tout en conservant un plan intérieur tout à fait fonctionnel.

Pages 114/115: Part of the architect's ambitious
projects to renew the warehouse areas of Culver
City, the curvilinear forms of the Ince Theater
contrast with the neighboring structures already
renovated by Moss.

Seite 114/115: Die kurvenförmigen Baukörper
des Ince Theater bilden einen Kontrast zu den
benachbarten, von Moss bereits renovierten
Gebäuden. Das Ganze ist Teil von Moss'
ehrgeizigen Sanierungsplänen für das Lagerhaus-
gebiet von Culver City.

Pages 114/115: Eléments d'un ambitieux projet
de réhabilitation des quartiers d'entrepôts de
Culver City, les formes courbes de l'Ince Theater
contrastent avec les constructions voisines, déjà
rénovées par Moss.

I.M. Pei

Ieoh Ming Pei

Pei's Rock & Roll Hall of Fame brings a touch of glamour to Cleveland's rather bland architecture.

Die von Pei entworfene Rock and Roll Hall of Fame verleiht Clevelands ansonsten wenig aufregender Architekturlandschaft einen Hauch von Glamour.

Le Rock and Roll Hall of Fame de I.M. Pei apporte une touche séduisante à l'architecture par ailleurs assez fade de Cleveland.

Since completing the Grand Louvre project in Paris, where he was more involved in the design of the Pyramid (completed in 1989) than in the Richelieu Wing (1992), I.M. Pei's first new building is the Rock and Roll Hall of Fame in Cleveland, Ohio. The obvious question that might come to mind would be "Why Cleveland?" Quite simply because the disk jockey Alan Freed coined the term Rock and Roll there in the 1950s, and because the city of Cleveland offered to pay half the costs. Although he was not responsible for the interior decoration and exhibition design of the building, it nonetheless has a distinctive Pei flavor, albeit in a more dramatic or "explosive" mode than was the case in his earlier work. "What is this music?" asks the architect. "It has a sense of rebellion, of breaking away from tradition. It has a dimension of energy. The generation that made rock music was much more transparent about their ideas than my generation. Everything is up front, whether you like it or not."

Die Rock and Roll Hall of Fame in Cleveland, Ohio ist I.M. Peis erstes neues Bauwerk seit der Fertigstellung des Grand Louvre-Projektes in Paris, wo Pei sich mehr mit dem Design der Pyramide (1989 fertiggestellt) als mit dem Richelieu-Flügel (1992) beschäftigte. Hier drängt sich die Frage auf: »Warum Cleveland?« Die Wahl fiel auf Cleveland, weil der Diskjockey Alan Freed in den 50er Jahren hier den Begriff »Rock and Roll« prägte und weil die Stadt Cleveland anbot, die Hälfte der Baukosten zu übernehmen. Obwohl Pei nicht für Innenausstattung und Ausstellungsräume des Gebäudes verantwortlich zeichnete, besitzt die Hall of Fame charakteristische Pei-Züge, wenn auch auf dramatischere Weise als bei all seinen früheren Werken. »Was sagt diese Musik aus?« fragte sich der Architekt. »Der Rock and Roll besitzt etwas Rebellisches; er verkörpert den Bruch mit der Tradition und strahlt eine ungeheure Energie aus. Die Generation der Rockmusik war erheblich ehrlicher in bezug auf ihre Ideen als meine Generation. Alles ist geradeheraus, ob es dir gefällt oder nicht.«

Le Rock and Roll Hall of Fame de Cleveland (Ohio), est le premier chantier important achevé par I.M. Pei depuis le Grand Louvre où il s'était davantage impliqué dans le dessin de la Pyramide (1989) que dans l'aile Richelieu (1992). Pourquoi Cleveland? Tout simplement parce que c'est ici que le disk jockey Alan Freed a inventé le terme de Rock'n' Roll dans les années 50, et que la ville proposait de financer la moitié des coûts du projet. Bien que la décoration intérieure et les salles d'exposition n'aient pas été confiées à I.M. Pei, le bâtiment porte indiscutablement sa «griffe» – en plus plus spectaculaire et exubérant que jusqu'à présent. «Qu'est-ce que cette musique?» s'est demandé l'architecte. «Elle traduit la rébellion, le rejet de la tradition. Elle est pleine de vitalité. La génération du rock avait des idées plus claires que la mienne. Tout est dit, que cela plaise ou non.»

Rock and Roll Hall of Fame, Cleveland, Ohio
1993–95

I.M. Pei may not have been the obvious choice to build a monument to Rock and Roll. As he candidly says, "I prefer jazz," but the 14000 square meter facility which he designed on the shores of Lake Erie is a tribute to the idea of architecture as "frozen music." Since the music in this case is exuberant or even violent at times, Pei's surprising, cantilevered asymmetrical volumes are too. The most evident features of the building are a 50 meter high concrete tower, which serves in part to support a 35 meter high triangular glass "tent" housing the spectacular entrance area. Inclined at a 45° angle, this glazed surface recalls numerous other Pei buildings, including the Louvre Pyramid. In an unusual configuration, some 3000 square meters of exhibition space are situated underground, beneath the public plaza, whereas the two cantilevered volumes, a trapezoid and a drum respectively contain a 125 seat theater and a dance area (still to be installed). A third floor café gives a view of the entrance volume, and the actual hall of fame is at the top of the tower in a space described by the *New York Times* as "lugubrious." Aside from defining the forms, Pei was not called on for the exhibition design, carried out by The Burdick Group of San Francisco. The Rock and Roll Hall of Fame is the center-piece of a $300 million development known as North Coast Harbor, which is also to contain a Science Museum and Aquarium designed by other architects.

Wahrscheinlich zählt I.M. Pei nicht zu den Architekten, an die man bei dem Entwurf eines Denkmals für den Rock and Roll zuerst denkt– und sogar er selbst bekannte freimütig, daß er Jazz bevorzugt. Aber das 14000m² große Bauwerk, das er am Ufer des Erie-Sees errichtete, ist ein Tribut an eine bestimmte Vorstellungsweise, die Architektur als »gefrorene Musik« betrachtet. Da es sich beim Rock and Roll um eine überschwengliche, bisweilen sogar gewalttätige Musik handelt, zeichnen sich Peis überraschende, vorkragende und asymmetrische Baukörper ebenfalls durch diese Eigenschaften aus. Kennzeichen der Hall of Fame ist ein 50 Meter hoher Betonturm, der teilweise als Stütze für das 35 Meter hohe, dreieckige Glas-»Zelt« dient, in dem sich der spektakuläre Eingangsbereich befindet. Seine um 45° geneigte, verglaste Oberfläche erinnert an zahlreiche von Pei entworfene Gebäude, u.a. an die Louvre Pyramide. 3000m² Ausstellungsfläche liegen unterhalb des öffentlichen Platzes im Tiefgeschoß, während die beiden vorkragenden Baukörper – ein Trapez und ein Zylinder – ein Theater mit 125 Plätzen und einen Tanzsaal (noch im Bau) beherbergen. Vom Café im dritten Geschoß bietet sich ein Blick auf den Eingangsbereich; die eigentliche »Ruhmeshalle« befindet sich in der Spitze des Turms in einem Raum, den die »New York Times« als »traurig« bezeichnete. Pei zeichnete nur für die Gestaltung der Bauformen, nicht jedoch für das Design der Ausstellung verantwortlich, das von The Burdick Group of San Francisco ausgeführt wurde. Die Rock and Roll Hall of Fame bildet das Kernstück eines 600 Millionen Dollar teuren Bauvorhabens namens North Coast Harbour, das außerdem ein (von anderen Architekten entworfenes) Wissenschaftsmuseum sowie ein Aquarium umfassen wird.

I.M. Pei n'était peut-être pas le choix le plus évident pour élever un monument au Rock and Roll. Comme il le précise honnêtement: «Je préfère le jazz», mais le projet de 14000m² qu'il vient de concevoir sur les rives du Lac Erié est un hommage à l'idée d'une architecture qui serait une sorte de «phrase musicale en suspens». Comme en l'occurrence la musique est exubérante, et même parfois violente, les volumes asymétriques en étonnants porte-à-faux le sont également. Le point fort du bâtiment est une tour de béton de 50 m de haut, qui sert notamment à soutenir une «tente» triangulaire de verre de 35 m de haut qui abrite l'impressionnante entrée de l'immeuble. Inclinée à 45°, cette surface de verre rappelle de nombreuses autres œuvres de Pei, y compris la Pyramide du Louvre. L'architecte a choisi des solutions peu conventionnelles: les espaces d'exposition (quelque 3000m²) sont en sous-sol, sous la plaza, tandis que les deux volumes en porte-à-faux—un trapézoïde et un tambour—abritent respectivement un théâtre de 125 places et une piste de danse (non encore installée). Au troisième niveau, un café donne sur le volume de l'entrée et la salle des stars du rock, le «Hall of Fame» se trouve au sommet de la tour dans un espace décrit par «The New York Times» comme «lugubre». La présentation de l'exposition est l'œuvre du Burdick Group, de San Francisco. Ce bâtiment est la pièce centrale d'un projet d'urbanisme de près de 300 millions de dollars appelé North Coast Harbor, qui comprend également un musée des sciences et un aquarium dessinés par d'autres architectes.

Pages 118–121: Despite the rather unusual forms of the structure, Pei nonetheless applies certain recurring themes of his architecture, such as triangles and large glassed atriums.

Seite 118–121: Trotz der eher ungewöhnlichen Form der Konstruktion integrierte Pei einige für seine Architektur typische Themen wie Dreiecke und große, verglaste Atrien.

Pages 118–121: Malgré les formes peu banales du bâtiment, Pei s'appuie ici sur des thèmes récurrents dans son œuvre: les triangles et les grands atriums de verre.

Cesar **Pelli**

Cesar Pelli

Pelli's House for an anonymous patron in the Western United States uses a vocabulary which is unusual for the architect, concentrating on wooden beams and columns.

Cesar Pellis Anwesen für einen anonymen Bauherrn im Westen der Vereinigten Staaten zeichnet sich durch eine für den Architekten ungewöhnliche Formensprache aus, die sich auf Holzbalken und -säulen konzentriert.

La maison de Pelli, pour un client de l'Ouest des Etats-Unis resté anonyme, fait appel à tout un vocabulaire de poutres et de colonnes de bois, inhabituel pour l'architecte.

Cesar Pelli, born in Tucuman, Argentina in 1926 is one of the outstanding figures of contemporary American architecture. On emigrating to the United States, he worked for 10 years in the office of Eero Saarinen. The list of major buildings designed by Pelli with his different firms – DMJM, Gruen Associates, and Cesar Pelli and Associates is impressive. They include the famous Pacific Design Center in Los Angeles (1975), the tower expansion of the Museum of Modern Art in New York (1977), the World Financial Center in New York (1980–88), and Canary Wharf Tower in London (1987–91). The private residence here may not be entirely typical of Cesar Pelli, but it shows the same strength and presence so obvious in his major corporate commissions. Pelli's current work includes twin 85-story towers for the Kuala Lumpur City Center Phase 1, Kuala Lumpur, Malaysia (1992–96). Recipient of the 1995 AIA Gold Medal, Pelli recently won a competion to design the $139 million Metropolitan Dade County Performing Arts Center in Miami.

Der 1926 in Tucuman, Argentinien geborene Cesar Pelli arbeitete nach seiner Auswanderung in die Vereinigten Staaten 10 Jahre für das Büro von Eero Saarinen. Zu den bekanntesten der von Pelli und seinen verschiedenen Firmen – DMJM, Gruen Associates und Cesar Pelli and Associates – entworfenen Gebäuden zählen das Pacific Design Center in Los Angeles (1975), die Erweiterung des Museum of Modern Art in New York (1977), das World Financial Center in New York (1980–88) oder der Canary Wharf Tower in London (1987–91). Das hier vorgestellte Privathaus zeigt ein für Cesar Pelli sehr ungewöhnliches und vielleicht atypisches Design, aber der Entwurf besitzt dieselbe Kraft und Präsenz, die auch in seinen Bauaufträgen für große Firmen zu finden ist. Zu Pellis gegenwärtigen Arbeiten zählen u.a. zwei 85-stöckige Türme für das Kuala Lumpur City Center Phase 1, die bis 1996 in der malaysischen Hauptstadt fertiggestellt werden sollen (Baubeginn 1992).

Cesar Pelli, né à Tucuman (Argentine), en 1926 est l'une de grandes figures de l'architecture américaine contemporaine. Immigré aux Etats-Unis, il travaille pendant 10 ans dans l'agence d'Eero Saarinen. La série de grands immeubles dessinés par Pelli pour ses différentes agences – DMJM, Gruen Associates et Cesar Pelli and Associates, constitue un palmarès extraordinairement prestigieux: Pacific Design Center de Los Angeles (1975), tour de l'extension du Museum of Modern Art de New York (1977), World Financial Center à New York (1980–88), Canary Wharf Tower à Londres (1987–91). La résidence privée illustrée ci-après est un projet très inhabituel et même atypique dans l'œuvre de Pelli, mais elle révèle une puissance et une présence égales. Pelli réalise actuellement deux tours jumelles de 85 étages pour la Phase 1 du centre ville de Kuala Lumpur, en Malaisie (1992–96). Titulaire de la médaille d'or de l'AIA (1995), il vient de remporter le concours d'un projet de 139 millions de dollars, le Metropolitan Dade County Performing Arts Center à Miami.

House for an anonymous patron, Western United States 1990–93

The spectacular two level main house and garage of this residence measure about 900 square meters, with a 150 square meter guest house. Both are located on a 40 hectare site. The main house is oriented to permit views of mountains. The guest house includes a bedroom loft, living room, kitchen, two full baths and a garage. Construction is post and beam with wire-brushed Douglas-fir beams, mortise-and-tenoned into hand-peeled Engleman spruce logs with a diameter of approximately 70 centimeters. The house has 55 log columns, harvested as standing dead trees, killed by beetles. Aside from the wooden columns, insulating glass and Mahogany-frame windows together with cedar siding make up the exterior of the structure. A "central spine" beneath a pitched roof serves to permit both vertical and horizontal movement through the house, with the public areas (living room, dining room, kitchen and study) located to the west of the spine, and bedrooms to the east. As Cesar Pelli's firm biography has it, "Mr. Pelli has avoided formalistic preconceptions in his designs. He believes that the aesthetic qualities of a building should grow from the specific characteristics of each project such as its location, its construction technology and its purpose. In search for the most appropriate response to each project, his designs have covered a wide range of solutions and materials."

Das spektakuläre zweigeschossige Haupthaus und die Garage dieser Residenz umfassen 900 m² Grundfläche, an die sich ein 150 m² großes Gästehaus anschließt. Beide Gebäude liegen auf einem 40 Hektar großen Gelände in der Nähe eines Bachs. Das Haupthaus ist so ausgerichtet, daß es eine Aussicht auf die naheliegenden Berge erlaubt. Das Gästehaus umfaßt ein Loft als Schlafzimmer, einen Wohnraum, eine Küche, zwei voll ausgestattete Bäder und eine eigene Garage. Das Haus ist in Ständerbauweise errichtet, mit drahtgebürsteten Balken aus Kiefernholz, die mit von Hand entrindeten Stämmen der Engleman-Fichte verzapft sind; diese Stämme haben einen Durchmesser von etwa 70 cm. Das Haus verfügt über 55 dieser Säulenstämme, die aus bereits durch Käferbefall abgestorbenen Stämmen gefertigt wurden. Neben den Baumstämmen bestimmen Verbundfensterglas und Fensterrahmen aus Mahagoni sowie eine Außenwandverkleidung aus Zedernholz das äußere Erscheinungsbild des Gebäudes. Eine »zentrale Wirbelsäule« unterhalb eines Pultdaches gestattet einen sowohl vertikalen als auch horizontalen Zugang zu allen Bereichen des Hauses, wie etwa zu den öffentlichen Räumen (Wohnraum, Eßzimmer, Küche und Atelier) im Westen der »Wirbelsäule« und den Schlafzimmern im Osten. In Cesar Pellis Firmenbiographie steht: »Mr. Pelli verzichtet in seinen Entwürfen weitestgehend auf formalistische Vorurteile. Er ist der Ansicht, daß die ästhetische Qualität eines Gebäudes aus den spezifischen Eigenschaften eines jeden Projekts – wie etwa seiner Lage, seiner Bauweise und seinem Verwendungszweck – erwachsen sollte. Stets auf der Suche nach den am besten geeigneten Maßnahmen für jedes Projekt, zeichnen sich seine Entwürfe durch eine große Bandbreite an individuellen Lösungen und Materialien aus.«

Cette spectaculaire résidence sur deux niveaux couvre, avec son garage, 900 m², sans compter une maison d'amis de 150 m². Elle est située sur un terrain de 40 hectares au bord d'une rivière. La vue de la maison principale est orientée vers les montagnes. La maison d'amis comprend une chambre mansardée, un salon, une cuisine, deux salles de bain et un garage. Construite en madriers en pin de Douglas et sapin Engelman de 70 cm de diamètre environ, la maison ne compte pas moins de 55 rondins, qui proviennent tous d'arbres tués par les insectes. L'extérieur est également marqué par la forte présence de verre isolant, de cadres de fenêtres en acajou et de panneaux de cèdres. Une «colonne vertébrale centrale» sous un toit pentu permet la circulation horizontale et verticale à travers la maison, les espaces communs (salon, salle à manger, cuisine et bureau) étant à l'ouest, et les chambres à l'est. Comme le précise la biographie de Cesar Pelli fournie par son agence: «M. Pelli évite les préjugés formels dans ses plans. Il pense que les qualités esthétiques d'un bâtiment doivent venir des caractéristiques spécifiques de chaque projet, comme, entre autres, le site, les techniques de construction, et l'objectif poursuivi. Ses plans et dessins font appel à un large éventail de solutions et de matériaux qui permettent de trouver la solution la mieux adaptée au projet.»

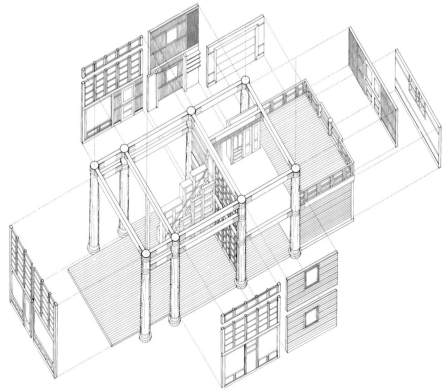

Pages 125–127: The massive log columns of this house recall the neighboring forest, the American tradition of indigenous wooden structures, and the very origins of architecture.

Seite 125–127: Das aus massiven Bäumen errichtete Haus erweckt Erinnerungen an das benachbarte Waldgebiet, an die traditionelle amerikanische Holzbauweise und an die Ursprünge der Architektur.

Pages 125–127: Les gros madriers-colonnes de cette maison rappellent la forêt toute proche, la tradition américaine des structures en bois, et les origines même de l'architecture.

Antoine **Predock**

Antoine Predock

Civic Arts Plaza, Laramie, Wyoming, 1989–94, detail.

Civic Arts Plaza, Laramie, Wyoming, 1989–94, Detail.

Civic Arts Plaza, Laramie, Wyoming, 1989–94, détail.

Architecture magazine recently wrote that "no contemporary American architect has done more to extend architecture's spiritual and symbolic range" than Antoine Predock. One of the most notable contributions of this star of the rising school of the southwest is that his analysis of a site and a project goes beyond strict programmatic and economic considerations. The large collages which he makes before completing his designs not only conjure up images related to the project, but also explore deeper connections to local history and geography. A wide variety of further influences on Predock's concepts includes popular culture as expressed for example in his curious fascination with Unidentified Flying Objects. Occasionally, as in the case of the American Heritage Center shown here, he strikes on a form which is clearly inspired by the mountainous surroundings of the site, but also by UFOs or even futuristic (or ancient) helmets. This type of profound connection between the present, past and future, may indeed be what contemporary architecture is searching for.

Das Magazin »Architecture« schrieb vor kurzem über Antoine Predock: »Kein zeitgenössischer amerikanischer Architekt hat die spirituellen und symbolischen Grenzen der Architektur weiter ausgelotet«. Zu den größten Stärken dieses Stararchitekten gehört, daß seine Analyse eines Baugeländes und eines Projekts weit über die strengen programmatischen und ökonomischen Erwägungen hinausgeht, die die meisten Architekten als hinderlich empfinden. Die großen Collagen, die Predock erstellt, bevor er seinen eigentlichen Entwurf abschließt, dienen nicht nur dazu, Bilder zu erzeugen, die mit dem Projekt in Beziehung stehen, sondern auch der Suche nach einer tieferen Verbindung mit der Geschichte und Geographie des Bauortes. Auch die populäre Kultur – die sich zum Beispiel in seiner seltsamen Faszination für UFOs zeigt – taucht immer wieder als Einfluß auf. Diese Art einer tiefgründigen Verbindung von Vergangenheit, Gegenwart und Zukunft könnte tatsächlich eine der Lösungen sein, nach denen die Architektur unserer Zeit sucht.

Le Magazine «Architecture» a récemment écrit de Predock: «Aucun architecte américain contemporain n'a autant fait pour élargir les horizons spirituels et symboliques de l'architecture.» L'une des contributions les plus notables de cette étoile montante de l'école du Sud-Ouest est que son analyse du site et du projet va au-delà des considérations programmatiques et économiques qui paralysent la plupart des architectes. Ses grands collages préparatoires ont pour but de visualiser le projet et de chercher un rapport plus étroit à l'histoire et à la géographie locales. D'autres influences sont sensibles dans l'œuvre de l'architecte. Ainsi la culture populaire est présente, par exemple, à travers cette curieuse fascination pour les OVNI. A l'occasion, comme pour l'American Heritage Center reproduit ici, Predock s'arrête sur une forme inspirée par le site montagneux du projet, mais aussi par des OVNI ou même un heaume futuriste, ou médiéval. L'architecture contemporaine est peut-être à la recherche de ces rapports profonds entre présent, passé et futur.

American Heritage Center, Laramie, Wyoming 1987–93

This 12000 square meter facility was built for $13.8 million. The axis of the project is aligned with two summits – Medicine Bow Peak and Pilot's Knob in the distant Snowy Range and the nearer Laramie Range. As Predock says, this "consciously monumental landscape abstraction represents a symbol for future campus growth... and a statement of the powerful spirit of Wyoming." Situated on a 10 hectare site, the complex includes the American Heritage Center and Fine Arts Museum. The patinated copper cone at the center of the building corresponds to a nearby round basketball arena, but also calls forth images of a UFO, one of the architect's recurring themes, and is equally reminiscent of a mountainous volcanic shape or for strange warrior's helmet. This example illustrates Predock's capacity to fuse sources of inspiration which can be at once geological and anchored in popular culture. The cone and its base house the American Heritage Center, a research facility for scholars. A long, terraced volume with flat roofs, trailing from the cone, houses the University of Wyoming Art Museum, with its collection of artifacts ranging from saddles to mineral maps and stills from Hollywood Westerns. The block-like elements of the museum, intended to recall the architecture of Pueblo Indians, are built with sandblasted concrete blocks specially formed with a coarse aggregate.

Auf etwa 13,8 Millionen Dollar beliefen sich die Baukosten für dieses 12000 m² große Zentrum, dessen Achse an zwei Berggipfeln ausgerichtet wurde: dem Medicine Bow Peak in den weiter entfernten Snowy Range und dem Pilot's Knob in der nähergelegenen Laramie Range. Predock beschrieb das Projekt so: »Diese bewußt monumentale Landschaftsabstraktion stellt ein Symbol des zukünftigen Wachstums des Campus dar... und dokumentiert den kraftvollen Geist des Staates Wyoming.« Der auf einem 10 Hektar großen Gelände gelegene Gebäudekomplex umfaßt das American Heritage Center und das Fine Arts Museum. Ein von Patina überzogener Kupferkegel im Zentrum des Gebäudes findet seine Entsprechung in einer nahegelegenen, runden Basketballarena, assoziiert aber auch Bilder eines UFOs – einem immer wiederkehrenden Thema des Architekten – und erinnert in gleicher Weise an einen Vulkan oder den Helm eines fremdartigen Kriegers. Dieses Beispiel illustriert Predocks Fähigkeit, unterschiedliche Inspirationsquellen – die zugleich geologischen Ursprungs als auch in der Popkultur verankert sein können – miteinander zu verschmelzen. Der Kegel und sein Fundament beherbergen das American Heritage Center, eine Forschungseinrichtung für Geisteswissenschaftler. Das University of Wyoming Art Museum mit seiner Sammlung von Artefakten und Gebrauchsgegenständen – wie etwa Sättel, Karten von Bodenschätzen oder Standfotos von Hollywood-Western – befindet sich dagegen in einem sich an den Kegel anschließenden langen, terrassenförmig abgestuften Komplex mit Flachdächern. Die blockartigen Elemente des Museums, die an die Architektur der Pueblo-Indianer erinnern sollen, wurden aus sandgestrahlten, speziell mit einem Grobzuschlagstoff gefertigten Betonblöcken errichtet.

Ce bâtiment de 12000 m² a coûté 13,8 millions de dollars. L'axe du projet est aligné sur deux sommets de la Snowy Range et de la Laramie Range – Medecine Bow Peak et Pilot's Knob. Comme le déclare Predock: «Cette abstraction monumentale et consciente d'un paysage est un symbole du développement futur du campus, et une affirmation de la puissante personnalité du Wyoming.» Implanté sur un terrain de 10 hectares, l'ensemble comprend l'American Heritage Center et le musée des Beaux-Arts. Le cône de cuivre patiné au centre du bâtiment fait écho à un stade circulaire de basketball voisin, mais rappelle également des images d'objets volants non identifiés (un des thèmes récurrents de l'architecte), une forme volcanique ou même le heaume d'un guerrier. Cet exemple illustre la capacité de Predock à fusionner des sources d'inspiration aussi bien géologique qu'ancrées dans la culture populaire. Le cône et son socle abritent l'American Heritage Center, un centre de recherche universitaire. Un long volume en terrasse et à toits plats, partant du cône, est occupé par le musée de l'Université du Wyoming, dont la collection va des selles de cheval aux cartes géologiques en passant par les photos de westerns hollywoodiens. Le musée est construit en blocs de béton à gros granulat passés au jet de sable. On pense évidemment ici à l'architecture des Indiens pueblo.

Pages 131–135: The central cone of the American Heritage Center is redolent with images ranging from a warrior's helmet to a UFO or a volcanic shape. Like an ancient observatory or temple, it seems to contain a symbolic significance in its forms and orientation.

Seite 131–135: Der zentrale Kegel des American Heritage Center erinnert gleichermaßen an den Helm eines Kriegers, an ein UFO und einen Vulkan. Wie eine antike Sternwarte oder ein Tempel erbaut, scheint es in Formen und Ausrichtung eine symbolische Bedeutung zu besitzen.

Pages 131–135: Le cône central de l'American Heritage Center évoque diverses images: heaume, OVNI, volcan. A la manière d'un temple ou d'un très ancien observatoire, il semble porter dans ses formes comme dans son orientation une signification symbolique.

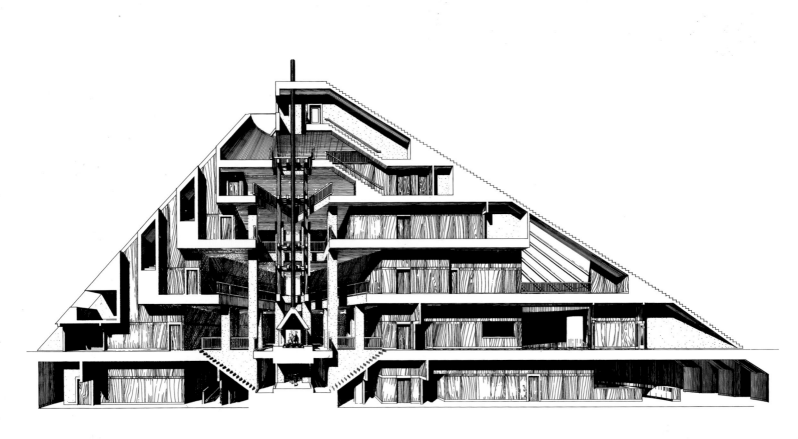

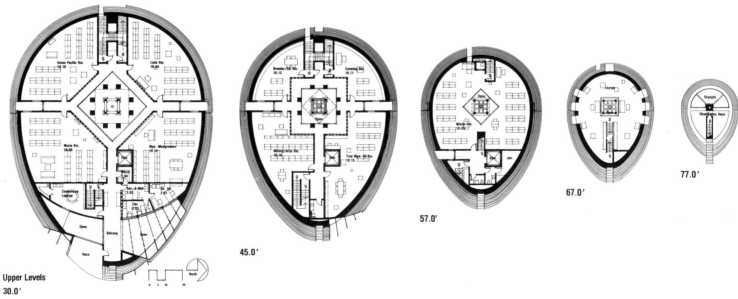

Upper Levels
30.0'

45.0'

57.0'

67.0'

77.0'

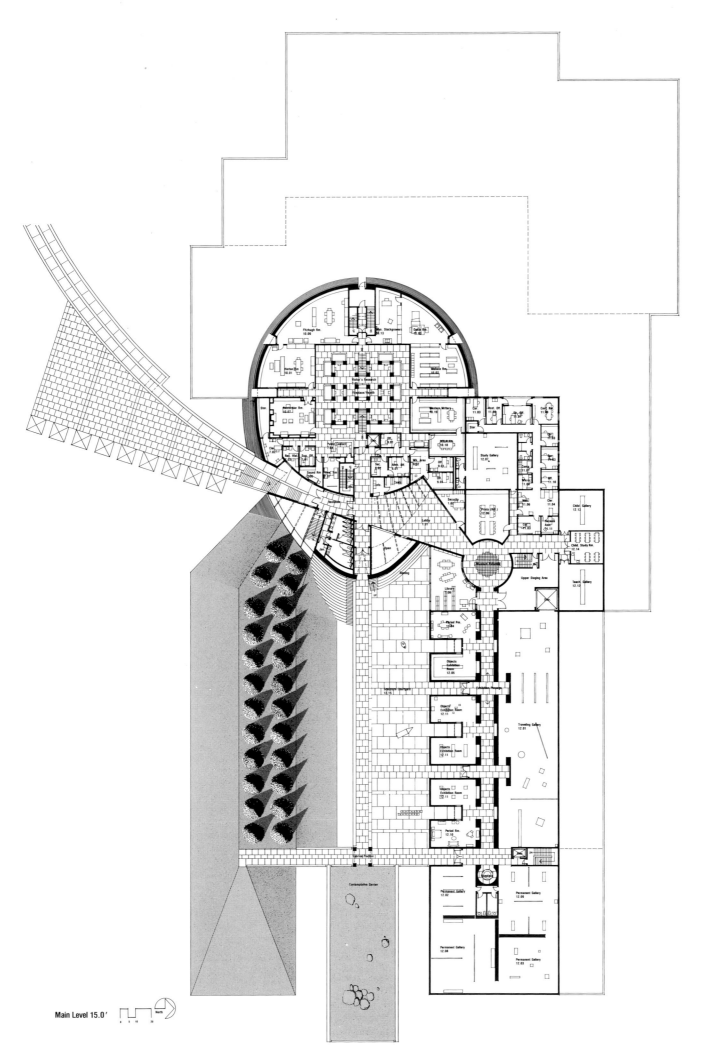

Main Level 15.0'

Civic Arts Plaza, Thousand Oaks, California 1989–94

Covering an area of about 17000 square meters, this structure cost $53 million. It includes offices for city administrative departments, a 398 seat theater, Council Chambers, an 1800 seat auditorium, gallery exhibition space, a 3 hectare community park, and an 850 space parking lot. "Bambi meets Godzilla" is how Antoine Predock describes this site bounded on the south by the busy Ventura Freeway, and on the north by Thousand Oaks Boulevard. The site is less than an hour's drive north from Los Angeles. The topography is further complicatd by a 25 meter change of grade from the level of the elevated freeway to that of the buildings. One of the interesting decorative features is the so-called "Pictograph Wall" made with acrylic tubes set in a wall to create a pattern of openings, intended as a stylized reference to the original inhabitants of the Coneyo Valley. Like most of Predock's buildings, the Thousand Oaks Civic Plaza is austere and closely related to the earth. His largest institutional project to date, it is also massive and complex.

Die Baukosten für das 17000 m² umfassende Civic Arts Plaza – zu dem Büroräume für die Stadtverwaltung, ein Theater mit 398 Plätzen, Ratssäle, ein Auditorium mit 1800 Plätzen, eine Galerie mit Ausstellungsflächen, ein 3 Hektar großer öffentlicher Park und ein Parkplatz mit 850 Stellplätzen gehören – betrugen 53 Millionen Dollar. »Bambi trifft Godzilla« – mit diesen Worten beschrieb Antoine Predock das Gelände, das im Süden an den vielbefahrenen Ventura Freeway und im Norden an den Thousand Oaks Boulevard grenzt und keine Autostunde nördlich von Los Angeles liegt. Die topographische Beschaffenheit des Grundstücks wird durch einen Höhenunterschied von 25 Metern zwischen dem Niveau des hochgelegten Freeways und dem des Gebäudes zusätzlich erschwert. Zu den herausragenden dekorativen Eigenschaften der Plaza gehört die sogenannte »Pictograph Wall«, die aus Acrylröhren gefertigt ist. Diese Röhren sind in die Wand eingelassen und bilden so ein Muster aus Röhrenöffnungen, das eine stilisierte Referenz an die ursprünglichen Bewohner des Coneyo Valley darstellen soll. Wie die meisten von Predock entworfenen Gebäude wirkt auch das nüchterne und sehr erdverbundene Thousand Oaks Civic Plaza – sein bis dato größtes Projekt für eine öffentliche Einrichtung – massiv und komplex.

Ce bâtiment de 17000 m² environ a coûté 53 millions de dollars. Il comprend des bureaux administratifs de la ville, un théâtre de 398 places, les salles du conseil municipal, un auditorium de 1800 places, un espace d'exposition, un parc de 3 hectares et un parking de 850 places. «Bambi et Godzilla», c'est ainsi que Predock décrit ce site limité au sud par l'autoroute très fréquentée de Ventura, et au nord par Thousand Oaks Boulevard. Le tout se trouve à moins d'une heure de voiture de Los Angeles. La topographie est rendue encore plus délicate par une différence de niveau de 25 m entre l'autoroute surélevée et les bâtiments. Le «Pictograph Wall», fait de tubes d'acrylique insérés dans un mur qui créent un motif d'ouvertures, référence stylisée aux habitants originaux de la Coneyo Valley, est l'un des éléments décoratifs les plus intéressants. Comme la plupart des réalisations de Predock, cet ensemble austère, massif et complexe est intimement lié à son site. C'est le plus important projet réalisé à ce jour par l'architecte.

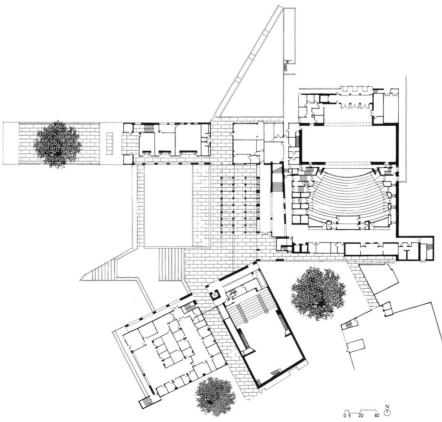

Despite his interest in local traditions related to the sites he works with, Antoine Predock is undoubtedly first and foremost concerned with meeting the programmatic requirements of the client, which were particularly complex in this case.

Trotz seines Interesses an lokalen Traditionen kümmert sich Antoine Predock in erster Linie um die programmatischen Anforderungen seines Kunden, die in diesem Fall sehr komplex waren.

Très intéressé par les traditions locales des sites sur lesquels il travaille, Antoine Predock est sans aucun doute d'abord et essentiellement intéressé par les exigences programmatiques de son client, particulièrement complexes en l'occurrence.

Ventata Vista Elementary School, Tucson, Arizona 1992—94

Surprisingly for a school, this stark structure is viewed by the architect as a direct confrontation with an inhospitable environment. Located near the Catalina Mountains and the Sonoran desert, it is constituted by a series of courts and passages arranged around the two story library. Predock makes no apology for the austerity of his architecture in this instance. He says, "the desert is about power and loneliness. The desert is not cute. Kids are smart; they understand this." Built for a cost of $7.7 million, or $85 per square foot, the building takes into account the smaller scale of children's bodies, and includes a "Solstice wall" designed so that the sun falls on plaques on the ground which make reference to significant days or events. Much as he wanted a form planned for the Santa Fe Hotel at EuroDisney to resemble a crashed UFO, Predock hoped to place the tail of a B-52 bomber in a courtyard of this school. A nearby Air Force base might justify this relic as a piece of "local color," but once again, Predock mixes references to his site in a geological sense to much more contemporary bits of culture.

Diese starre Konstruktion betrachtet der Architekt als eine direkte Konfrontation mit einer wenig einladenden Umgebung – ein für ein Schulgebäude ungewöhnlicher Ansatz. Die in der Nähe der Catalina Mountains und der Sonora-Wüste gelegene Grundschule besteht aus einer Reihe von Innenhöfen und Verbindungsgängen rund um das zweigeschossige Bibliotheksgebäude. Predock sieht keine Notwendigkeit, sich für das nüchtern-strenge Erscheinungsbild seiner Architektur zu entschuldigen: »Die Wüste steht für Macht und Einsamkeit, eine Wüste ist nicht niedlich. Die Kinder sind nicht dumm und verstehen das sehr genau.« Das Gebäude, dessen Baukosten 7,7 Millionen Dollar oder 915 Dollar pro Quadratmeter betrugen, wurde speziell auf die geringere Körpergröße von Kindern zugeschnitten und verfügt über eine »Sonnenwend-Mauer«, die so konzipiert ist, daß die Sonne auf im Boden eingelassene Platten fällt, die jeweils zu einem besonderen Tag oder Ereignis gehören. Predocks Vorliebe für Flugkörper zeigt sich nicht nur bei seinem Entwurf für das Hotel Santa Fe in EuroDisney, das teilweise an ein abgestürztes UFO erinnert, sondern auch bei dieser Schule, in deren Innenhof er das Heck eines B 52-Bombers integrieren wollte. Aufgrund des nahegelegenen Air Force-Stützpunktes könnte man dieses Relikt als ein Stück »Lokalkolorit« rechtfertigen, aber auch hierbei ging es Predock nur um eine Kombination geologischer, das Gelände betreffender Bezüge mit sehr viel zeitgenössischeren Elementen unserer Kultur.

Surprenante pour une école, cette puissante construction a représenté pour l'architecte une confrontation directe avec un environnement inhospitalier. Située non loin des Catalina Mountains et du désert de Sonora, elle comprend une succession de cours et de passages disposés autour d'une bibliothèque à deux niveaux. Dans un tel contexte, Predock ne cherche pas à s'excuser de l'austérité de son architecture: «Le désert pose les problèmes du pouvoir et de la solitude. Le désert n'a rien de charmant. Les enfants sont intelligents, il comprennent.» Le bâtiment a côuté 7,7 millions de dollars, soit 915 dollars le m². Il a été conçu à l'échelle des enfants et comprend un «mur du solstice» qui dirige les rayons du soleil sur des plaques fixées au sol où sont inscrits les jours ou événements importants. Un peu comme il avait voulu une forme d'OVNI écrasé au sol pour son Santa Fe Hotel d'EuroDisney, il souhaitait placer la queue d'un bombardier B-52 dans la cour de cette école. La présence d'une base aérienne militaire dans la région aurait pu justifier l'ajout de cette relique au nom de la «couleur locale». Une fois encore, Predock mélange les références géologiques à celles de la culture contemporaine.

FLOOR PLAN - LEVEL ONE

Pages 138/139: As the plan shows, this school is far from the kind of rectilinear layout usually expected in such facilities. According to Predock, the system of linked courtyards suggests "ageless ruins."

Seite 138/139: Der Grundriß zeigt deutlich, daß sich diese Schule erheblich von der sonst üblichen geradlinigen Aufteilung solcher öffentlichen Einrichtungen unterscheidet. Laut Predock erinnert das System untereinander verbundener Schulhöfe an »zeitlose Ruinen«.

Pages 138/139: Comme on le voit ici, cette école est très éloignée des plans rectilignes conventionnels de ce type d'établissement. Selon Predock, le système des cours communicantes évoque «les ruines immémoriales».

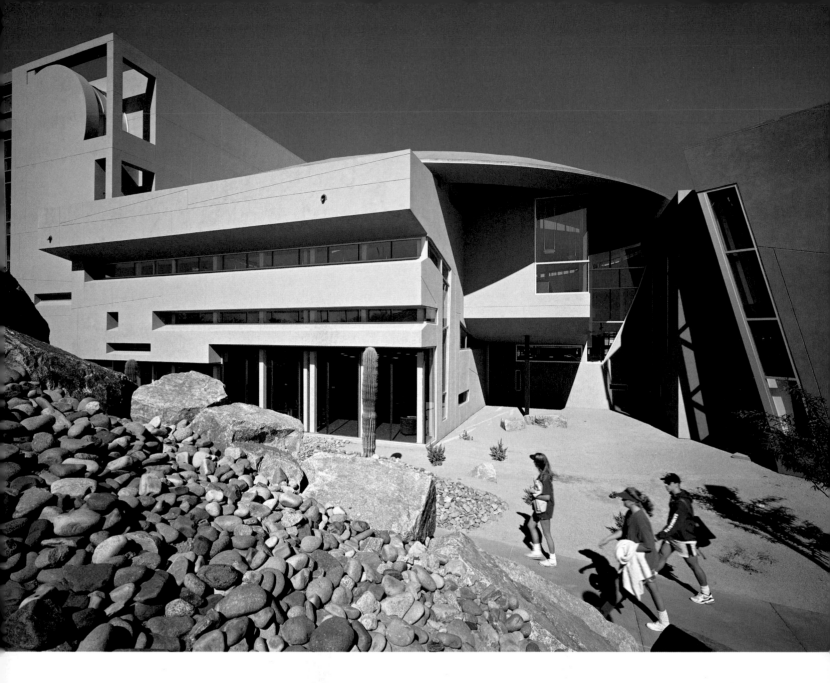

140 Ventata Vista Elementary School

Pages 140/141: Classroom areas are designed with the age of the children in each class in mind. Predock evokes the "tent-like white canvas structure... emerging from the low-lying silhouette" as a reminder of the "nomadic occupation of the desert".

Seite 140/141: Die Klassenräume wurden dem jeweiligen Alter der Schüler entsprechend konzipiert. Laut Predock dient die »zeltartige Konstruktion aus weißem Segeltuch..., die aus der eher niedrigen Silhouette herausragt«, als Erinnerung an »die nomadische Besiedelung der Wüste«.

Pages 140/141: Les classes sont conçues en fonction de l'âge des enfants qui les utiliseront. Predock considère la «structure en forme de tente de toile blanche émergeant d'une silhouette basse» comme un rappel de l'ancienne «occupation nomade du désert».

Bart **Prince**

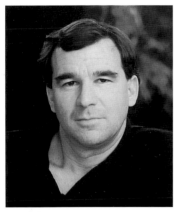

Bart Prince

Mead/Penhall Residence, Albuquerque, New Mexico, 1992–93, detail.

Mead/Penhall Residence, Albuquerque, New Mexico, 1992–93, Detail.

Mead/Penhall Residence, Albuquerque, Nouveau Mexique, 1992–93, détail.

Unlike many of the other well-known "local" architects who have established residence in the southwest, Albuquerque-born Bart Prince also can boast that his work as an assistant to Bruce Goff from 1968 to 1973 established his credentials as the most legitimate representative of a strong regional tradition of organic architecture. His often complex, undulating forms frequently have a strong natural connotation without being specifically anthropomorphic. The Mead/Penhall residence shown here is something of an exception in the work of Bart Prince, because of the small lot and limited budget available. The architect shows here that his capacities for invention are not impaired by the use of exposed concrete or galvanized metal, and he also achieves a degree of privacy for the clients without sacrificing light and views toward the mountains. Another of Bart Prince's current projects, the Hight Residence (Mendocino County, CA), returns with its spectacular undulating surfaces of wood, copper and glass to a more familiar mode for this talented, and unexpected architect.

Der in Albuquerque geborene Bart Prince hat durch seine Arbeit als Assistent von Bruce Goff (1968–73) bewiesen, daß er unter den rechtmäßigen Vertretern einer starken regionalen Tradition organischer Architektur führend ist. Seine vielfach komplexen Wellenformen besitzen häufig starke Bezüge zur Natur, ohne dabei bewußt anthropomorph zu wirken. Die Mead/Penhall Residence stellt in Bart Princes Œuvre die Ausnahme von der Regel dar, was hauptsächlich dem kleinen Baugelände und dem schmalen Budget zuzuschreiben ist. Prince beweist hier, daß sein Einfallsreichtum nicht durch die Verwendung von unverputztem Beton oder Zinkblech beeinträchtigt wird; sein Entwurf bietet seinen Kunden einen hohen Grad von Intimität, ohne den Lichteinfall oder den Ausblick auf die Berge einzuschränken. Dagegen weist ein anderes von Princes gegenwärtigen Projekten, die Hight Residence (Mendocino County, Kalifornien), wieder die gewellten Oberflächen aus Holz, Kupfer und Glas auf, die für diesen begabten Architekten so charakteristisch sind.

Né à Albuquerque, à la différence d'autres célèbres architectes «locaux» nouvellement installés dans le Sud-Ouest, Bart Prince peut aussi se targuer d'avoir été l'assistant de Bruce Goff de 1968 à 1973, ce qui fait de lui l'un des représentants les plus légitimes d'une puissante tradition régionale d'architecture organique. Ses lignes complexes, souvent ondulées, évoquent irrésistiblement les formes naturelles, sans être spécifiquement anthropomorphiques. La résidence Mead/Penhall illustrée ici est une sorte d'exception à la règle, Prince travaillant d'habitude sur des projets et des budgets plus importants. Il prouve ici que sa capacité d'invention n'est pas gênée par l'utilisation du béton brut ou du métal galvanisé, et parvient à offrir à ses clients une réelle intimité sans sacrifier la lumière et la vue sur les montagnes. Parmi ses autres projets actuels, la High Residence (Mendocino County, Californie) aux surfaces ondulées de bois, de cuivre et de verre marque le retour à une inspiration plus familière pour cet architecte talentueux et souvent inattendu.

Mead/Penhall Residence, Albuquerque, New Mexico 1992–93

Designed with a very low construction budget and simple materials such as exposed, sandblasted concrete block for the walls around the carport, wood framing finished either with stucco and sheetrock or galvanized metal on the exterior and rough-sawn cedar plywood panels on the interior, this house sits on a lot which is only 20 x 41 meters in size. Houses on nearby lots are one and two story contractor designed frame/stucco structures, with a carport in front of each one. The design here was completed with the idea of providing space for a collection of photographs, paintings and 19th century furniture. There is a continuous curving ceiling made with exposed joists and metal. A series of covered and uncovered decks on the roof level emphasizes the distant mountain views to the north and east. Bart Prince, a former colleague of Bruce Goff, is best known for his Japanese pavilion at the Los Angeles County Museum of Art, which he completed after Goff's death, and for a large number of spectacular private residences. It is particularly interesting to see his efficient and visually spectacular approach to a low-budget project.

Das mit einem sehr niedrigen Budget und schlichten Materialien – unverputzte, sandgestrahlte Betonblocksteine für die Mauern um den Carport, eine von außen mit Putz und Steinplatten oder Zinkblech verkleidete und von innen mit sägerauhen Zedernsperrholzplatten versehene Holzrahmenkonstruktion – errichtete Haus liegt auf einem nur 20 x 41 Meter großen Gelände. Die Häuser der umliegenden Grundstücke sind ein- oder zweigeschossige, von Bauunternehmen geplante Tragrahmen/Putzbauten mit jeweils einem Carport davor. Der Entwurf für die Mead/Penhall Residence entstand mit dem Hintergedanken, daß das Gebäude ausreichend Raum für eine Sammlung von Photographien, Gemälden und Möbeln aus dem 19. Jahrhundert bieten sollte. Über das gesamte Gebäude erstreckt sich eine gewölbte Deckenkonstruktion aus freiliegenden Unterzügen und Metall. Eine Reihe von offenen und überdachten Terrassen auf Dachniveau betont die Aussicht auf Berge im Norden und Osten. Bart Prince wurde bekannt durch seinen japanischen Pavillon im Los Angeles County Museum of Art, den er nach Goffs Tod fertigstellte, sowie durch eine große Anzahl aufsehenerregender Privathäuser.

Cette résidence construite à peu de frais utilise avec bonheur des matériaux banals: parpaings bruts sablés pour l'abri voitures, bois de charpente habillé de panneaux crépis ou de métal galvanisé (pour les façades) et des panneaux de cèdre brut (pour les murs intérieurs). Le terrain ne mesure que 20 x 41 m. Les maisons voisines sont des réalisations de promoteurs à un ou deux niveaux, en bois et crépi, avec un abri à voiture devant chacune d'entre elles. L'idée était d'aménager dans la Mead/Penhall Residence un espace suffisament vaste pour contenir une collection de photographies, de peintures et de mobilier du XIXe siècle. La charpente métallique du plafond incurvé reste apparente. Une série de «ponts» couverts ou découverts au niveau du toit donnent sur le panorama des montagnes, au nord et à l'est. Bart Prince, ancien confrère de Bruce Goff, est surtout connu pour avoir réalisé le pavillon japonais du Los Angeles County Museum of Art, qu'il a terminé après le décès de Goff, et pour un grand nombre de résidences privées. Il est ici particulièrement intéressant de le voir atteindre un résultat aussi efficace que spectaculaire pour un budget aussi réduit.

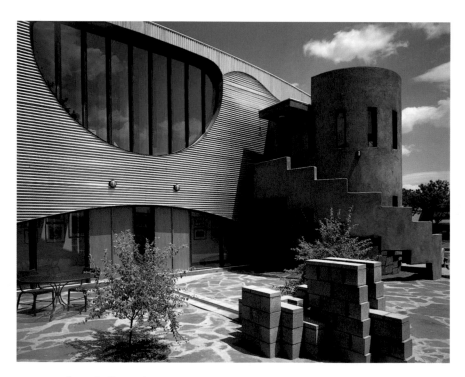

Pages 144–147: Although not overtly anthropomorphic, this house does in some respects bring to mind a living creature, or perhaps an ark.

Seite 144–147: Obwohl dieses Haus nicht offenkundig anthropomorph ist, weckt es dennoch Assoziationen an ein lebendiges Wesen oder an eine Arche.

Pages 144–147: Sans être ouvertement anthropomorphique, cette maison évoque à certains égards une créature vivante, ou peut-être une arche.

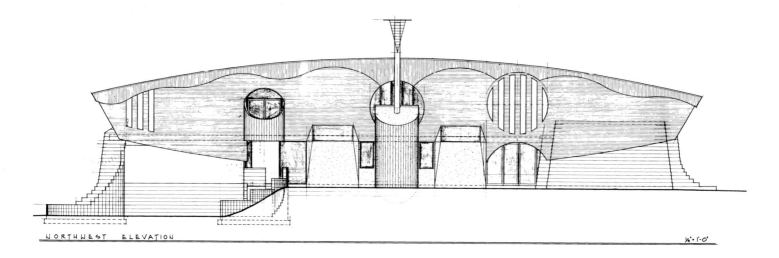

NORTHWEST ELEVATION   1/4" = 1'-0"

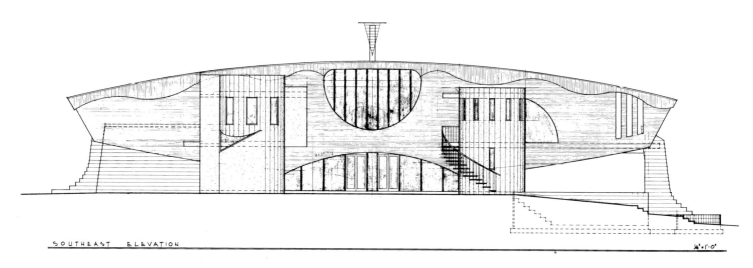

SOUTHEAST ELEVATION   1/4" = 1'-0"

Pages 148/149: Though the design is intended to preserve the privacy of the owners, the house admits substantial amounts of natural light. Simple, inexpensive materials are used throughout.

Seite 148/149: Trotz des Designs, das die Privatsphäre des Besitzers wahren soll, fällt viel Tageslicht in das Gebäude ein, das aus schlichten und preiswerten Materialien gefertigt wurde.

Pages 148/149: Si la maison est conçue pour préserver l'intimité de ses propriétaires, elle profite néanmoins d'un abondant éclairage naturel. Elle fait partout appel à des matériaux simples et bon marché.

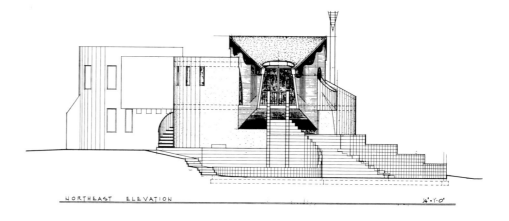

NORTHEAST ELEVATION   1/4" = 1'-0"

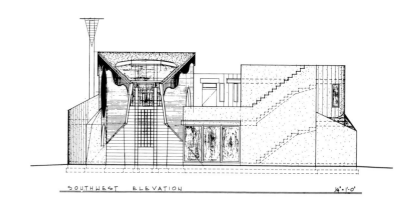

SOUTHWEST ELEVATION   1/4" = 1'-0"

Scogin Elam and Bray

Mark Scogin, Merrill Elam and
Lloyd Bray

John J. Ross – William Blakley Law
Library, Tempe, Arizona, 1991–93,
detail.

John J. Ross – William Blakley Law
Library, Tempe, Arizona, 1991–93,
Detail.

John J. Ross – William Blakley Law
Library, Tempe, Arizona, 1991–93,
détail.

Despite their Georgia back-grounds, Mark Scogin, Chairman of the Department of Architecture at the Harvard Graduate School of Design, and his design partner Merrill Elam have entered fully into the spirit of the southwest with their John J. Ross – William C. Blakley Law Library at Arizona State University. They speak of the anomalies of vision and appearance in a desert environment to describe their project, and define it in terms of the intense Arizona sunlight. Despite this foray into the desert, most of the firm's current projects, such as their Bridge over Highway 41 in Atlanta, the Riverdale Branch Library (Riverdale, GA) and private residences in Lake Norman, NC, Moreland, GA, Dillard, GA and Stoneham, ME are concentrated on the East Coast. Although it does cite features of the western desert, the Ross – Blakley Library is further evidence of a trend in contemporary architecture towards distinctly defined volumes conceived in non-Cartesian terms. The new modernism clearly breaks with the geometric determinism of its immediate forbears.

Obwohl sie ursprünglich aus Georgia stammen, haben Mark Scogin, Vorsitzender des Department of Architecture der Harvard Graduate School of Design, und seine Partnerin Merrill Elam ihren Entwurf für die John J. Ross – William C. Blakley Law Library an der Arizona State University ganz im Geiste des Südwestens gestaltet. Bei der Beschreibung ihres Projekts sprechen sie von den optischen Täuschungen, die für eine Wüste typisch sind, und sie definieren ihr Bauwerk mit Bezug auf das intensive Sonnenlicht Arizonas. Trotz dieses Ausflugs in die Wüste konzentriert sich der Großteil aller gegenwärtigen Projekte des Büros – eine Brücke über den Highway 41 in Atlanta, die Riverdale Branch Library (Riverdale, Georgia) sowie Privathäuser in Lake Norman, North Carolina, Moreland, Georgia, Dillard, Georgia und Stoneham, Maine – auf die amerikanische Ostküste. Obwohl ihr Erscheinungsbild Bezüge zur Wüstenlandschaft enthält, ist die Ross – Blakley Library ein weiterer Beweis für einen Trend der zeitgenössischen Architektur hin zu eindeutig definierten Räumen.

Bien qu'originaires de l'Etat de Géorgie, Mark Scogin, président du département d'architecture de la Harvard Graduate School of Design, et son associé Merrill Elam ont su pleinement se pénétrer de l'esprit du Sud-Ouest, comme le montre cette Bibliothèque John J. Ross – William C. Blakley pour la faculté de droit de l'Arizona State University. A propos de leur projet, ils parlent de la puissante luminosité de l'Arizona et des anomalies de vision qu'elle provoque dans cet environnement désertique. Cette escapade dans le désert n'empêche pas la majorité des projets actuels de l'agence d'être concentrée sur la côte Est: pont sur l'autoroute 41 à Atlanta, Riverdale Branch Library (Riverdale, Géorgie), et résidences particulières à Lake Norman (Caroline du Nord), Moreland et Dillard (Géorgie), Stoneham (Maine). La Ross – Blakley Library montre une fois de plus le goût de l'architecture contemporaine pour les volumes bien définis et conçus dans un esprit non cartésien. Ce nouveau modernisme rompt avec le déterminisme géométrique de ses prédécesseurs.

John J. Ross – William Blakley Law Library Arizona State University, Tempe, Arizona, 1991–93

Completed in the summer of 1993, this is a law library expansion and renovation. Roughly 6000 square meters of new construction and 1500 square meters of renovation are involved, with a budget of $7.37 million. Located on the fringe of the Arizona State University campus, the project represents a reaction to the neighboring Armstrong Hall, but these Georgia architects seem to have been seduced by the very particular climatic and geographic conditions in this area. As they write, "the Arizona desert landscape provokes mis-readings. Plants look like animals, animals look like rocks, rocks look like animals... eye foolers. The sun bursts over the horizon not bothering with some filtering effect of east coast greenery, but immediately filling an enormous sky with incredible light. Textures and colors vibrate." Aside from the architectural environment, the unexpected forms of this library take their clue from the spectacular desert landscape. The architects call part of the structure the "magic mountain." Named for two prominent Phoenix attorneys, the library has a collection of over 300000 volumes and microfilm volume equivalents. There is a thirty station computer lab, and 27 meeting and study rooms. The building is a steel frame on concrete foundations, with exterior materials which include synthetic stucco and metal roofing.

Bei diesem im Sommer 1993 fertiggestellten Sanierungs- und Erweiterungsprojekt einer juristischen Bibliothek wurden bei einem Budget von 7,37 Millionen Dollar 6000m² neue Fläche dazugewonnen und 1500m² renoviert. Das am Rande des Campus der Arizona State University gelegene Gebäude stellt zwar eine Reaktion auf die benachbarte Armstrong Hall dar, aber die Architekten aus Georgia scheinen den Versuchungen der sehr spezifischen klimatischen und geographischen Bedingungen dieser Gegend erlegen zu sein: »Die Wüstenlandschaft Arizonas provoziert Fehlinterpretationen. Pflanzen sehen aus wie Tiere, Tiere wie Steine, Steine wie Tiere... alles optische Täuschungen. Die Sonne steigt plötzlich am Horizont hoch, ohne sich lange durch den Filtereffekt einer üppigen Pflanzenwelt wie an der Ostküste aufhalten zu lassen, und sie erfüllt den gewaltigen Himmel sofort mit unglaublichem Licht. Farben und Strukturen vibrieren.« Neben der architektonischen Umgebung diente die aufsehenerregende Wüstenlandschaft als weitere Inspirationsquelle für die ungewöhnlichen Formen der Bibliothek. Die Architekten bezeichnen einen Teil der Konstruktion als den »magischen Berg«. Die nach zwei berühmten Anwälten der Stadt Phoenix benannte Bibliothek umfaßt eine Sammlung von über 300000 Bänden und den entsprechenden Mikrofilmen; darüber hinaus verfügt sie über einen Lesesaal mit 30 Computerterminals sowie 27 Konferenz- und Arbeitsräume. Bei diesem Gebäude handelt es sich um eine Stahlskelettkonstruktion auf einem Betonfundament, die von außen mit synthetischem Putz und einer Dacheindeckung aus Metall versehen ist.

Ce projet achevé à l'été 1993 est en fait l'extension et la rénovation de la bibliothèque de droit: 6000m² de constructions nouvelles, 1500m² de rénovation pour un budget de 7,37 millions de dollars. Elle est située en bordure du campus de l'Arizona State University, et se démarque délibérément de l'Armstrong Hall voisin. Venus du sud-est des Etats-Unis, ses architectes semblent avoir été séduits par les conditions climatiques et géographiques particulières de la région: «Le paysage désertique de l'Arizona déroute la vision. Les plantes ont l'air d'animaux, les animaux font penser à des rochers, les rochers évoquent des animaux... autant d'illusions d'optique. Le soleil déboule à l'horizon sans être filtré par un quelconque écran végétal comme dans l'Est, et il emplit instantanément le ciel immense d'une lumière incroyable. Les matières et les couleurs vibrent.» Par un double mouvement d'attraction/opposition, les formes du bâtiment renvoient donc à la fois à l'architecture environnante et aux paysages spectaculaires du désert. Les architectes ont surnommé une partie du bâtiment «la montagne magique». Dédiée à deux grands juristes de Phoenix, la bibliothèque possède une collection de plus de 300000 volumes et microfilms, 30 postes de travail informatisés, et 27 salles de réunion et d'étude. Le bâtiment est à structure métallique sur fondations en béton, avec, à l'extérieur, des matériaux comme l'enduit synthétique et une toiture métallique.

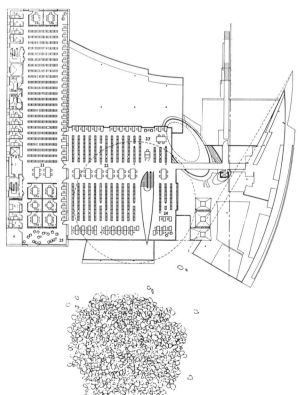

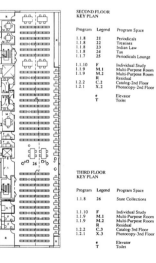

SECOND FLOOR
KEY PLAN

Program	Legend	Program Space
1.1.8	21	Periodicals
1.1.8	22	Treatises
1.1.8	23	Indian Law
1.1.8	24	Tax
1.1.7	25	Periodicals Lounge
1.1.10	F	Individual Study
1.1.9	M.1	Multi-Purpose Room
1.1.9	M.2	Multi-Purpose Room
	R	Residual
1.2.2	C.2	Catalog-2nd Floor
1.2.1	X.2	Photocopy-2nd Floor
	e	Elevator
	T	Toilet

THIRD FLOOR
KEY PLAN

Program	Legend	Program Space
1.1.8	26	State Collections
1.1.10	F	Individual Study
1.1.9	M.1	Multi-Purpose Room
1.1.9	M.2	Multi-Purpose Room
	R	Residual
1.2.2	C.3	Catalog-3rd Floor
1.2.1	X.3	Photocopy-3nd Floor
	e	Elevator
	T	Toilet

Pages 153–155: A second floor plan shows that in spite of apparently unusual exterior forms, the library facilities are laid out in an extremely straightforward way.

Seite 153–155: Der Grundriß des zweiten Stocks zeigt, daß die Funktionen und Versorgungswege der Bibliothek – ungeachtet der ungewöhnlichen äußeren Formen – extrem gradlinig konzipiert wurden.

Pages 153–155: Le plan du second étage montre que, malgré des formes extérieurs peu courantes, les fonctions de la bibliothèque sont traitées de manière très directe.

SITE

James Wines

Watercolor by James Wines showing his "phytoremediation" scheme for the Trawsfynydd Nuclear Power Station in Wales.

Diese Aquarellstudie von James Wines zeigt sein »Phyto-Remediation«-System für die Trawsfynydd Nuclear Power Station in Wales.

Aquarelle de James Wines montrant son projet de «phyto-traitement» pour la centrale nucléaire de Trawsfynydd, au Pays de Galles.

James Wines retains the biting humor that in a sense defines the work of SITE. Although they may have shifted to a more thoroughly environmental approach in recent years, Wines and his associates have long been critics in built form of the various forms of incoherence and inconsistency in architecture and modern society. With their Trawsfynydd Nuclear Power Station Decommissioning Project, published here, SITE undoubtedly enters new terrain, both because of the extremely sensitive nature of the problem which they seek to resolve at least partially, and logically because their work thus takes on something of the *gravitas* of the site itself. It is highly unlikely that this particular North Wales project will indeed be carried out, especially because it was initiated not by the power company but by a television station. Yet if James Wines can succeed in drawing some attention to a neglected aspect of the architectural heritage of the 20th century his efforts will have been well worth while.

James Wines hat sich den beißenden Humor bewahrt, der in gewisser Hinsicht auch die Arbeiten von SITE kennzeichnet. Obwohl sie in den letzten Jahren zu einem noch stärkeren ökologischen Architekturansatz gelangt sind, beziehen Wines und seine Partner mit ihren Bauten schon seit langem kritisch Stellung gegen die verschiedenen Formen von Zusammenhangslosigkeit und Inkonsistenz, die in der Architektur und der heutigen Gesellschaft auftreten. Mit ihrem hier vorgestellten Trawsfynydd Nuclear Power Station Decommissioning Project, einem Konzept für die Stillegung eines Atomkraftwerks, betritt SITE ohne Zweifel Neuland. Allerdings ist es sehr unwahrscheinlich, daß dieses Projekt in Nordwales jemals zur Ausführung gelangen wird, da der Auftrag für das Konzept nicht von der Betreibergesellschaft, sondern von einer Fernsehstation kam. Aber wenn es James Wines gelingt, diesem bisher vernachlässigten Aspekt des architektonischen Erbes des 20. Jahrhunderts etwas mehr Aufmerksamkeit zukommen zu lassen, hat dies die Mühe gelohnt.

James Wines a conservé l'humour mordant qui, dans un sens, définit l'œuvre de SITE. Même s'ils ont évolué ces dernières années vers une approche plus résolument écologique, Wines et ses associés critiquent depuis longtemps les multiples incohérences et contradictions de l'architecture et de la société actuelles. Avec le projet de démantèlement de la centrale nucléaire de Trawsfynydd, publié dans ces pages, SITE pénètre dans un domaine entièrement nouveau, à la fois par la nature extrêmement sensible du problème qu'il a cherché à résoudre, au moins partiellement, et parce que son travail s'appuie en partie sur la *gravitas* du site lui-même. Il est hautement improbable que ce projet pour le nord du Pays de Galles soit mené à bien, en particulier parce qu'il émane non pas de la société d'exploitation de la centrale mais d'une chaîne de télévision. Cependant, si James Wines peut attirer l'attention sur un aspect négligé de l'héritage architectural du XXème siècle, ses efforts n'auront pas été vains.

Tennessee Aquarium Imax Building, Chattanooga, Tennessee 1993 (project)

Adjacent to SITE's 1992 Ross's Landing Plaza and Park, this design is intended as a "visual and functional microcosm of the city's most identifiable features – the river and mountains, the materiality and scale of early waterfront industrial buildings, and certain recent architectural and urbanistic commitments that have begun to define the new regional ambiance." The Imax project is also located near the site of the Tennessee Aquarium, the world's only aquarium dedicated to fresh-water aquatic life, designed by the Cambridge Seven Architects. Seven lateral walls, built out of a combination of brick, stone concrete block undulate through the site, providing for extensive planting on the upper surfaces. Almost apologizing for a rather non-ecological atrium, required in the project, SITE President James Wines nonetheless managed to include stainless steel screening capable of reflecting 90 % of the sun's undesirable rays. The rest of the project is conceived to be as respectful of the environment as possible, taking into account "the ecological effects of mining, harvesting, transportation, manufacturing and packaging as they relate to renewable sources," as well as the "minimalization of building materials that generate pollution... and the specification of materials and systems that avoid health hazards."

Dieses an das 1992 von SITE errichtete Gebäude Ross's Landing Plaza and Park angrenzende Projekt soll einen »optischen und funktionalen Mikrokosmos der herausragendsten Kennzeichen der Stadt« darstellen: »den Fluß und die Berge, die Stofflichkeit und den Maßstab der frühen Industriebauten des Hafenviertels sowie bestimmte architektonische und städtebauliche Projekte, die seit einiger Zeit das Bild der Region zu prägen beginnen.« Das Imax-Projekt befindet sich in der Nähe des Tennessee Aquarium, dem weltweit einzigen Süßwasseraquarium, das von Cambridge Seven Architects enworfen wurde. Sieben aus einer Kombination von Ziegelstein, Naturstein und Betonblockstein errichtete Querwände erstrecken sich wellenförmig durch das Gelände und bieten die Möglichkeit für eine intensive Bepflanzung der Oberflächen. Den Architekten von SITE, dessen Leiter James Wines sich für das weniger umweltfreundliche Atrium, das die Bauauflagen verlangten, fast schon entschuldigt, gelang es, einen Edelstahl-Sonnenschutz zu integrieren, der 90 Prozent der unerwünschten Sonnenstrahlung reflektiert. Der Rest des Projektes wurde so umweltfreundlich wie möglich konzipiert und berücksichtigt »die ökologischen Auswirkungen des Bergbaus, der Landwirtschaft, des Transportwesens sowie der Fertigungs- und der Verpackungsindustrie in bezug auf nachwachsende Rohstoffe.« Darüber hinaus achtete man auf »eine Minimalisierung von umweltbelastenden Baumaterialien... und eine Spezifizierung der Materialien und Systeme, die keine gesundheitlichen Risiken darstellen.«

Adjacent au Ross's Landing Plaza and Park, également dû à SITE (1992), ce projet se propose d'être «un microcosme visuel et fonctionnel des caractéristiques les plus identifiables de la ville – la rivière et les montagnes, la matérialité et l'échelle des bâtiments industriels des quais, et certains partispris architecturaux et urbanistiques qui ont commencé à définir un nouvel esprit régional». Le projet Imax se trouve non loin de l'Aquarium du Tennessee, un des seuls aquariums au monde consacré à la vie aquatique en eau douce conçu par Cambridge Seven Architects. Les sept murs qui s'incurvent en gradins le long du site, et qui associent la brique, la pierre et le béton, retiennent des jardins suspendus. S'excusant presque d'avoir dessiné un atrium assez peu écologique, mais demandé dans le cahier des charges, le président de SITE, James Wines, n'en a pas moins réussi à y incorporer des écrans d'acier inoxydables capables de réfléchir 90% des rayons solaires. Le reste du projet est aussi respectueux de l'environnement qu'il est possible, prenant en compte «les effets écologiques de la mine, des moissons, des transports, de la fabrication industrielle et des emballages, dans leur relation avec les richesses renouvelables», ainsi que «la réduction au minimum des matériaux de construction polluants et le choix de matériaux et de systèmes sans risques pour la santé».

Page 159: James Wines and SITE were amongst the first architects in the United States to consistently privilege environmental factors, as evidenced in their increasingly plant-covered designs.

Seite 159: James Wines und sein Architekturbüro SITE zählen zu den ersten Architekten in den Vereinigten Staaten, die umweltfreundlichen Faktoren generell den Vorzug geben – wie ihre zunehmend von Pflanzen überwucherten Entwürfe zeigen.

Page 159: James Wines et SITE ont été l'une des premières agences d'architecture aux Etats-Unis à privilégier avec constance les facteurs environnementaux, comme le montrent leurs projets de plus en plus recouverts de végétation.

Trawsfynydd Nuclear Power Station Decommissioning, North Wales 1994 (project)

In the fall of 1994, SITE, together with Arup Associates, Alsop & Störmer, and Ushida-Findlay was asked by a BBC-sponsored television producer to develop a proposal for the decommissioning of a 1959 nuclear power station in North Wales. The two part concept evolved by SITE consisted first in a proposal for the use of robotics and "phyto-remediation" in the decommissioning of the existing facility, and second in the design of an International Energy Communications Center "for the study of decommissioning and alternative energy sources for the future." Phyto-remediation would entail "a massive greening of the entire area, lake shore, and nuclear electric buildings, using moss, rages weed and ivy as a means of removal of toxins from soil and water through the bio-chemical reaction of certain natural vegetation to radioactive materials." The Study Center design is a combination of a Celtic cross, and "the typical layered mounds of a Neolithic monument," both of which are closely related to the history of North Wales. Though this project has all the less hope of being realized since it calls for a very costly "rapid decommissioning" through the use of sophisticated robots to remove deadly radioactive materials, it has the virtue of calling attention to the enormous problem posed by the estimated 400 nuclear power plants scheduled to be taken out of production within the next twenty years.

Im Herbst 1994 trat ein von der BBC gesponsorter Fernsehproduzent an die Architekturbüros SITE, Arup Associates, Alsop & Störmer und Ushida-Findlay mit der Bitte heran, einen Entwurf für die Stillegung eines 1959 gebauten Atomkraftwerks in Nordwales zu entwickeln. Das von SITE erarbeitete zweiteilige Konzept beinhaltete die Verwendung von Robotern und eines als »Phyto-Remediation« bezeichneten technischen Verfahrens zum Abbau des bestehenden Kraftwerks sowie den Entwurf eines International Energy Communications Center »zur Erforschung von Demontage-Arbeiten und alternativer Energiequellen für die Zukunft«. Die sogenannte »Phyto-Remediation« würde eine »massive Bepflanzung des gesamten Gebietes, des Uferbereichs und der Kernkraftgebäude vorsehen, um mit Moosen, Kreuzkraut und Efeu den Boden und das Grundwasser von Giftstoffen zu befreien. Das Ganze basiert auf biochemischen Reaktionen, die einige Pflanzen gegenüber radioaktiven Materialien zeigen.« Bei dem Design des Study Center handelt es sich um die Kombination eines keltischen Kreuzes und »den auf typische Weise aufgehäuften Erdhügeln neolithischer Monumente«, die beide in engem Zusammenhang mit der Geschichte von Nordwales stehen. Obwohl bei diesem Projekt kaum Hoffnung auf eine Realisierung besteht, weil es eine sehr teure »schnelle Demontage« beinhaltet, bei der hochentwickelte Roboter die tödlichen radioaktiven Stoffe entfernen, gebührt ihm die Ehre, die Öffentlichkeit auf das gewaltige Problem aufmerksam gemacht zu haben, das die schätzungsweise 400 Atomkraftwerke darstellen, die in den kommenden zwanzig Jahren stillgelegt werden müssen.

A l'automne 1994 un producteur de télévision financé par la BBC, demandait à SITE, Arup Associates, Alsop & Störmer et Ushida-Findlay d'étudier le démantèlement d'une centrale nucléaire construite en 1959 dans le nord du Pays de Galles. Le concept mis au point par SITE comporte deux parties: le recours à la robotique et au «phyto-traitement» pour le démantèlement des installations, et la réalisation d'un Centre international d'information sur l'énergie «pour l'étude du démantèlement des centrales et de la recherche de sources d'énergie alternatives pour le futur». Le phyto-traitement consiste à couvrir l'ensemble du site, les rives du lac et les bâtiments de la centrale, de mousses, d'herbes et de lierre afin de diminuer la contamination du sol et de l'eau au moyen d'une réaction chimique de certains végétaux soumis à radiation. Le plan du Centre d'études évoque à la fois la croix celtique et le tumulus néolithique, éléments tous deux liés à l'histoire de la région. Même s'il a peu de chances d'être réalisé, le projet a le mérite d'attirer l'attention sur le gigantesque problème posé par les quelque 400 centrales nucléaires qui seront mises hors service dans les vingt prochaines années.

Page 161 bottom: A photo of the Power Station as it currently exists in its site. Page 161 top: A watercolor by James Wines showing how the buildings could be covered with plants which absorb radiation. Pages 162/163: Plan section and watercolor drawings by James Wines of the proposed International Energy Communications Center.

Seite 161 unten: Eine Fotografie der bislang unveränderten Power Station. Seite 161 oben: Diese Aquarellstudie von James Wines zeigt, wie das Gebäude von Pflanzen überwuchert werden könnte, die ihrerseits radioaktive Strahlung absorbieren. Seite 162/163: Querschnitt und Aquarellstudien des geplanten International Energy Communications Center (von James Wines).

Page 161 en bas: Photo de la centrale nucléaire dans son état acuel. Page 161 en haut: Une aquarelle de James Wines montrant la façon dont la construction pourrait être recouverte de plantes absorbant les radiations. Pages 162/163: Plan de section et dessins à l'aquarelle de James Wines, pour le Centre international d'information sur l'énergie.

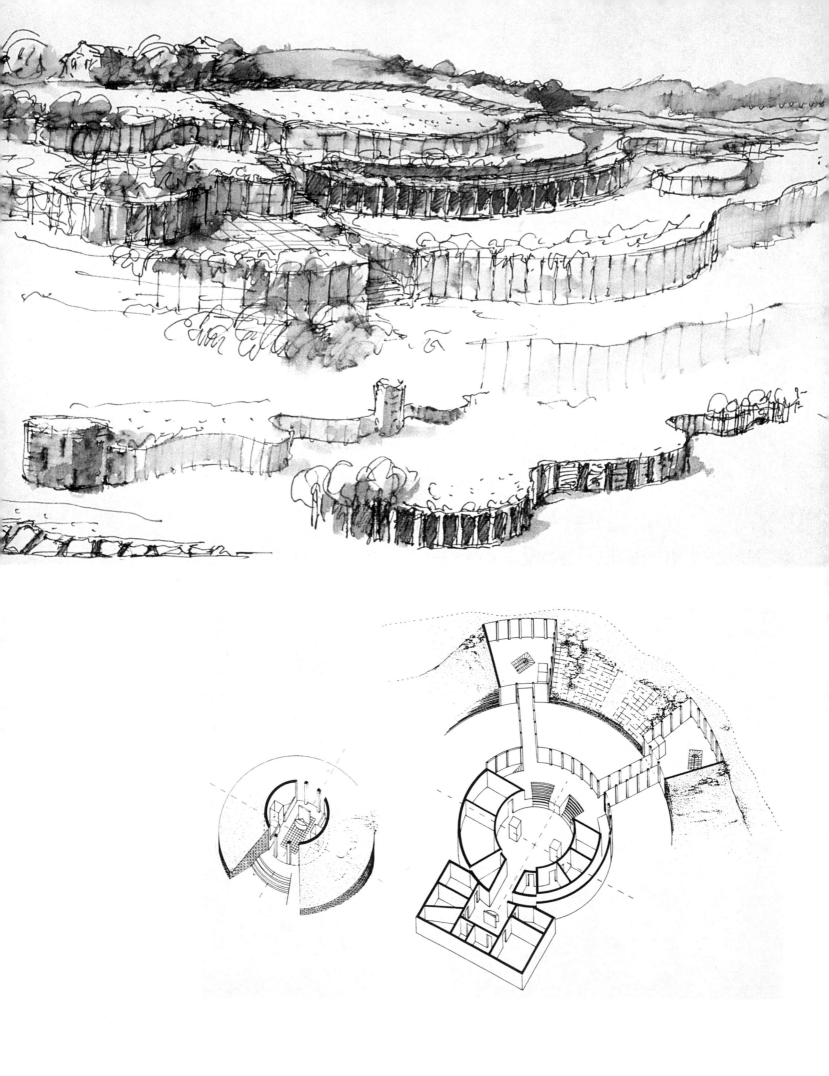

162 Trawsfynydd Nuclear Power Station Decommissioning

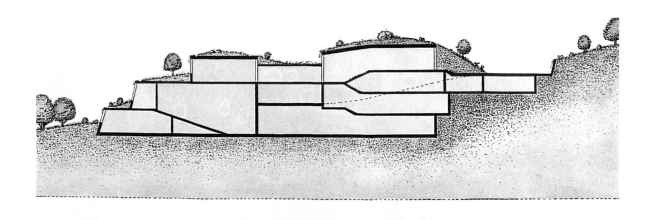

Simon **Ungers**

Simon Ungers

T-House, Wilton, New York, 1988–94, designed with Tom Kinslow. The upper, library area.

T-House, Wilton, New York, 1988–94, gemeinsam mit Tom Kinslow gestaltet. Der Bibliotheksbereich im oberen Teil des T-House.

T-House, Wilton, New York, 1988–94, construite avec Tom Kinslow. La bibliothèque dans la partie supérieure de la maison.

Simon Ungers is an unusual figure in that he arrived in the United States at the age of 22, and went on work as much in installation art as architecture. As he says, "conceived as a conflation of architecture, sculpture and painting, this work informs and directs my architecture and vice versa." It is clear that his T-House, built with Tom Kinslow, is very much a piece of large-scale sculpture, built entirely out of weathering steel. Despite its apparent affinity for monumental works of artists like Richard Serra, and indeed for Ungers' own untitled sculptural installation at Hunter's Point, New York (1988), the form of this house was in fact dictated by the needs of the client. It would seem that the difficulty faced by traditional sculpture and painting to evolve in the face of modern society is partially resolved by the more and more frequent relationship which has developed between architecture and art. Simon Ungers promises to be a leading figure in this trend.

Simon Ungers kam im Alter von 22 Jahren in die USA und arbeitet als Installationskünstler und als Architekt. »Ich betrachte diese Arbeit als Verschmelzung von Architektur, Bildhauerei und Malerei, die sich wechselseitig durchdringen und leiten.« Daher ist es auch kein Wunder, daß Ungers T-House, das er, zusammen mit Tom Kinslow, ausschließlich aus verwittertem Stahl erbaute, sehr stark an eine groß angelegte Skulptur erinnert. Trotz des Bezugs zu monumentalen Arbeiten von Künstlern wie Richard Serra und der eigenen, unbetitelten skulpturalen Installation in Hunter's Point, New York (1988), wurde die Form des hier vorgestellten Hauses eindeutig von den Bedürfnissen des Kunden diktiert. Es hat den Anschein, als ob die Schwierigkeiten, denen die Entwicklung der zeitgenössischen Bildhauerei und Malerei innerhalb der heutigen Gesellschaft begegnet, zumindest teilweise durch die immer stärkeren Bindungen ausgeglichen werden, die sich zwischen Architektur und Kunst entwickeln. Und Simon Ungers verspricht, eine der führenden Persönlichkeiten dieses Trends zu werden.

Simon Ungers a eu un parcours original: Il est arrivé aux Etats-Unis à 22 ans, et a autant travaillé comme artiste que comme architecte. Il explique volontiers que ses installations, à la confluence de l'architecture et de la peinture, éclairent et guident son travail d'architecte, et vice-versa. Il est évident que sa T-House en acier, construite avec Tom Kinslow, a tout de la sculpture. Si elle peut faire penser à certaines œuvres d'artistes comme Richard Serra, et à l'une des installations d'Ungers à Hunter's Point, New York (1988), sa forme a en fait été dictée par les besoins du client. Il semblerait que les difficultés d'évolution de la sculpture et de la peinture traditionnelles face à la société moderne soient en passe d'être résolues par les relations de plus en plus fréquentes qui s'établissent entre l'art et l'architecture. Simon Ungers promet d'être une figure majeure de cette tendance.

T-House, Wilton, New York
1988–94

Apparently the first house ever built out of weathering steel, the T-House, designed by Simon Ungers and Tom Kinslow, is intended to reflect the program of the client, with a 13 meter long library for 10000 books cantilevered over the living areas. As Simon Ungers writes, "the plasticity of the form is a result of a complex three dimensional extrapolation of a very simple cruciform plan. For the concept and form to be understood as clearly as possible it was critical to use a material that would permit a homogeneous monolithic surface without joints or differentiation of vertical and horizontal surfaces." The material involved is a shell, brought to the site in six pieces, and made of 1/4 inch thick steel, whose nickel and chromium finish was oxidized to create a vibrant rust color. The use of this material underlines the similarity of the T-House to a large sculpture, a fact which is confirmed by Simon Ungers' frequent involvement with installation art. Set on an 18 hectare plot of forested land, the house was built on the site of a former sand excavation pit. Its maximum height of 12.8 meters required a local zoning variance. A series of windows 2.4 meters high and 60 centimeters wide offer a view on the Berkshire Mountains. Despite the usually ephemeral nature of installation art, this sculptural presence seems firmly anchored, giving an impression of great solidity and permanence.

Dieses Haus aus verwittertem Stahl, entworfen von Simon Ungers und Tom Kinslow, reflektiert das Programm des Bauherrn: es besitzt eine 13 Meter lange Bibliothek mit 10000 Bänden, die freitragend über den Wohnbereichen liegt. Laut Ungers »ist die Plastizität der Form das Ergebnis einer komplexen dreidimensionalen Extrapolation eines sehr einfachen kreuzförmigen Plans. Um das Konzept bzw. die Form so eindeutig wie möglich zu verstehen, war es ungeheuer wichtig, ein Material zu verwenden, das eine homogene monolithische Oberfläche ohne Fugen und ohne Differenzierung von vertikalen und horizontalen Oberflächen ermöglicht.« Es handelt sich um eine Schalenkonstruktion, die in sechs separaten Teilen auf das Gelände transportiert wurde. Sie besteht aus 6 mm dickem Stahl, dessen Nickel- und Chromoberfläche man oxidieren ließ, damit sie einen leuchtenden Rostton annahm. Das Material unterstreicht die Ähnlichkeit des T-House mit einer großen Skulptur – ein Faktum, das Simon Ungers regelmäßiges Engagement im Bereich der Installationskunst bestätigt. Das auf einem 18 Hektar großen, bewaldeten Grundstück gelegene Haus entstand auf dem Gelände einer ehemaligen Sandgrube, und seine max. Höhe von 12,8 Metern erforderte eine Ausnahmegenehmigung der örtlichen Bauhöhenvorschriften. Die 2,4 Meter hohen und 60 Zentimeter breiten Fenster bieten eine direkte Aussicht auf die Berkshire Mountains. Trotz des eher vergänglichen Charakters der Installationskunst wirkt dieses skulpturale Bauwerk fest verankert und vermittelt den Eindruck großer Solidität und Beständigkeit.

Première maison sans doute entièrement construite en acier patinable, la T-House (réalisée de Simon Ungers et Tom Kinslow) et sa bibliothèque de 13 m de long en porte-à-faux, répond aux attentes du commanditaire, qui possède quelque 10000 livres. Comme l'écrit Simon Ungers : «La plasticité de la forme résulte d'une extrapolation complexe en trois dimensions d'un plan cruciforme très simple. Pour comprendre aussi clairement que possible le concept formel, il était indispensable de faire appel à un matériau permettant une surface homogène unie, sans joints, ni différenciation des surfaces verticales et horizontales.» Le matériau en question se présente sous la forme d'une coquille, transportée sur place en six morceaux, et faite d'un acier de près de 60 cm d'épaisseur dont la surface traitée au nickel et au chrome a pris un chaleureux ton rouille en s'oxydant. L'emploi de ce matériau souligne la parenté de la T-House avec la sculpture, ce qui n'étonnera guère quand on sait qu' Ungers est aussi un artiste dont les installations sont largement appréciées. La T-House a été construite au milieu d'un bois de 18 hectares, sur le site d'une ancienne sablière. Sa hauteur maximum de 12,8 m a nécessité une dérogation à la réglementation locale. Une série d'ouvertures de 2,4 m de haut et de 60 cm de large donne sur les Berkshire Mountains. Cette présence sculpturale qui semble fermement ancrée dans le sol donne une impression de solidité et de permanence.

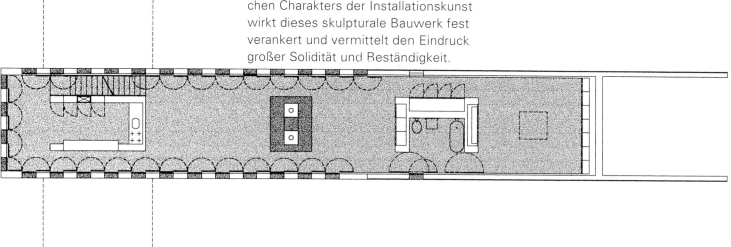

Pages 166–169: Monolithic and sculptural in its unusual appearance, the T-House is the rigorous expression of the client's wishes in terms of the spatial division of the library (above) and living areas (below).

Seite 166–169: Das monolithisch und skulptural erscheinende T-House mit seinen ungewöhnlichen Formen bildet die rigorose Umsetzung des Wunsches der Bauherren, die Bibliothek (oben) und die Wohnräume (unten) räumlich voneinander zu trennen.

Pages 166–169: D'aspect monolithique et sculptural, la T-House est l'expression rigoureuse des souhaits du client, qui voulait séparer la bibliothèque (en haut) et les espaces d'habitation (en bas).

Biographies
Biographien

Agrest and Gandelsonas

Diana Agrest, born in Buenos Aires (1944), studied at University of Buenos Aires and Ecole Pratique des Hautes Etudes, Paris. Designed and built Pierre Cardin Store, Buenos Aires (1970), and Urban Fragments, Buildings 1, 2, 3, 4, 5 Buenos Aires (1977–83). Co-founded Agrest and Gandelsonas, New York (1980). Professor adjunct of architecture, Columbia University since 1989. Mario Gandelsonas, born in Buenos Aires (1938) studied at University of Buenos Aires and Ecole Pratique des Hautes Etudes, Paris. Agrest and Gandelsonas summer house, Easthampton, 1985, Visiting professor, Yale School of Architecture (1988–91). Designed house on Sag Pond, Southampton. Professor of Architecture at Princeton University since 1991.

Diana Agrest wurde 1944 in Buenos Aires geboren. Sie studierte an der Universität Buenos Aires und an der Ecole Pratique des Hautes Etudes in Paris. Agrest entwarf und erbaute den Pierre Cardin Store (1970) sowie die Urban Fragments, Buildings 1, 2, 3, 4, 5 (1977–83), beide in Buenos Aires. Sie ist Mitbegründerin von Agrest and Gandelsonas in New York (1980) und seit 1989 als außerordentliche Professorin für Architektur an der Columbia University tätig. Mario Gandelsonas, 1938 in Buenos Aires geboren, studierte an der Universität Buenos Aires und an der Ecole Pratique des Hautes Etudes in Paris. Entwurf für das Agrest and Gandelsonas Summer House, Easthampton (1985), Gastprofessor an der Yale School of Architecture (1988–91). Entwurf für das House on Sag Pond, Southampton, New York. Seit 1991 Professor für Architektur an der Princeton University.

Diana Agrest, née à Buenos Aires (1944). Ecole d'architecture de l'Université de Buenos Aires et Ecole Pratique des Hautes Etudes, Paris. A dessiné et réalisé à Buenos Aires la boutique Pierre Cardin (1970), et Urban Fragments, immeubles 1, 2, 3, 4, 5 (1977–83). Co-fondatrice de l'agence Agrest et Gandelsonas, New York (1980). Professeur-adjoint d'architecture à Columbia University, depuis 1989. Mario Gandelsonas, né à Buenos Aires (1938). Ecole d'architecture de l'Université de Buenos Aires, puis études à l'Ecole Pratique des Hautes Etudes. 1985: maison d'été Agrest/Gandelsonas, Easthampton. 1988–91: professeur invité, Yale School of Architecture. Maison sur Sag Pond, Southampton. Depuis 1991, professeur d'architecture à Princeton University.

Agrest and Gandelsonas
740 Broadway, 10th Floor
New York, NY 10003
Tel: (212) 260-9100
Fax: (212) 260-5661

Arquitectonica

Bernardo Fort-Brescia was born in Lima, Peru in 1951. B. Arch., Princeton, 1973. M. Arch., Harvard, 1975. Principal of Arquitectonica since founding in 1977 in Miami. Laurinda Hope Spear was born in Rochester, Minnesota in 1950. M. Arch. Columbia, 1975. Master in City Planning, M.I.T. Principal of Arquitectonica with her husband since its founding. Major projects: Spear House, Miami (1976–78), The Palace, Miami (1979–82), The Atlantis, Miami (1980–82), Mulder House, Lima, Peru (1983–85), Banco de Crédito, Lima, Peru (1983–88), North Dade Justice Center, Miami (1984–87), Center for Innovative Technology, Herndon, VA (1985–88), Banque de Luxembourg Headquarters, Luxembourg, 1994.

Bernardo Fort-Brescia wurde 1951 in Lima, Peru geboren. Bachelor of Architecture, Princeton 1973; Master of Architecture, Harvard 1975. Er leitet Arquitectonica seit der Gründung 1977 in Miami. Laurinda Hope Spear wurde 1950 in Rochester, Minnesota geboren. Master of Architecture, Columbia University 1975, Master of City Planning am Massachusetts Institute of Technology. Leitet Arquitectonica seit der Gründung zusammen mit ihrem Mann. Bekannteste Projekte: Spear House, Miami (1976–78); The Palace, Miami (1979–82); The Atlantis, Miami (1980–82); Mulder House, Lima, Peru (1983–85); Banco de Crédito, Lima, Peru (1983–88); North Dade Justice Center, Miami (1984–87); Center for Innovative Technology, Herndon, Virginia (1985–88); Zentrale der Banque de Luxembourg, Luxemburg, 1994.

Bernardo Fort-Brescia est né à Lima, au Pérou, en 1951. B. Arch. à Princeton, 1973, M. Arch., Harvard, 1975. Responsable d'Arquitectonica depuis sa fondation en 1977 à Miami.
Laurinda Hope Spear est née à Rochester, Minnesota, en 1950. M. Arch. Columbia, 1975. Maîtrise d'urbanisme, M.I.T. Co-responsable d'Arquitectonica avec son époux depuis sa fondation. Principales réalisations: Spear House, Miami (1976–78), The Palace, Miami (1979–82), The Atlantis, Miami (1980–82), Mulder House, Lima, Pérou (1983–85), Banco de Crédito, Lima, Pérou (1983–88), Palais de Justice de North Dade County, Miami (1984–87), Center for Innovative Technology, Herndon, Virginie (1985–88), siège de la Banque de Luxembourg, Luxembourg, 1994.

Arquitectonica
426 Jefferson Avenue
Miami Beach, FL 33139
Tel: (305) 672-0690
Fax: (305) 672-0096

Will Bruder

Born in Milwaukee, Wisconsin in 1946, Will Bruder has a BA degree in Sculpture from the University of Wisconsin-Milwaukee and is self trained as an architect. He apprenticed under Paolo Soleri and Gunnar Birkerts. He obtained his architecture licence in 1974 and created his own studio the same year. He studied at the American Academy in Rome for six months in 1987. He has taught and lectured at SCI-Arc, Yale, Taliesin West and Georgia Tech. Current projects include Teton County Library, Jackson, Wyoming; Riddell Advertising, Jackson, WY; Temple Kol Ami, Scottsdale, AZ; Deer Vallery Rock Art Center, Phoenix, AZ; and residences in Boston, Colorado, Arizona, Canada and Australia as well as a restaurant in Manhattan.

Will Bruder wurde 1946 in Milwaukee, Wisconsin, geboren. Er studierte Bildhauerei an der University of Wisconsin-Milwaukee und ist als Architekt Autodidakt. Bruder lernte bei Paolo Soleri und Gunnar Birkerts, erlangte 1974 seine Zulassung als Architekt und gründete im gleichen Jahr sein eigenes Büro. 1987 studierte er sechs Monate an der American Academy in Rom. Bruder hielt Vorlesungen und unterrichtete am SCI-Arc, in Yale, Taliesin West und am Georgia Tech. Zu seinen gegenwärtigen Projekten zählen: Teton County Library, Jackson, Wyoming; Riddell Advertising, Jackson, Wyoming; Temple Kol Ami, Scottsdale, Arizona; Deer Vallery Rock Art Center, Phoenix, Arizona; Privathäuser in Boston, Colorado, Arizona, Kanada und Australien sowie ein Restaurant in Manhattan.

Né à Milwaukee, Wisconsin, en 1946, Will Bruder possède un BA de sculpture de l'University of Wisconsin-Milwaukee et s'est formé lui-même à l'architecture. Il a fait son apprentissage avec Paolo Soleri et Gunnar Birkerts. Il a obtenu sa licence d'architecte en 1974 et a créé sa propre agence la même année. Il a étudié à l'American Academy de Rome pendant six mois en 1987. Il a enseigné et donné des conférences à SCI-Arc, Yale, Taliesin West et Georgia Tech. Parmi ses projets en cours: la bibliothèque du comté de Teton, Jackson, Wyoming, l'agence de publicité Riddel Advertising, Jackson, Wyoming, Temple Kol Ami, Arizona, Deer Valley Rock Art Center, Phoenix, Arizona, et des résidences privées à Boston, dans le Colorado, en Arizona, au Canada et en Australie, ainsi qu'un restaurant à Manhattan.

bruder DWLarchitects
1314 West Circle Mountain Road
New River, AZ 85027
Tel: (602) 465-7399
Fax: (602) 465-0109

Peter Eisenman

Born in New York in 1932, B. Arch. Cornell, M. Arch. Columbia, Masters and Ph.D. degrees, University of Cambridge, England. Peter Eisenman has taught at Cambridge, Princeton, Yale and Harvard as well as the University of Illinois and Ohio State University. Main buildings: Wexner Center for the Visual Arts, Ohio State University, Columbus OH (1982–89), Koizumi Sangyo Building, Tokyo Japan (1987–89), Greater Columbus Convention Center, Columbus, OH (1989–93). Current projects include the Center for the Arts, Emory University, Atlanta, GA; and the Arnoff Center for Design and Art, University of Cincinnati, OH.

Geboren 1932 in New York. Bachelor of Architecture, Cornell University, Master of Architecture, Columbia University, Magister and Promotion, University of Cambridge. Peter Eisenman lehrte in Cambridge, Princeton, Yale und Harvard, an der Universität von Illinois sowie an der Ohio State University. Wichtige Bauten: Wexner Center for the Visual Arts, Ohio State University, Columbus, Ohio (1982–89); Koizumi Sangyo Building, Tokio, Japan (1987–89); Greater Columbus Convention Center, Columbus, Ohio (1989–93). Zu seinen gegenwärtigen Projekten zählen das Center for the Arts, Emory University, Atlanta, Georgia, sowie das Arnoff Center for Design and Art, University of Cincinnati, Ohio.

Né à New York en 1932, B. Arch. Cornell, M. Arch. Columbia, Masters et Ph.D. de l'Université de Cambridge, en Grande-Bretagne, Peter Eisenman a enseigné à Cambridge, Princeton, Yale, Harvard, University of Illinois et Ohio State University. Principales réalisations: Wexner Center for the Visual Arts, Ohio State University, Columbus, Ohio (1982–89), immeuble Koizumi Sangyo, Tokyo, Japon (1987–89), Greater Columbus Convention Center, Columbus, Ohio (1989–93). Il travaille actuellement sur le Center for the Arts, Emory University, Atlanta (Géorgie), et l'Arnoff Center for Design and Art, University of Cincinatti (Ohio).

Eisenman Architects
41 West 25th Street
New York, NY 10010
Tel: (212) 645-1400
Fax: (212) 645-0726

Peter Forbes

Born in Berkeley, California, in 1942, B. Arch. University of Michigan (1966); M. Arch. Yale (1967). Project designer for Skidmore, Owings and Merrill, Chicago (1965–66); Associate Partner PARD Team, Inc., Boston (1967–71); President, Forbes Hailey Jeas Erneman, Boston (1972–80); President, Peter Forbes and Asociates, Inc., Boston and Southwest Harbor, ME (1980 to present). Recent projects include houses in Massachusetts, New York, Washington and Maine, and stores for Origins Natural Resources in Massachusetts, New York, Connecticut and California.

Peter Forbes wurde 1942 in Berkeley, Kalifornien geboren. Bachelor of Architecture, University of Michigan (1966); Master of Architecture, Yale (1967). Projektdesigner für Skidmore, Owings & Merrill, Chicago (1965–66); Teilhaber PARD Team, Inc., Boston (1967–71); Präsident von Forbes Hailey Jeas Erneman, Boston (1972–80); Präsident von Peter Forbes and Associates, Inc., Boston und Southwest Harbor, Maine (1980 bis heute). Zu den gegenwärtigen Projekten zählen Häuser in Massachusetts, New York, Washington und Maine sowie Ladenlokale für Origins Natural Resources in Massachusetts, New York, Connecticut und Kalifornien.

Peter Forbes est né à Berkeley (Californie) en 1942. B. Arch., University of Michigan (1966); M. Arch., Yale (1967). Dessinateur de projets pour Skidmore, Owings & Merrill, Chicago (1965–66); partenaire associé de PARD Team, Inc., Boston (1969–71); président de Forbes Hailey Jeas Erneman, Boston (1972–80), président de Peter Forbes & Associates, Inc., Boston and Southwest Harbor, Maine (1980–). Parmi ses récents projets: des maisons dans le Massachusetts, l'Etat de New York, de Washington, le Maine; magasins pour Origins Natural Resources dans le Massachusetts, l'État de New York, le Connecticut et la Californie.

Peter Forbes and Associates
70 Long Wharf
Boston, MA 02110
Tel: (617) 523-5800
Fax: (617) 523-5810

Frank O. Gehry

Born in Toronto, Canada in 1929, Frank O. Gehry, studied at the University of Southern California, Los Angeles (1949–51), and at Harvard (1956–57). Principal of Frank O. Gehry and Associates, Inc., Los Angeles, since 1962, he received the 1989 Pritzker Prize. Some of his main projects are, the Loyola Law School, Los Angeles (1981–84); the Norton House , Venice, California (1982–84); California Aerospace Museum, Los Angeles (1982–84); Schnabel House, Brentwood (1986–89); Festival Disney, Marne-la-Vallée, France (1988–92); University of Toledo Art Building, Toledo, Ohio (1990–92); American Center, Paris, France (1988–93); Disney Concert Hall, Los Angeles (construction temporarily halted), and the Guggenheim Museum, Bilbao Spain (under construction).

Frank O. Gehry wurde 1929 in Toronto, Kanada geboren und studierte an der University of Southern California, Los Angeles (1949–51) sowie in Harvard (1956–57). Als Leiter von Frank O. Gehry and Associates, Inc., Los Angeles (seit 1962) erhielt er 1989 den Pritzker Preis. Zu seinen wichtigsten Projekten gehören die Loyola Law School, Los Angeles (1981–84); Norton Residence, Venice, Kalifornien (1982–84); California Aerospace Museum, Los Angeles (1982–84); Schnabel House, Brentwood (1986–89); Festival Disney, Marne-la-Vallée, Frankreich (1988–92); University of Toledo Art Building, Toledo, Ohio (1990–92); American Center, Paris, Frankreich (1988–93); Disney Concert Hall, Los Angeles (zeitweiliger Baustopp) sowie das Guggenheim Museum, Bilbao, Spanien (im Bau befindlich).

Né à Toronto (Canada), en 1929, Frank O. Gehry a étudié à USC (University of Southern California, Los Angeles, 1949–51), et Harvard (1956–57). Responsable de Frank O. Gehry & Associates, Inc., Los Angeles depuis 1962, il a reçu le prix Pritzker en 1989. Parmi ces réalisations les plus connues: Loyola Law School, Los Angeles (1981–84), la Norton House, Venice, Californie (1982–84), California Aerospace Museum, Los Angeles (1982–84); Schnabel House, Brentwood (1986–89); Festival Disney, Marne-la-Vallée, France (1988–92); University of Toledo; Art Building, Toledo, Ohio (1990–92); American Center, Paris (1988–93); Disney Concert Hall, Los Angeles (construction arrêtée pour l'instant) et le Guggenheim Museum, Bilbao, Espagne (en construction).

Frank O. Gehry and Associates, Inc.
1520-B Cloverfield Blvd.
Santa Monica, CA 90404
Tel: (310) 828-6088
Fax: (310) 828-2098

Steven Holl

Born in 1947 in Bremerton, Washington. B. Arch., University of Washington, 1970, in Rome and at the Architectural Association in London (1976). Began his career in California and opened his own office in New York in 1976. Has taughtat the University of Washington, Syracuse University, and, since 1981 at Columbia University. Notable buildings: Hybrid Building, Seaside, FL (1984–88); Berlin AGB Library, Berlin, Germany, competition entry (1988); Void Space/Hinged Space, Housing, Nexus World, Fukuoka, Japan (1989–91); Stretto House, Dallas, TX (1989–92); Makuhari Housing, Chiba, Japan (1992–97); Museum of Contemporary Art, Helsinki, Finland (1993–97).

Geboren 1947 in Bremerton, Washington. Bachelor of Architecture, University of Washington 1970; Studium in Rom und an der Architectural Association in London (1976). Holl begann seine Laufbahn in Kalifornien und eröffnete 1976 sein eigenes Büro in New York. Er lehrte an der University of Washington, an der Syracuse University und seit 1981 an der Columbia University. Bekannteste Bauten: Hybrid Building, Seaside, Florida (1984–88); Berliner AGB Bibliothek, Berlin, Wettbewerbsbeitrag (1988); Void Space/Hinged Space Wohnhäuser, Nexus World, Fukuoka, Japan (1989–91); Stretto House, Dallas, Texas (1989–92); Makuhari Wohnhäuser, Chiba, Japan (1992–97); Museum für zeitgenössische Kunst, Helsinki, Finnland (1993–97).

Né en 1947 à Bremerton (Washington), B. Arch., University of Washington (1970), études à Rome et à l'Architectural Association, Londres (1976). Débute sa carrière en Californie et ouvre sa propre agence à New York en 1976. Enseignant à University of Washington, Syracuse University, et, depuis 1981, à Columbia University. Principales réalisations: Hybrid Building, Seaside (Floride, 1984–88); participation au concours de la Bibliothèque AGB, Berlin (1988); immeuble d'appartements Void Space/Hinged Space, Nexus World, Fukuoka, Japon (1989–91); Stretto House, Dallas (Texas, 1989–92); immeuble d'habitation Makuhari, Chiba, Japon (1992–97); Musée d'Art Contemporain, Helsinki, Finlande (1993–97).

Steven Holl Architects
435 Hudson Street 4th FL
New York, NY 10014
Tel: (212) 989-0918
Fax: (212) 463-9718

Richard Meier

Born in Newark, New Jersey in 1934. Richard Meier received his architectural training at Cornell University, and worked in the office of Marcel Breuer (1960–63) before establishing his own practice in 1963. Pritzker Prize, 1984; Royal Gold Medal, 1988. Notable Buildings: The Atheneum, New Harmony, Indiana (1975–79); Museum for the Decorative Arts, Frankfurt, Germany (1979–84); High Museum of Art, Atlanta, Georgia (1980–83); Canal+ Headquarters, Paris, France (1988–91); City Hall and Library, The Hague, Netherlands (1990–95); Barcelona Museum of Contemporary Art, Barcelona, Spain (1988–95); Getty Center, Los Angeles, California (1984–96).

Geboren 1934 in Newark, New Jersey. Meier erhielt seine Ausbildung an der Cornell University und arbeitete im Büro von Marcel Breuer (1960–63), bevor er 1963 sein eigenes Büro eröffnete. 1984 gewann er den Pritzker Preis, 1988 die Royal Gold Medal. Wichtige Bauten: The Atheneum, New Harmony, Indiana (1975–79); Museum für Kunsthandwerk, Frankfurt a.M. (1979–84); High Museum of Art, Atlanta, Georgia (1980–83); Zentrale von Canal+, Paris (1988–91); Rathaus und Zentralbibliothek, Den Haag, Niederlande (1990–95); Museum für zeitgenössische Kunst, Barcelona, Spanien (1988–95); Getty Center, Los Angeles, Kalifornien (1984–96).

Né à Newark (New Jersey), en 1934, Richard Meier a étudié à Cornell University, et travaillé dans l'agence de Marcel Breuer (1960–63), avant de se mettre à son compte en 1963. Pritzker Prize, 1984; Royal Gold Medal, 1988. Principales réalisations: The Atheneum, New Harmony, Indiana (1975–79); Musée des Arts Décoratifs de Francfort-sur-le-Main (1979–1984); High Museum of Art, Atlanta, Géorgie (1980–83); Siège de Canal+, Paris (1988–91); Hôtel de ville et bibliothèque, La Haye (1990–95); Musée d'art contemporain de Barcelone (1988–95); Getty Center, Los Angeles (Californie, 1984–96).

Richard Meier & Partners
475 Tenth Avenue
New York, NY 10018
Tel: (212) 967-6060
Fax: (212) 967-3207

Eric Owen Moss

Born in Los Angeles, California in 1943, Eric Owen Moss received his BA degree from UCLA in 1965, and his M. Arch. in 1968. He also received a M. Arch. degree at Harvard in 1972. He has been a Professor of Design at the Southern California Institute of Architecture since 1974. He opened his own firm, in Culver City in 1976. His built work includes the Central Housing Office, University of California at Irvine, Irvine (1986–89); Lindblade Tower, Culver City (1987–89); Paramount Laundry, Culver City (1987–89); Gary Group, Culver City (1988–90), The Box, Culver City (1990–94) and the IRS Building, also in Culver City (1993–94).

Eric Owen Moss wurde 1943 in Los Angeles, Kalifornien geboren und erhielt 1965 seinen Bachelor of Arts und 1968 seinen Master of Architecture an der UCLA sowie 1972 seinen Master of Architecture in Harvard. Seit 1974 ist Moss als Professor of Design am Southern California Institute of Architecture tätig. 1976 gründete er in Culver City seine eigene Firma. Zu seinen Arbeiten zählen das Central Housing Office, University of California at Irvine, Irvine (1986–89); Lindblade Tower, Culver City (1987–89); Paramount Laundry, Culver City (1987–89); Gary Group, Culver City (1988–90); The Box, Culver City (1990–94) und das IRS Building, ebenfalls in Culver City (1993–94).

Né à Los Angeles (Californie), en 1943, Eric Owen Moss passe son BA à UCLA en 1965, un M. Arch. en 1968, et un autre à Harvard en 1972. Professeur de design au Southern California Institute for Architecture depuis 1974, il ouvre sa propre agence à Culver City en 1976. Son œuvre construit comprend le Central Housing Office, University of California at Irvine, Irvine (1986–89); Lindblade Tower, Culver City (1987–89); Paramount Laundry, Culver City (1987–89); Gary Group, Culver City (1988–90); The Box, Culver City (1990–94); l'IRS Building, toujours à Culver City (1993–94).

Eric Owen Moss Architects
8557 Higuera Street
Culver City, CA 90232
Tel: (310) 839-1199
Fax: (310) 839-7922

Ieoh Ming Pei

Born in 1917 in Canton (now Guangzhou), China. Pei came to the United States in 1935. B. Arch., M.I.T. (1940) ; M. Arch., Harvard (1946). Formed I.M. Pei & Associates, 1955. AIA Gold Medal, 1979; Pritzker Prize, 1983; Praemium Imperiale, Japan, 1989. Notable buildings: National Center for Atmospheric Research, Boulder, CO (1961–67); Federal Aviation Agency Air Traffic Control Towers, 50 buildings, various locations (1962-70); John F. Kennedy Library, Boston, MA (1965–79); National Gallery of Art, East Building, Washington, D.C. (1968–78); Bank of China Tower, Hong Kong (1982–89); Grand Louvre, Paris (1983–93); Rock and Roll Hall of Fame, Cleveland, OH (1993–95). Current projects include a museum for Shinji Shumeikai, Shiga, Japan.

Pei wurde 1917 in Kanton (heute Guangdschou), China geboren und kam 1935 in die Vereinigten Staaten. B. Arch., M.I.T. (1940); M. Arch., Harvard (1942); Promotion, Harvard (1946). Gründete 1955 I.M. Pei Associates. AIA Goldmedaille, 1979; Pritzker Preis, 1983; Praemium Imperiale, Japan, 1989. Wichtige Bauten: National Center for Atmospheric Research, Boulder, Colorado (1961–67); 50 Flugüberwachungstürme für die Federal Aviation Agency an zahlreichen Orten (1962–70); John F. Kennedy Library, Boston, Massachusetts (1965–79), National Gallery of Art, East Building, Washington, D.C. (1968–78); Bank of China Tower, Hongkong (1982–89); Grand Louvre, Paris (1983–93); Rock and Roll Hall of Fame, Cleveland, Ohio (1993–95). Zu seinen gegenwärtigen Projekten zählen u.a. ein Museum für Shinji Shumeikai, Shiga, Japan.

Né en 1917 à Canton (Chine), Pei arrive aux Etats-Unis en 1935. B. Arch., M.I.T. (1940); M. Arch., Harvard, 1942; Doctorat, Harvard, 1946. Crée I.M. Pei & Associates en 1955. Médaille d'or AIA, 1979; Pritzker Prize, 1983; Prix impérial, Japon, 1989. Réalisations les plus connues: National Center for Atmospheric Research, Boulder (Colorado, 1961–67); 50 tours de contrôle de trafic aérien pour la Federal Aviation Agency (divers lieux, 1962–70); bibliothèque John Kennedy, Boston (Massachusetts, 1965–79); bâtiment est de la National Gallery of Art, Washington D.C. (1968–78); tour de la banque de Chine, Hong Kong (1982–89); Grand Louvre, Paris (1983–93); Rock and Roll Hall of Fame, Cleveland (Ohio, 1993–95). Parmi ses projets actuels, un musée pour Shinji Shumeikai (Shiga, Japon).

I.M. Pei Architect
600 Madison Avenue
New York, NY 10022
Tel: (212) 872-4010
Fax: (212) 872-4222

Cesar Pelli

Born in 1926 in Tucuman, Argentina, studied at Tucuman University, Dip. Arch. (1949). Emigrated to the U.S. (1952) and attended University of Illinois, M.Arch. (1954). Worked in office of Eero Saarinen and Associates, Bloomfield Hills, Michigan and New Haven, Connecticut (1954–64), project designer for the TWA Terminal, Kennedy International Airport, New York, and Vivian Beaumont Theater at Lincoln Center, New York. In 1964, joined DMJM, Los Angeles as director (1964–66) then vice-president of design (1966–68). From 1968 to 1977, Pelli was partner in charge of design at Gruen Associates, Los Angeles. Notable buildings completed by Gruen Associates under Pelli's direction include the Pacific Design Center in Los Angeles (1975) and U.S. Embassy in Tokyo, Japan (1976). After becoming Dean of the School of Architecture at Yale in 1977, Pelli opened his own office, Cesar Pelli and Associates in New Haven, Connecticut. Notable structures include: Residential tower and gallery expansion, Museum of Modern Art, NY (1977); Four Leaf Towers, Houston, TX (1983–85), World Financial Center, NY (1980–88), Canary Wharf Tower, London, 1987–91, NTT Shinjuku Headquarters Building, Tokyo, Japan (1990–95); Kuala Lumpur City Center Phase 1, Malaysia (1992–96).

Geboren 1926 in Tucuman, Argentinien. Studierte an der Universität Tucuman; Diplomarchitekt 1949. Nach Auswanderung in die USA (1952) Besuch der University of Illinois; Master of Architecture 1954. Arbeitete für das Büro von Eero Saarinen and Associates in Bloomfield Hills, Michigan und New Haven Connecticut (1954–64); Projektdesigner für das TWA Terminal, Kennedy International Airport, New York sowie für das Vivian Beaumont Theater im Lincoln Center, New York. 1964 wechselte Pelli zu DMJM nach Los Angeles, zunächst als Direktor (1964–66), danach als Bereichsleiter für Design (1966–68). Von 1968 bis 1977 war er für das Design verantwortlicher Partner bei Gruen Associates, Los Angeles. Zu den bedeutendsten Bauten, die unter Leitung Pellis von Gruen Associates fertiggestellt wurden, zählen das Pacific Design Center in Los Angeles (1975) und die amerikanische Botschaft in Tokio, Japan (1976). Nachdem er 1977 zum Dekan der School of Architecture in Yale ernannt worden war, gründete Pelli in New Haven, Connecticut sein eigenes Büro, Cesar Pelli and Associates. Wichtigste Bauten: Wohnturm und Erweiterung des Museum of Modern Art, New York (1977); Four Leaf Towers, Houston, Texas (1983–85); World Financial Center, New York (1980–88); Canary Wharf Tower, London (1987–91); NTT Shinjuku Headquarters Building, Tokio, Japan (1990–95); Kuala Lumpur City Center Phase 1, Malaysia (1992–96).

Né en 1926 à Tucuman, Argentine. Diplôme d'architecture de l'université de Tucuman (1949). Émigre aux États-Unis (1952), et passe son M. Arch. en 1954 (University of Illinois). Travaille pour Eero Saarinen & Associates, Bloomfield Hills (Michigan) et New Haven (Connecticut, 1954–64), dessinateur de projet pour le terminal TWA de l'aéroport Kennedy, New York, et le Vivian Belmont Theater au Lincoln Center, New York. En 1964, il devient directeur de DMJM, à Los Angeles (1964–66), puis vice-président en charge de la conception (1966–68). De 1968 à 1977, Pelli est associé chargé de la conception chez Gruen Associates, Los Angeles. Parmi les réalisations remarquées de Gruen Associates sous la direction de Pelli: le Pacific Design Center à Los Angeles (1975) et l'ambassade américaine à Tokyo (1976). Devenu doyen de l'école d'architecture de Yale en 1977, il ouvre sa propre agence, Cesar Pelli & Associates à New Haven, Connecticut. Parmi ses réalisations importantes: tour d'appartements et extension du musée, Museum of Modern Art, New York (1977): les quatre Leaf Towers, Houston (Texas, 1983–85), le World Financial Center, New York (1980–88); Canary Wharf Tower, Londres (1987–91); Siège de NTT Shinjuku, Tokyo (1990–95); Kuala Lumpur City Center Phase 1, Malaisie (1992–96).

Cesar Pelli and Associates
1056 Chapel Street
New Haven, CT 06510
Tel: (203) 777-2515
Fax: (203) 787-2856

Antoine Predock

Born in 1936 in Lebanon, Missouri, educated at the University of New Mexico and Columbia University, B. Arch. 1962. Antoine Predock has been the principal of his own firm since 1967. He has taught at UCLA and California State Polytechnic University. Notable buildings: Nelson Fine Arts Center, Arizona State University, Tempe AZ (1986–89); Zuber House, Phoenix, AZ (1986–89); Hotel Santa Fe, Euro Disney, Marne-la-Vallée, France (1990–92), Classroom/Laboratory/Administration Building, California Polytechnic University, Pomona, CA (1993); American Heritage Center, Laramie, WY (1987–93); Civic Arts Plaza, Thousand Oaks, CA (1989–94); Ventata Vista Elementary School, Tucson, AZ (1992–94).

1936 in Lebanon, Missouri, geboren, erhielt Antoine Predock seine Ausbildung an der University of New Mexico und der Columbia University (Bachelor of Architecture 1962). Seit 1967 leitet er sein eigenes Büro. Predock lehrte an der UCLA sowie an der California State Polytechnic University. Wichtige Bauten: Nelson Fine Arts Center, Arizona State University, Tempe, Arizona (1986–89), Zuber House, Phoenix, Arizona (1986–89); Hotel Santa Fe, Euro Disney, Marne-la-Vallée, Frankreich (1990–92); Klassenzimmer/Labor/Verwaltungsgebäude der California Polytechnic University, Pomona, Kalifornien (1993); American Heritage Center, Laramie, Wyoming (1987–93); Civic Arts Plaza, Thousand Oaks, Kalifornien (1989–94); Ventata Vista Elementary School, Tucson, Arizona (1992–94).

Né en 1936 à Lebanon (Missouri), études à University of New Mexico et Columbia University. B. Arch. en 1962. Antoine Predock a créé son agence en 1967. Il a enseigneé à UCLA et à la California State Polytechnic University. Principales réalisations: Nelson Fine Arts Center, Arizona State University, Tempe, Arizona (1986–89); Zuber House, Phoenix, Arizona (1986–89); Hôtel Santa Fé, EuroDisney, Marne-la-Vallée, France (1990–92); Immeuble de salles de cours, laboratoires et bureaux, California Polytechnic University, Pomona, Californie (1993); American Heritage Center, Laramie, Wyoming (1987–93); Civic Arts Plaza, Thousand Oaks, Californie (1989–94); Ventata Vista Elementary School, Tucson, Arizona (1992–94).

Antoine Predock Architect
300 12th Street NW
Albuquerque, NM 87102
Tel: (505) 843-7390
Fax: (505) 243-6254

Bart Prince

Born in Albuquerque, New Mexico in 1947. B. Arch., Arizona State University (1970). Worked with Bruce Goff from 1968 to 1973, assisted him in the design of the Pavilion for Japanese Art, Los Angeles County Museum of Art, Los Angeles, CA (1978–89), and completed the building after Goff's death in 1982. Opened his own architectural practice in 1973. Main buildings: Bart Prince Residence and studio, Albuquerque, NM (1983), Joe Prince Residence, Corona del Mar, CA (1986), Brad and June Prince House, Albuquerque, NM (1988), Nollan Residence, Taos, NM (1993), Mead/Penhall Residence, Albuquerque, NM (1994); Hight Residence, Mendocino County, CA (1995).

Geboren 1947 in Albuquerque, New Mexico. 1970 Bachelor of Architecture an der Arizona State University. Von 1968 bis 1973 arbeitete Prince mit Bruce Goff zusammen, assistierte ihm beim Entwurf des Pavillons für japanische Kunst des Los Angeles County Museum of Art, Los Angeles, Kalifornien (1978–89) und stellte das Gebäude nach Goffs Tod 1982 fertig. Eröffnete 1973 ein eigenes Büro. Wichtige Bauten: Bart Prince Residence and Studio, Albuquerque, New Mexico (1983); Joe Price Residence, Corona del Mar, Kalifornien (1986); Nollan Residence, Taos, New Mexico (1993); Mead/Penhall Residence, Albuquerque, New Mexico (1994); Hight Residence, Mendocino County, Kalifornien (1995).

Né à Albuqerque, Nouveau Mexique en 1947. B. Arch. Arizona State University (1970). Travaille avec Bruce Goff de 1968 à 1973, et l'assiste dans la conception du pavillon de l'art japonais du Los Angeles County Museum of Art, Los Angeles (1978–89), qu'il achèvera après la mort de Goff en 1982. Ouvre sa propre agence en 1973. Principales réalisations: Bart Prince Residence and studio, Albuquerque, Nouveau-Mexique (1983), Joe Prince Residence, Corona del Mar (Californie, 1986); Brad and June Prince House, Albuquerque (Nouveau-Mexique, 1988); Nollan Residence, Taos (Nouveau-Mexique, 1993), Mead/Penhall Residence, Albuquerque (Nouveau-Mexique, 1994); Hight Residence, Mendocino County (Californie, 1995).

Bart Prince architect
3501 Monte Vista N.E.
Albuquerque, NM 87106
Tel: (505) 256-1961
Fax: (505) 268-9045

Scogin Elam and Bray

Mark Scogin was born in 1943 in Atlanta, Georgia. B. Arch., Georgia Institute of Technology (1967). He is presently Chairman of the Department of Architecture at the Harvard Graduate School of Design. Prior to founding Scogin Elam and Bray (1984), he was with Heery and Heery in Atlanta for 17 years, as President, Chief Operating Officer and Director of Design.
Merrill Elam was born in 1943 in Nashville, Tennessee. She received her B. Arch. at Georgia Institute of Technology (1971) and an M.B.A. at Georgia State University (1983). She has taught at the University of Illinois, the University of Virginia and Rice University. Lloyd Bray was born in Atlanta, Georgia in 1951. He received his B. Arch. at Tulane University (1976). Project architect at Heery and Heery until leaving to become one of the founding principals of Scogin Elam and Bray. Projects include private residences in North Carolina, Massachusetts and Georgia, a bridge and an art gallery in Atlanta, and a branch library in Riverdale, Georgia.

Mark Scogin wurde 1943 in Atlanta, Georgia geboren. Bachelor of Architecture am Georgia Institute of Technology 1967. Scogin ist heute Vorsitzender des Department of Architecture der Harvard Graduate School of Design. Vor der Gründung von Scogin Elam and Bray (1984) arbeitete er 17 Jahre bei Heery and Heery in Atlanta, als Präsident, Technischer Direktor und Bereichsleiter für Design.
Merrill Elam wurde 1943 in Nashville, Tennessee geboren. Sie erwarb 1971 ihren Bachelor of Architecture am Georgia Institute of Technology und 1983 ihren Master of Business Administration an der Georgia State University. Elam unterrichtete an der University of Illinois, der University of Virginia und der Rice University. Lloyd Bray wurde 1951 in Atlanta, Georgia geboren. Bachelor of Architecture an der Tulane University (1976). Bray arbeitete als Projektarchitekt bei Heery and Heery, bevor er Scogin Elam and Bray mitbegründete. Zu den gegenwärtigen Projekten zählen Privathäuser in North Carolina, Massachusetts und Georgia, eine Brücke und eine Kunstgalerie in Atlanta sowie eine Bücherei in Riverdale, Georgia.

Mark Scogin est né à Atlanta (Géorgie) en 1943. B. Arch. au Georgia Institute of Technology (1967). Il est actuellement président du département d'architecture de l'Harvard Graduate School of Design. Avant de fonder Scogin Elam and Bray (1984), il travaille pour Heery & Heery à Atlanta pendant 17 ans, comme directeur de la conception, responsable des opérations et président.
Merrill Elam est née à Nashville (Tennessee) en 1943. B. Arch. au Georgia Institute of Technology (1971) et M.B.A. à Georgia State University (1983). Elle a enseigné à l'Université de l'Illinois, l'Université de Virginie et Rice University. Lloyd Bray est né à Atlanta (Géorgie) en 1951. B. Arch. de Tulane University (1976). Responsable de projets chez Heery & Heery qu'il quitte pour fonder Scogin Elam and Bray. Parmi ses projets: des résidences privées en Caroline-du-Nord, au Massachusetts et en Géorgie, un pont, une galerie d'art à Atlanta, et une bibliothèque à Riverdale, en Géorgie.

Scogin Elam and Bray
434 Marietta Street NW
Atlanta, GA 30313
Tel: (404) 525-6869
Fax: (404) 525-7061

SITE

James Wines, founding principal of SITE (Sculpture in the Environment) was born in Chicago, IL and studied art and art history at Syracuse University, BA 1956. Between 1965 and 1968, he was a sculptor. Alison Sky, also a founding principal was born in New York and received a degree in fine arts from Adelphi University. Notable buildings include: Indeterminate Facade Showroom, Houston, TX (1975); Ghost Parking Lot, Hamden, CT (1978); Highway 86, World Exposition, Vancouver, British Columbia, Canada (1986); Four Continents Bridge, Hiroshima, Japan (1989); Avenida 5, Universal Exhibition, Seveille, Spain (1992) and Ross's Landing Plaza and Park, Chattanooga, TN (1992).

James Wines, Gründer von SITE (Sculpture in the Environment), wurde in Chicago, Illinois, geboren und studierte Kunst und Kunstgeschichte an der Syracuse University (Bachelor of Architecture 1956). Zwischen 1965 und 1967 arbeitete er als Bildhauer. 1970 gründete Wines zusammen mit Alison Sky und Michelle Stone die Gruppe SITE. Wichtige Bauten: Indeterminate Facade Showroom, Houston, Texas (1975); Ghost Parking Lot, Hamden, Connecticut (1978); Highway 86, Weltausstellung, Vancouver, British Columbia, Kanada (1986); Four Continents Bridge, Hiroshima, Japan (1989); Avenida 5, Expo, Sevilla, Spanien (1992) und Ross's Landing Plaza and Park, Chattanooga, Tennessee (1992).

James Wines, principal fondateur de SITE (Sculpture In The Environment) est né à Chicago (Illinois) et a étudié l'art et l'histoire de l'art à Syracuse University. BA en 1956. Sculpteur de 1965 à 1967. Il crée SITE avec Alison Sky et Michelle Stone en 1970. Réalisations notables: Indeterminate Facade Showroom, Houston, Texas (1975); parking Ghost, Hamden, Connecticut (1978); Highway 86, World Exposition, Vancouver, Colombie-Britannique, Canada (1986); pont des quatre continents, Hiroshima (1989); Avenida 5, Expo 92, Séville, et Ross's Landing Plaza et Parc, Chattanooga, Tennessee (1992).

SITE
632 Broadway
New York, NY 10012
Tel: (212) 254-8300
Fax: (212) 353-3086

Simon Ungers and Tom Kinslow

Born in 1957 in Cologne, Germany, emmigrated to the United States in 1979. B. Arch., Cornell 1979. Founding partner of UKZ (1981), Assistant Professor of Architecutre at Syracuse University, New York, 1981–86. Hobbs Residence, Lansing, NY (1982); Honorable Mention, Japan Opera House Competition, 1986; Assistant Professor of Architecture at Rensselaer Polytechnic Institute (1986–92). Numerous installations – Gallery Sophia Ungers, Cologne Germany, 1993, Sandra Gering Gallery, New York 1992. 1995 First Prize in Holocaust Memorial Competition, Berlin, Germany. Tom Kinslow was born in Baldwinsville, NY in 1957. Syracuse University, M. Arch. 1988. From 1984 to 1986, he worked with UKZ in Ithaca, NY. Since 1992, he has had his own practice.

Simon Ungers wurde 1957 in Köln geboren und wanderte 1979 in die Vereinigten Staaten aus. Bachelor of Architecture, Cornell 1979. Mitbegründer von UKZ (1981), Lehrbeauftragter für Architektur an der Syracuse University, New York (1981–86). Hobbs Residence, Lansing, New York (1982); Ehrenvolle Erwähnung, Japan Opera House Competition (1986); Lehrbeauftragter für Architektur am Rensselaer Polytechnic Institute (1986–92). Zahlreiche Installationen – Galerie Sophia Ungers, Köln (1993), Sandra Gering Gallery, New York (1992). 1995 Erster Preis beim Wettbewerb Denkmal für den Holocaust, Berlin. Tom Kinslow wurde 1957 in Baldwinsville, New York geboren. Master of Architecture, Syracuse University 1988. Von 1984–86 arbeitete Kinslow für UKZ in Ithaca, New York. Seit 1992 hat er sein eigenes Architekturbüro.

Né en 1957 à Cologne (Allemagne), et émigre aux États-Unis en 1979. B. Arch. à Cornell University (1979). Fondateur associé de UKZ (1981). Assistant en architecture à Syracuse University (New York, 1981–86). Hobbs Residence, Lansing, New York (1982); mention honorable au concours pour l'opéra du Japon (1986); assistant en architecture à Rensselaer Polytechnic Institute (1986–92). Nombreuses installations: Galerie Sophia Ungers, Cologne (1993), Sandra Gering Gallery, New York (1992). Premier prix au concours pour le Mémorial de l'Holocauste, Berlin (1995). Tom Kinslow est né à Baldwinsville (New York), en 1957. M. Arch. de Syracuse University (1988). De 1984 à 1986, travaille pour UKZ, à Ithaca (New York). Il ouvre sa propre agence en 1992.

Simon Ungers architect
17 Jay Street
New York City, NY 10013
Tel: (212) 941-7757
Fax: (212) 941-1823

Bibliography
Bibliographie

Agrest and Gandelsonas, Works. Introduction by Anthony Vidler. New York: Princeton Architectural Press, 1995.

Antoine Predock, Architect. Compiled by Brad Collins and Juliette Robbins, New York: Rizzoli, 1994.

Arquitectonica. Foreword by Philip Johnson. Washington, D.C.: American Institute of Architects Press, 1991.

Cesar Pelli. Introduction by Michael Crosbie. Images Publishing, 1993.

Dixon, John Morris: "The Santa Monica School. What's Its Lasting Contribution?" *Progressive Architecture*, May 1995.

Eric Owen Moss, 1974–1994. Architecture and Urbanism (A+U), 94:11. Tokyo: A+U Publishing.

Ghiradro, Diane. "Eisenman's Bogus Avant-Garde". *Progressive Architecture*, November 1994.

Glancey, Jonathan. "Ideas beyond the nuclear station." *The Independent*, April 12, 1995.

Goldberger, Paul: "The Masterpieces They Call Home." *The New York Times Magazine*, March 12, 1995.

Jencks, Charles ed. *Frank O. Gehry, Individual Imagination and Cultural Conservatism*. London: Academy Editions, 1995.

Muschamp, Herbert. "Building on the Ruins of Temples to Nuclear Power." *The New York Times*, April 2, 1995.

Muschamp, Herbert. "A Flare for Fantasy: 'Miami Vice' Meets 42nd Street." *The New York Times*, May 21, 1995.

Noever, Peter ed. *The End of Architecture?* Munich: Prestel 1993.

Steven Holl. GA Architect N°11. Tokyo: A.D.A. Edita, 1993.

Steven Holl. Introduction by Kenneth Frampton, essay by Fréderic Migayrou. Zürich: Artemis, 1994.

Sudjic, Deyan. *Banque de Luxembourg*. Blueprint Extra n° 12. London: Wordsearch, 1994.

Index

Photographic credits
Fotonachweis
Crédits photographiques

The publisher and editor wish to thank each of the architects and photographers for their kind assistance.

p. 2	© Photo: Paul Warchol
p. 6-9	© Photo: Joshua White
p. 10	© Photo: Paul Warchol
p. 11	© Photo: Paul H. Groh
p. 12	© Photo: Scott Frances/Esto
p. 13	© Photo: Cesar Pelli & Associates
p. 14-15	© Photo: Timothy Hursley
p. 16	© Photo: Paul Warchol
p. 17	© SITE
p. 19	© Photo: Richard Bryant/Arcaid
p. 20-21	© Photo: Eisenman Architects
p. 22-25	© Photo: Paul Warchol
p. 26	© Simon Ungers
p. 27	© Photo: Arch Photo Eduard Hueber
p 28-31	© Photo: Richard Bryant/Arcaid
p. 32	© Photo: Timothy Hursley
p. 33	© Antoine Predock
p. 35	© Photo: Timothy Hursley
p. 39	© SITE
p. 43	© Photo: Richard Bryant/Arcaid
p. 44	© Will Bruder
p. 45	© Photo: Timothy Hursley
p. 50	© Photo: Paul Warchol
p. 51	© Photo: Jesse Frohman
p. 52	© Agrest & Gandelsonas
p. 53 top	© Photo: Paul Warchol
p. 53 bottom	© Agrest & Gandelsonas, Architects
p. 54/55	© Photo: Scott Frances/Esto
p. 56 bottom	© Agrest & Gandelsonas, Architects
p. 56/57 top	© Photo: Scott Frances/Esto
p. 57 bottom	© Photo: Scott Frances/Esto
p. 58	© Photo: Richard Bryant/Arcaid
p. 59	© Arquitectonia International
p. 61	© Photo: Richard Bryant/Arcaid
p. 62 top	© Photo: Richard Bryant/Arcaid
p. 62 bottom	© Jacques Wirtz
p. 63	© Photo: Richard Bryant/Arcaid
p. 65	© Arquitectonica International
p. 66	© Photo: Timothy Hursley
p. 67	© Will Bruder
p. 69 top	© Photo: Timothy Hursley
p. 69 bottom	© Will Bruder
p. 70-72	© Photo: Timothy Hursley
p. 73 top	© Will Bruder
p. 73 bottom	© Photo: Timothy Hursley
p. 74	© Photo: Jochen Littkemann
p. 75	© Peter Eisenman
p. 77 top	© Photo: Jochen Littkemann
p. 77 bottom	© Photo: Jochen Littkemann
p. 78	© Photo: Paul Warchol
p. 79	© Photo: Clark Quin
p. 81 top	© Photo: Paul Warchol
p. 81 bottom	© Peter Forbes
p. 82	© Photo: Paul Warchol
p. 83 top	© Photo: Paul Warchol
p. 83 bottom	© Peter Forbes
p. 84	© Photo: Richard Bryant/Arcaid
p. 85	© Photo: Brian S.U. Woo
p. 87	© Photo: Richard Bryant/Arcaid
p. 88 top	© Photo: Richard Bryant/Arcaid
p. 88 bottom	© Frank O. Gehry & Associates, Inc.
p. 89	© Photo: Richard Bryant/Arcaid
p. 91 top	© Photo: Joshua White
p. 91 bottom	© Frank O. Gehry & Associates, Inc.
p. 92/93 top	© Photo: Joshua White
p. 92 bottom	© Frank O. Gehry & Associates, Inc.
p. 93 bottom	© Photo: Joshua White
p. 94	© Photo: Paul Warchol
p. 95-96	© Steven Holl Architects
p. 97-98	© Photo: Paul Warchol
p. 99	© Steven Holl Architects
p. 101	© Photo: Paul Warchol
p. 102 top	© Photo: Paul Warchol
p. 102 bottom	© Steven Holl Architects
p. 103	© Photo: Paul Warchol
p. 104	© Photo: Richard Bryant/Arcaid
p. 105	© Luca Vignelli
p. 107 top	© Photo: Richard Bryant/Arcaid
p. 107 bottom	© Richard Meier & Partners Architects
p. 108	© Richard Meier & Partners Architects
p. 109	© Photo: Richard Bryant/Arcaid
p. 110	© Photo: Paul H. Groh
p. 111	© Eric Owen Moss
p. 113-115	© Photo: Paul H. Groh
p. 116	© Photo: Timothy Hursley
p. 117	© Photo: Serge Hambourg
p. 118-121	© Photo: Timothy Hursley
p. 122	© Photo: Scott Frances/Esto
p. 123	Photo: Hank Morgan
p. 125 top	© Photo: Scott Frances/Esto
p. 125 bottom	© Cesar Pelli & Associates
p. 126/127 top	© Photo: Scott Frances/Esto
p. 127 bottom	© Cesar Pelli & Associates
p. 128	© Photo: Timothy Hursley
p. 129	© Photo: Robert Reck
p. 131 top	© Antoine Predock
p. 131 bottom	© Photo: Timothy Hursley
p. 132/133	© Photo: Timothy Hursley
p. 134 top	© Photo: Timothy Hursley
p. 134 bottom	© Antoine Predock
p. 135	© Antoine Predock
p. 137 top	© Photo: Timothy Hursley
p. 137 bottom	© Antoine Predock
p. 138	© Antoine Predock
p. 139-141	© Photo: Timothy Hurslcy
p. 142	© Photo: Michele M. Penhall
p. 143	© Photo: Alan Weintraub
p. 144-147	© Photo: Michele M. Penhall
p. 148	© Bart Prince
p. 149	© Photo: Michele M. Penhall
p. 150	© Photo: Timothy Hursley
p. 151	© Photo: Dot Griffith
p. 153 top	© Photo: Timothy Hursley
p. 153 bottom	© Scogin Elam and Bray
p. 154/155	© Photo: Timothy Hursley
p. 156	© SITE
p. 157	© Andreas Sterzing
p. 159	© SITE
p. 161 top	© SITE
p. 161 bottom	© Nuclear Electric
p. 162-163	© SITE
p. 164	© Photo: Arch Photo Eduard Hueber
p. 165	© Simon Ungers
p. 166	© Simon Ungers
p. 167-169	© Photo: Arch Photo Eduard Hueber